The OS/2 Programming Environment

David A. Schmitt

Prentice Hall
Englewood Cliffs, New Jersey 07632

Library of Congress Cataloging-in-Publication Data

Schmitt, David A.
The OS/2 programming environment / by David A. Schmitt.
p. cm.
Includes index.
ISBN 0-13-642927-0
1. OS/2 (Computer operating system) 2. MS-DOS (Computer operating system) I. Title.
QA76.76.063S38 1989
005.265--dc19 88-29759
CIP

Editorial/production supervision: Jacqueline A. Jeglinski
Cover design: Photo Plus Art
Manufacturing buyer: Mary Ann Gloriande

To Karen--

For the inspiration, the time, and her constant encouragement.

The publisher offers discounts on this book when ordered in bulk quantities. For more information, write:

Special Sales/College Marketing
Prentice-Hall, Inc.
College Technical and Reference Division
Englewood Cliffs, NJ 07632

Printed in the United States of America

10 9 8 7 6 5 4 3 2 1

ISBN 0-13-642927-0

Prentice-Hall International (UK) Limited, *London*
Prentice-Hall of Australia Pty. Limited, *Sydney*
Prentice-Hall Canada Inc., *Toronto*
Prentice-Hall Hispanoamericana, S.A., *Mexico*
Prentice-Hall of India Private Limited, *New Delhi*
Prentice-Hall of Japan, Inc., *Tokyo*
Simon & Schuster Asia Pte. Ltd., *Singapore*
Editora Prentice-Hall do Brasil, Ltda., *Rio de Janeiro*

Table of Contents

Foreword

The unprecedented explosion in Personal Computers in the early 1980s was due in large part to the thousands of innovative application programs which were developed for the DOS operating system. At first, it seemed that the capabilities of the PC were limitless. But as the environment matured, PC programmers soon started running into the inherent limitations of the DOS architecture. The 640 KB physical address space, its single tasking structure, and the lack of reasonable protection mechanisms make life very difficult for application developers.

In many ways, the PC software industry of 1988 is being throttled by the capabilities of DOS. The increasingly sophisticated features of today's personal computer hardware cannot be harnessed using an operating system which was never intended to support these new machines. To further complicate things, as the hardware has evolved, so has the PC user community. Users are demanding more and more sophisticated application programs which better exploit their hardware investment. The PC application developers are stuck in the middle of the tempest. Truly supporting the new hardware systems means that application developers must spend more time and effort making DOS do "unnatural acts" and less time making their applications state-of-the-art programs.

The DOS engine which so successfully fueled the PC revolution is rapidly running out of steam. But this is not an indictment of DOS as much as it is an acknowledgement that the underlying hardware is developing in ways which were inconceivable in 1981. DOS is rooted in older hardware technologies which have little support for the large memory or protection that is required by responsive, predictable, multitasking environments.

In April, 1987, the IBM and Microsoft Corporations announced *Operating System/2*, the fruit of a joint software development venture. OS/2 is a new system which was built with programmers in mind. While designing the system we tried to listen to the common complaints of DOS programmers. In fact, the design team which defined the OS/2 architecture was composed of some of the best PC minds in the industry today. This joint Microsoft/IBM group brought their collective experience to the project to attempt what many called a "mission impossible" – building a system which addresses the weaknesses of the DOS environment while striving to maintain overall responsiveness and flexibility. Did the team succeed? Well, the ultimate judge will not be any of us who worked on the project. The ultimate judge is you, the programmers who will use the system facilities to build a new generation of exciting application programs and system extensions. We have done our job, but our appraisals will come from you.

As the president of the Lattice corporation, Dave Schmitt has been involved in the OS/2 project for quite some time. His company was one of the first to acknowledge the possibilities of the system by porting their products onto the new platform. I first met Dave at the OS/2 announcement in 1987 where he enthusiastically gave me a first hand report on what we were doing right, and more importantly, what we were doing wrong. His commentary was incisive. It was clear to me then that Dave really understood the PC business and why OS/2 was needed. Since then, I have spoken to him on many occasions. He has always provided me with clear feedback, which was invaluable input to difficult design trade-offs.

Dave puts this understanding to work in this book. As I read through the text, I could see OS/2 through different eyes. What you will read here is the OS/2 system from the perspective of an experienced programmer who has gone through the conversion from DOS to OS/2. His commentary is sometimes kind, sometimes not, but always honest. He does a good job putting the system's capabilities into perspective. I enjoyed reading this book, as I am sure you will.

Ed Iacobucci

Preface

I never met an operating system I didn't like, going all the way back to the early 1960s when I worked with the primitive I/O Control System (IOCS) on the IBM 1401 computer. During subsequent years I was a designer and programmer for four operating systems (which we called central control programs) used in electronic telephone switching systems, culminating with a three-year stint in the early 1980s on the fault-tolerant version of UNIX known as DMERT.

If I've learned anything during twenty-five years studying operating systems, it is how to distinguish the good ones from the stinkers. The good ones are a pleasure to use because they are efficient, understandable, and logically consistent. The stinkers are a pain to use because they're sluggish, arcane, and constantly surprise you with their inconsistencies.

If you smell anything around OS/2, it's the sweet smell of success. This is probably the most complex operating system ever crammed into a microprocessor, but for all of its features, it is remarkably efficient and is quite approachable. You don't need to be an operating system guru to use most of the OS/2 features.

In some ways, OS/2 is a compendium of the good operating system ideas that have evolved during the past twenty-five years. While writing this book about the new technology of OS/2, I've had a lot of fun discovering those old nuggets and seeing how they've been shined up for use in the personal computing environment.

Many thanks to the fine people at IBM who gave me the opportunity to play with OS/2 while it was under development: Joe Carusillo, Steve Hancock, Ed Iacobucci, Tom Peters, Emmet Wainwright, and many others. I also owe a lot to the programming staff at Lattice who provided valuable insight as OS/2 users, especially Glenn Musial, Tom Prodehl, and John Pruitt. And finally, thanks to Ed Moura, Jackie Jeglinski, and the others at Prentice-Hall who sweated through this book with me, and to Ed Yourdon who delivered the kick in the pants that got me started.

David A. Schmitt

Introduction

Remember the early days of the IBM PC? Programming this little beast wasn't much fun. The original PC was just an anemic 16-bit replacement for the 8-bit CP/M computers then in vogue, and DOS (i.e., Microsoft's MS-DOS and IBM's PC-DOS) didn't do much to correct the deficiencies of CP/M. Furthermore, the Intel 8088 was a nasty chip to program in assembly language, and there weren't many tools available to support programming in higher-level languages.

But within a few years, the PC hardware had improved markedly, and a large number of excellent software development tools were available at reasonable prices. PC programming became a pleasant experience, because these high-level tools provided a smooth ride over the many 8088 potholes. Furthermore, DOS had evolved well beyond its CP/M roots, but it remained an unobtrusive little operating system that could be pushed aside whenever you wanted to get "down and dirty" with the hardware. PC programmers had found something that mainframe and minicomputer programmers dream about: *an environment in which the programmer had total control.*

Unfortunately, the people who pay us programmers to indulge our passion wouldn't let us rest comfortably in this pleasant environment. They saw what we could do with the PC and wanted more: more color, more graphics, more interaction, bigger spreadsheets, better help systems, and on and on. The hardware folks thought this was great. After all, they get their kicks by building systems with more memory, bigger disks, faster processors, and more exotic peripherals. IBM and the other computer manufacturers enjoyed this trend too, since they make most of their money selling hardware.

But those of us who develop PC application software for a living were getting more and more uncomfortable. The software solutions that our customers and managers wanted could only be provided with huge and complex packages that banged up solidly against some DOS limitations that were not so easy to overcome. We found ourselves wasting a lot of time bending, folding, and mutilating our programs so they would fit within the 640-kilobyte memory limit. Many programmers spent long midnight hours devising bizarre schemes to thwart the DOS single-tasking architecture, so we could then develop those essential pop-up utilities, background communication handlers, and other multitasking features.

This constant tussle with DOS took a lot of the fun out of PC programming. Of course, as an old and wise manager once told me, nobody said that programmers are supposed to have fun. But in this case, the pleasure disappeared because PC programming was becoming a slow and tedious process, with constant delays as we figured out how to get around yet another DOS limit. This decrease in efficiency was certainly of great concern to managers as well as programmers. By late 1987, it became apparent that many PC programming projects were in states of crisis, experiencing the delays and setbacks that have often plagued software development projects on larger systems.

But fortunately, December of that year saw the marriage of IBM and Microsoft produce OS/2, an offspring destined to lead us all into a brave new world of PC programming, free of the many problems and constraints in the DOS world. This fancy new operating system combines the best features of DOS and UNIX to give us a programming environment that (at least today) appears to be limitless. We can now wallow in a one-gigabyte address space. We can create entire armies of cooperating processes busily going about their assigned tasks. And with the Presentation Manager, we can finally write sophisticated interactive graphical applications that don't bring the system to its knees.

Well.....maybe OS/2 doesn't really warrant this kind of purple prose; after all, it's really just another in a long string of operating systems, and like all the others, it will probably cure some old problems and create some new ones. So, as an application programmer, you'll be better off if you don't completely convert to the *OS/2 religion*. Learn as much as you can about it, develop an understanding of its strong and weak points, and understand how it relates to its predecessors, especially DOS and UNIX. But remain a free thinker, because OS/2 will not make these other systems obsolete. Furthermore, you'll probably see an even better operating system during your career. Perhaps it will be called OS/3.

This is not the first OS/2 programming book, and it certainly won't be the last. Are these books necessary, or should you just buy the *OS/2 Technical Reference Manual* from IBM or Microsoft? Well, there are several texts which, for the most part, duplicate information that can be found in the reference manual. I suppose these would appeal to someone who doesn't want to lay out $200 for the manual.

Other books, most notably *The OS/2 Programmer's Guide* by Ed Iacobucci and *Inside OS/2* by Gordon Letwin, were written by members of the OS/2 design team in order to explain how and why this new operating system was developed. But while these books explain how OS/2 works, they don't tell you much about writing application programs for the new operating system. Iacobucci's book does contain a thorough treatment of the OS/2 Application Program Interface, but it concentrates on assembly language programming, just like the *OS/2 Technical Reference*.

And that's where this text comes in. Rather than present a history of OS/2 or simply summarize the information contained in the reference manual, I've tried to focus on the transition from DOS to OS/2 for programmers who are working in a high-level language such as C. Most people who will write programs for OS/2, especially in its early years, have some experience with DOS. Indeed, many of you will be converting DOS programs to run under OS/2; you're probably less concerned about using the new OS/2 features and more concerned with minimizing your conversion effort. So, I will present OS/2 in just that way. First we'll examine the features it shares with DOS and explain how to use them. Then we'll see how to improve your DOS programs by making use of new OS/2 features such as multitasking.

Here's a brief summary of the book's contents:

- Chapter 1 explains why OS/2 was developed – basically a lengthier treatment of the preceding paragraphs.
- Chapter 2 explains the different ways that DOS and OS/2 utilize the Intel processors.

- Chapter 3 gives a quick overview of the OS/2 feature set.
- Chapter 4 compares the DOS and OS/2 Application Program Interfaces.
- Chapter 5 gives some guidelines for converting existing DOS programs to run in OS/2 protected mode.
- Chapter 6 explains the OS/2 File System, which is very similar to that of DOS and also has some useful new features.
- Chapters 7, 8, and 9 describe the OS/2 techniques for accessing the screen, keyboard and mouse, which are much different and, in some ways, better than the DOS techniques.
- Chapters 10, 11, and 12 discuss OS/2's multitasking, memory management, and interprocess communication features. Then Chapter 13 covers some advanced I/O topics not discussed in Chapter 6.
- Chapter 14 covers the OS/2 features that support country-independent programming.
- Chapter 15 describes how to use the OS/2 "family-mode" capability to produce software that can run under DOS or OS/2 and utilize the best features of both operating systems.

The Appendix is a quick reference to the functions that constitute the Application Program Interface for IBM OS/2 Standard Edition 1.0, which is essentially identical to Microsoft OS/2 Version 1.0.

You should have no trouble with this book if you are reasonably familiar with DOS and the C language, and if you are at least comfortable with short stretches of Intel assembly-language code. Those who do not know DOS and/or C may have a harder time, but none of the examples are complicated or arcane, and so you should get in the groove after the first few chapters.

One area that gave me some trouble was the representation of hexadecimal numbers. In C, the hexadecimal form of the decimal number 256 is 0x100, while the assembly language form is 100H. I finally decided to use both formats, depending on which one seemed to make the most sense at the time. In many cases, such as when writing addresses in the *segment:offset* or *selector:offset* form, I write the plain hexadecimal numbers with no prefix or suffix, since the meaning is clear.

Incidentally, although neither Microsoft nor IBM like to state this directly, C is the preferred language for programming high-performance OS/2 applications. If you review the OS/2 reference manuals, you'll find a lot of C-related examples and jargon, and the OS/2 Presentation Manager can't really be used effectively from any other language. So if you are not already a C programmer, I hope this book will help you get your OS/2 "C legs."

Chapter 1

The Need for OS/2

1.1 The Personal Computer Revolution

Odd matings often produce interesting and unexpected results. In 1981 IBM, one of the world's largest and best-managed companies, joined with Microsoft, a group of brash young microcomputer hackers, to produce a simple personal computer and disk operating system. Who could have predicted that this coupling would give rise to a multibillion dollar PC hardware and software industry in less than five years? Or that this computer architecture would be so resilient that it would find use in every facet of domestic and international business? Or that the IBM PC and its clones would almost totally eclipse the then-dominant CP/M, Apple, and Commodore computers?

Those early PCs were small machines by today's standards – an anemic 8088 microprocessor, less than 256 kilobytes of main memory, one or two low-density floppy disks, and only a few I/O adaptors. But the PC and DOS designers at IBM and Microsoft were either extraordinarily foresighted or unusually lucky, because their basic design decisions survived more than five years of rapid change – the so-called *personal computer revolution*.

Today's PC is likely to sport at least 640 kilobytes of memory, a high performance 80286 or 80386 microprocessor, a hard disk storing at least 20 megabytes, and a multitude of I/O devices. In addition to the keyboard, many systems have advanced input devices such as mice, trackballs, bar code readers, document scanners, and even speech recognizers. High-resolution color graphic displays, high-speed modems, and laser printers are becoming *de rigueur*. PC-to-mainframe communication is commonplace, and PC-to-PC interconnection via local area networks (LANs) is finally happening as more people need to share PC data with their fellow workers.

Of course, much of this hardware evolution has been driven by and has, at the same time, provided fuel for an explosive PC software industry.

1.2 Standardized Software: A New Industry

Before the PC brought substantial computing power to the desktop, interactive software tended to be sluggish and quite hostile to all but expert users. Full screen interfaces, menus, context sensitive help, pointing devices, and other user convenience features were rare. Software documentation was often incomplete, inaccurate, or out of date – further barring the casual user from access to the computer. There were few industry-wide human-interface standards, because much of that era's software was custom designed by in-house programming staffs or by contract programming houses.

But when IBM put its seal of approval on a microcomputer system, businesses started buying PCs, and software product developers began to examine the possibilities for personal computing in the workplace. They soon discovered that, whether by accident or by design, the IBM PC was an ideal platform for highly interactive business software. The Intel 8088 processor, while no speed demon, was fairly powerful and, with its 16-bit addressing, could support much more memory than earlier 8-bit microcomputers. The PC keyboard and screen were well-matched to the 8088, easy to program, and could give very snappy performance when driven directly by the software. And DOS, being little more than a disk file manager, could be easily pushed out of the way by the application software to achieve this level of performance.

Certain products, such as Lotus 1-2-3, took early advantage of the IBM PC architecture and achieved dominant positions. Their human interface techniques quickly became *de facto* standards for the other software vendors to imitate. Within a few years thousands of software companies were disgorging a glut of PC products ranging from simple *desktop accessories* to complex multistation *transaction processing systems*. And with each new product, the human interfaces improved and the PC became a little easier to use.

1.3 Conspicuous Consumption

However, these new interactive software products were voracious consumers of the PC's computing resources, thereby forcing rapid evolution of the hardware. IBM was able to answer the demand for more and faster bulk storage by introducing the PC-XT with its 10-megabyte hard disk. At the same time, they wisely introduced DOS Version 2 with a multilevel file system.

When the 8088 ran out of gas, IBM introduced the PC-AT with an 80286 processor and 20 megabytes of disk storage. The request for higher quality color displays was met with with the Enhanced Graphics Adaptor (EGA), and the desire for PC-to-PC communication led to several LAN adaptors and to DOS Version 3. IBM provided PC-to-mainframe links via the specialized and expensive 3270-PC and also via an assortment of hardware and software packages for the normal PC line.

Finally, IBM streamlined this motley assortment of technologies and introduced the PS/2 family. At its high end, the PS/2 family increased the performance of IBM hardware by introducing the 80386 processor and high-speed disks with capacities greater than 100 megabytes. At the low end, the PS/2 family included reasonably-priced replacements for the PC and the XT designed to appeal to students and residential users.

Meanwhile IBM's nemesis, the clone-makers, were busily mimicking every step IBM took, and they achieved impressive success with low-priced alternatives to the AT. In fact, because of these powerful and inexpensive clones, IBM was only able to claim about one-third of the AT market.

1.4 The Limits of DOS

The DOS developers at Microsoft and IBM did not sit still during this period of hardware evolution. But even though DOS had reached Version 3 by evolving along with the hardware, more and more software developers were venturing far beyond its inherent limits. DOS was designed to provide fairly good file management services to one application program at a time, running within a one-megabyte address space. Since IBM usurped 384 kilobytes (i.e., 384K) of that space for the PC's Basic I/O Subsystem, or BIOS, an application program had 640K to share with DOS. So, when DOS Version 3 checked in with about 128K of baggage, the typical PC had about 512K available for applications.

In earlier and simpler times, 512K was considered to be a huge amount of memory. For instance, during the 1960s an IBM 360 Model 50 with 512K was *big time computing*. During the 1970s it was rare for a minicomputer to go beyond 256K, and yet these machines often supported a dozen users running independent applications from their terminals. And even though today's mainframes and minicomputers usually have several megabytes of memory, they typically share this among many users and applications.

But the highly-interactive, graphically-oriented applications being hosted on the PC demanded megabytes, not just kilobytes. Furthermore, PC users had become accustomed to having instant access to *pop-up programs* which, when activated via a *hot key*, provided such services as telephone lists, notepads, calculators, and so on. These pop-up programs not only consumed a significant portion of the available 512K, but they also stressed another DOS limitation: *They forced it to multitask.*

Since most mainframes and minicomputers must support several users at the same time, their operating systems are designed to manage several application programs at once, a feature called *multitasking*. On the other hand, DOS, as we mentioned earlier, was originally envisioned as a single-user system handling only one application program at a time.

Why, the DOS designers asked, would any PC user want to run several programs at the same time? After all, a personal computer is only serving one person at a time, not dozens of people like minicomputers and mainframes must do.

The PC users quickly answered. They loved the pop-up utilities, which forced DOS to perform unnatural acts in order to provide a shaky form of multitasking. They also began to make heavy use of local area networks, which required that DOS support the LAN communication manager as a background task.

Unfortunately, the multitasking feature is at the heart of any operating system and must be designed in from the beginning; it is extremely difficult to add as an afterthought. But because DOS had become so popular, IBM and Microsoft did the best they could to make it multitask without introducing drastic changes to its user and programmer interfaces.

IBM released a multitasking add-on package called *Topview*, which performed the neat trick of allowing existing PC application programs to share the computer, with no changes required in those applications. But *Topview* died a quick death because it consumed too much memory and did not provide good support for pop-up programs and for graphically-oriented software.

Microsoft came out with a much more ambitious multitasking feature, called *Windows*, which included an impressive graphical interface and a sophisticated memory manager. However, existing PC programs had to be completely re-designed in order to use these advanced features. Furthermore, Microsoft lost a lot of credibility when they delayed the initial release of *Windows* until almost two years after their original announcement. To make matters worse, they tinkered with the design during several subsequent releases, causing much frustration among the software developers who were trying to use *Windows*. As a result, *Windows*, which was too strong to die, became a bit of a zombie, its graphical interface being used by a few desktop publishing and charting programs, but its multitasking feature being generally spurned.

Ingenious though they may have been, *Topview*, *Windows*, and similar multitasking packages such as *Desqview* were all fairly shaky compromises. The fundamental problem was DOS, and all of these packages were built on top of it. As long as DOS was around, its limitations would continue to inhibit PC programmers from developing the sophisticated, resource-hungry, interactive applications that were the next logical stage of the personal computer revolution.

1.5 Introducing OS/2

I'm not saying that IBM, Microsoft, and other companies didn't recognize the need to replace DOS. It's just that nobody saw how to introduce the necessary improvements without making a lot of perfectly usable PC hardware and software obsolete.

For instance, after seeing the weak acceptance of *Windows*, Microsoft designed a multitasking operating system that they called DOS Version 4. Unlike *Windows*, Version 4 would run on all existing PC hardware and support most existing PC software packages. In effect, they took the multitasking feature from *Windows*, cleaned it up, and embedded it right in DOS. However, although DOS Version 4 could support a bank-switched extended memory system (EMS), it still limited an individual program to about 512K.

Because of this limit, Microsoft's largest customer, IBM, did not think Version 4 was the significant step that the market needed. And so, Version 4 wound up being used by only a few of Microsoft's European customers for turnkey applications.

In another attempt to provide a better PC environment, IBM introduced a DOS-compatible multitasking operating system called the 3270 PC Control Program. This system enabled the 3270 PC user to run one or more DOS applications while also having one or more terminal sessions active on an IBM mainframe. Unlike DOS Version 4, which was purely a software solution, the 3270 PC included special hardware that allowed DOS programs and 3270 sessions to share the keyboard and screen. Unfortunately, this extra hardware was expensive, and so the 3270 PC appealed only to the relatively small community of mainframe computer users who also wanted to run DOS applications.

After these and other experiments, IBM and Microsoft decided that it would not be possible to substantially improve DOS if the resulting operating system had to run on the original PC hardware. So, with some reluctance, they decided to abandon the 8086-class machines and concentrate on the 80286 and 80386 processors. Industry rumors have hinted that Microsoft wanted to jump right to the 80386, which has the ability to emulate several 8086 processors while also supporting new large applications in its large addressing mode. But IBM was adamant about not abandoning the IBM AT, which used the 80286. After all, IBM had long promised that the AT would eventually receive an *Advanced DOS*, thereby eliminating the 640K barrier and providing true multitasking.

The joint IBM and Microsoft development of this Advanced DOS, or ADOS, took more than three calendar years and hundreds of person-years. In addition to the ADOS acronym, it was also called, at various times, DOS Version 5, 286DOS, and Protected DOS. IBM finally decided that this new operating system was potentially as important to personal computing as their OS/360 had been to the mainframe world, and so they chose a similar name: Operating System/2, or OS/2.

1.6 A Compromising Situation

OS/2, like most other good engineering, is a result of many compromises. For example, while OS/2 cannot run on the PC's original 8086-class hardware, it can switch into 8086 mode to run most DOS-based applications. And while the 80386 can easily provide several of these 8086 partitions, OS/2 took the more difficult path of providing a single 8086 partition on the older 80286 machines, of which there are millions. For new applications, OS/2 provides a large addressing mode, called protected mode, which gives each program a 30-bit address space. This allows immediate access to the 16 megabytes of memory that can be hung on an 80286, and in the future it will allow OS/2 applications to access much more memory on the 80386.

Despite their need to compromise, the OS/2 designers never lost sight of their original mission: to overcome the DOS 640K memory barrier and introduce true multitasking. They accomplished both of these with style and elegance. OS/2 is one of the most sophisticated operating systems ever put into production, and its features are so well designed that it can be expected to find use in an even broader range of applications than DOS. Furthermore, its concepts are general enough that it should evolve gracefully as future processor generations come along.

For example, OS/2 defines an Application Program Interface, or API, that can be called directly from high-level languages such as C and Pascal. The API makes it possible to write entire applications without resorting to assembly-language routines that are difficult to maintain and to adapt to new processors. The API forms the basis for a plethora of standard OS/2 services, such as task management, task-to-task communication, and I/O. Furthermore, the API can be easily extended through dynamic link libraries and new I/O drivers, which need not come only from Microsoft or IBM. This ability to be extended and customized makes OS/2 ideal for turnkey applications such as point-of-sale systems, factory automation, and message switching.

And so, in attempting to overcome the limitations of DOS, the OS/2 designers made a giant step forward. DOS, of course, will live on in lap-held, educational, and home computers. But as hardware prices continue to decline and the demand for personal computing power continues to increase, OS/2 will undoubtedly become the preferred PC operating system for business computing of all kinds.

In the remaining chapters of this book, we'll examine OS/2 from a programmer's viewpoint, with particular attention to the similarities and differences between DOS and OS/2. First comes a brief review of the Intel processor family, followed by a quick tour of OS/2. Then we'll cover the various OS/2 programming features in detail.

Chapter 2

Intel Processors

OS/2 is designed for the Intel 80286 processor and its successors. If you intend to do all of your OS/2 application programming in a high-level language such as C, you won't need to know a whole lot about the 80286. But if you will be working in assembly language, or if you just want to become more familiar with the OS/2 hardware environment, some 80286 knowledge is essential.

This chapter gives a quick overview of the following 80286 topics that pertain to OS/2 programming:

- Intel Processor Architecture
- Real Addressing Mode
- Protected Addressing Mode

As you can see, this is by no means an exhaustive treatment of the 80286; for example, there's no review of the instruction set. See the Bibliography for several references that provide all the details.

2.1 Intel Processor Architecture

The Intel *iAPX* processor family includes the 8086, 80186, 80286, and 80386, as well as the 8088 and 80188, which are variations of the 8086 and 80186, respectively. These processors all share some basic 8086 features of interest to both DOS and OS/2 programmers:

- Eight 16-bit general purpose registers and four 16-bit segment registers, as shown in Figure 2-1;
- Ability to generate 20-bit memory addresses, providing access to one megabyte of program/data memory;
- Ability to generate 16-bit I/O addresses, providing access to 65,536 I/O ports.

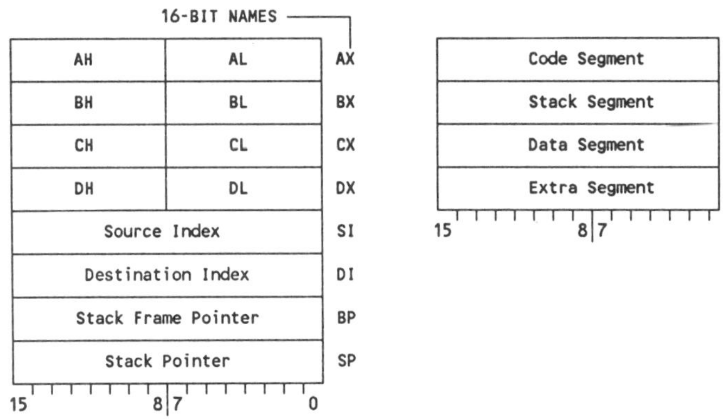

Figure 2-1. 8086 Register Set

The 80286 and 80386 are advanced members of this family, offering much higher throughput and many additional features, such as 24-bit memory addressing on the 80286 and 32-bit addressing on the 80386. The 80386 also adds two more segment registers and extends the general registers to 32 bits, as shown in Figure 2-2.

So far, IBM has built machines using the 8086, 8088, 80286, and 80386. Other manufacturers have used the 80186 and 80188 in their DOS-based systems. But regardless of which processor is used, DOS and its applications are generally restricted to the common 8086 feature set. For example, the primary advantage you get if you replace an IBM PC with an IBM AT is a faster processor. There is no easy way for DOS applications on an AT to take advantage of the 80286's ability to address 16 megabytes. Similarly, DOS applications cannot conveniently use the 32-bit capabilities of the 80386.

OS/2 was designed specifically to overcome the limitations of the 8086 architecture, especially in the area of memory capacity. Therefore, the new operating system requires at least an 80286, and preferably a faster version of that

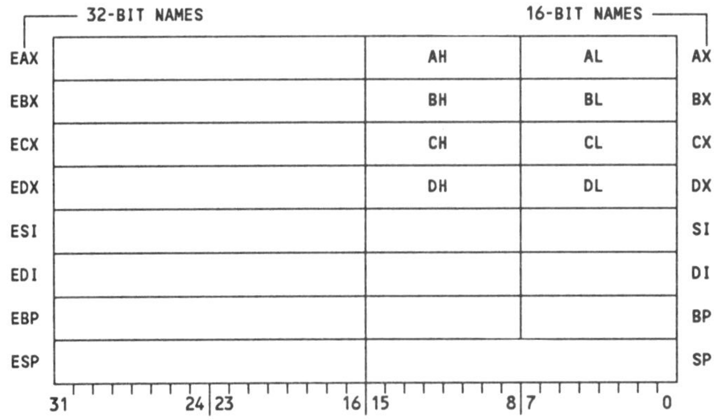

Figure 2-2. 80386 Register Set

chip than is normally used in the IBM AT. OS/2 will also run on an 80386, but only in 80286 mode; many of the 32-bit features of the 80386 are still denied to OS/2 applications. (Perhaps there will be an OS/3 in the future.)

Since the *raison d'etre* of OS/2 has largely to do with 8086 memory limitations, it's important to understand how the 8086 and 80286 differ in this area. The 8086 addressing method is called *real mode*, while the 80286 uses a method called *protected mode*. Next we'll examine each method in detail.

2.2 Real Addressing Mode

When the 8086 was being designed in the late 1970s, it was envisioned as a 16-bit version of the 8085, the most advanced member of Intel's 8080 microprocessor family. That is, the 8086 was to have a full set of 16-bit registers, whereas the 8085 had mostly 8-bit registers. The 8085, however, could generate 16-bit memory addresses, and that would continue to be the case with the 8086.

But somewhere along the way, the 8086 designers decided to expand its addressing capability, while preserving its 16-bit register structure. They accomplished this by defining a *segmented* addressing scheme and adding four *segment registers* to the processor. So, for each memory reference, the processor automatically performs the computation shown in Figure 2-3, producing a 20-bit address capable of spanning one megabyte of memory. The procedure to do this requires the following steps:

- Choose the 16-bit *segment* value. Unless an explicit segment register is

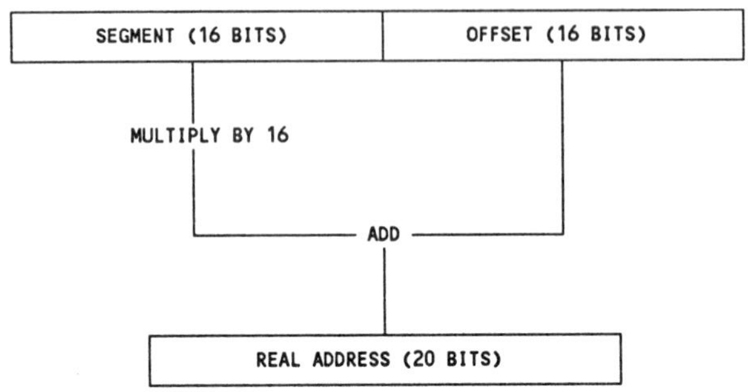

Figure 2-3. Real-Mode Address Computation

specified in the current instruction, this choice is made via the following rules:

- Use CS for instruction fetches.
- Use DS for data fetches.
- Use SS for stack access, including pushing, popping, and addressing via the BP register, which normally points to the current stack frame.
- Use ES for the destination address in string instructions.

- Choose or compute the 16-bit *offset* value. This can come directly from the instruction pointer, a register, or the data portion of the current instruction. It can also be the result of a computation involving some or all of these.
- Shift the segment value left four bits, that is, multiply it by 16.
- Add the offset value.
- Use only the rightmost 20 bits of this computation as the target memory address.

This method of address computation is called *real mode* because the segment registers contain real addresses. That is, the value in a segment register refers directly to a 16-byte area, often called a *paragraph*, in the one-megabyte address space. In protected mode, as we'll see later, the value in the segment register has no direct relationship to the "real" address of the data.

A real-mode address is conventionally written as a pair of hexadecimal numbers separated by a colon. This is called the *segment:offset* form, since the first number is the segment and the second is the offset. An interesting characteristic of *segment:offset* addressing is that each byte in memory has 4096 valid addresses. For example, 0040:0000, 0000:0400, 0001:03F0, and 0002:03E0 all refer to the same location. If you perform the real-mode address calculation as I just described, these combinations all produce a 20-bit address whose hexadecimal value is 00400. This final result is called the *physical address*, while the *segment:offset* form is called a *logical address*.

The fact that each physical address has 4096 logical addresses is used by many 8086 programs to avoid problems with segment boundaries. Suppose, for example, that you want to copy a block of data using the 8086 "move string" instruction. If the source *segment:offset* address is in the DS:SI registers, the destination address is in ES:DI, and the number of bytes is in CX, it would seem that you could simply execute these two instructions:

```
CLD                 ; clear direction flag
REP MOVSB           ; move the string of bytes
```

The first instruction clears the direction flag, thereby causing subsequent string instructions to increment the SI and/or DI registers. The second instruction moves bytes from the source to the destination, incrementing SI and DI after each byte is moved.

Now this is deceptively simple, because these two lines of code will not work correctly in many cases. For instance, take the case where CX contains a hexadecimal value of 100 (i.e., 256 decimal) and DS:SI contains 0000:FFF0, which means that the source block extends from 0000:FFF0 to 1000:00EF. Since the block start address is only 16 bytes from the end of a segment, DS:SI will contain 0000:0000 after the first 16 bytes have been moved, because the 8086 *never* increments or decrements segment registers automatically. So, the processor stupidly continues to copy 240 more bytes from locations 0000:0000 through 00EF, which is not at all what you want. This is known as a *segment overrun* bug.

To avoid segment overruns, DOS compilers and careful programmers working in assembly language usually test *segment:offset* addresses at appropriate points in the program. And to simplify these tests, the addresses are first *normalized* to the form whose offset value is less than 16, thereby ensuring that up to 65520 bytes can be addressed without changing the segment register. In other words, you normalize by choosing, from the 4096 possibilities, the address whose offset portion has its upper 12 bits reset. Here's the previous example with code introduced to avoid a segment overrun:

```
MOV     AX,SI           ; get high 12 bits of DS:SI offset
SHR     AX,1            ; right adjust them
SHR     AX,1
SHR     AX,1
SHR     AX,1
MOV     BX,DS           ; add to DS:SI segment
ADD     AX,BX
MOV     DS,AX
AND     SI,15           ; reset high 12 bits of offset
MOV     AX,DI           ; get high 12 bits of ES:DI offset
SHR     AX,1            ; right adjust them
SHR     AX,1
SHR     AX,1
SHR     AX,1
MOV     BX,ES           ; add to ES:DI segment
ADD     AX,BX
MOV     ES,AX
AND     DI,15           ; reset high 12 bits of offset
CMP     CX,65520        ; check block size
JA      ERROR           ; error if above 65520
JCXZ    ERROR           ; error if full 64K
CLD                     ; clear direction flag
REP MOVSB               ; move the string of bytes
```

Notice that once both addresses have been normalized, it's very easy to check if the block size in CX will cause a segment overrun. That is, if the block size is less than 65520, then no normalized address will cause a segment overrun.

This topic of segment overruns and normalization is very important when you convert programs from the DOS real-mode environment to the OS/2 protected-mode environment. Many DOS programs are rife with normalization code, but it's totally useless in protected mode. In fact, if you tried to run this example in protected mode, the program would either get aborted because of a memory addressing error, or else it would mutilate some portion of your address space. And yet, you must be just as careful about segment boundaries in protected mode, as we'll see next.

2.3 Protected Addressing Mode

When operating in protected mode, the 80286 processor can access up to 16 megabytes of memory, using a 24-bit physical address. Figure 2-4 shows how these 24 bits are derived from the 32-bit logical addresses used by the software.

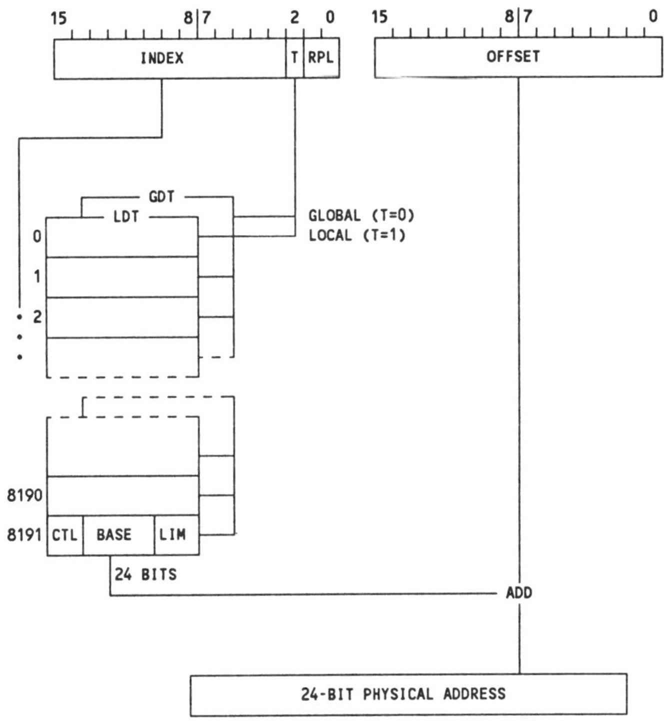

Figure 2-4. Protected-Mode Address Computation

As with real mode, a logical address consists of 16 bits from a segment register and a 16-bit offset, which can come from the instruction pointer, a general register, the current instruction, or a memory location. But while the segment register for real mode is simply the address of a 16-byte paragraph, in protected mode it contains three components, which together are called the *segment selector* or the *selector*, for short.

Examining Figure 2-4, note that only two of the three selector components are actually used to determine the physical address. First the *Table Identifier*

(T) in bit 2 selects one of the two *segment descriptor tables*. Then the *Segment Index* (INDEX) in bits 3 through 15 selects one of the possible 8192 *segment descriptors* in that table.

Figure 2-5 shows that the descriptor is eight bytes long and contains, among other things, the 24-bit base address of the segment. The processor adds the offset from the logical address to the base address from the descriptor, thereby producing the 24-bit physical address.

Now we'll examine this address translation procedure in more detail, including the various accessing checks that are made along the way. Memory access checks enable the operating system to erect barriers between itself and the applications that are sharing the system, as well as between the applications themselves. This prevents application programs from intentionally or accidentally interfering with the operating system or with each other, which is why this addressing method is called *protected mode*.

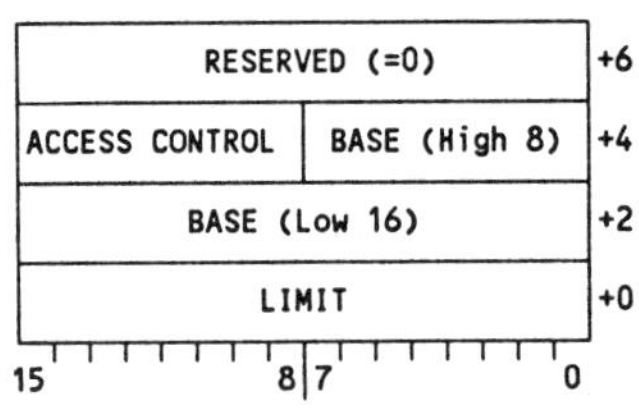

Figure 2-5. Segment Descriptor

2.3.1 Segment Descriptor Tables

Figure 2-4 shows that the Table Index bit selects one of two descriptor tables. OS/2 uses the *General Descriptor Table*, or GDT, for public information that is available, with appropriate accessing restrictions, to all programs. The *Local Descriptor Table*, or LDT, then refers to segments that are of interest only to a single program or to a set of closely cooperating programs. Each time OS/2 switches to a different program, it also switches to a different LDT. Most of the addresses you'll see as an OS/2 application programmer will have the T bit set, because application programs generally use "local addresses" mapped through the LDT rather than the "global addresses" mapped through the GDT.

Incidentally, in OS/2 jargon an active program is called a *process*, which is the term we will use from now on. The next chapter covers this and other OS/2 naming conventions.

As I mentioned earlier, the GDT and LDT can each be up to 64 kilobytes (i.e., one segment) long and can be located anywhere in the 16-megabyte physical address space. The operating system tells the processor how to find the GDT by loading the *GDT register*, or GDTR, which is shown in Figure 2-6. This register contains the 24-bit physical address of the GDT and a 16-bit item specifying the GDT size in bytes.

The location of the LDT is also specified by a register, which in this case is called the LDTR. Referring to Figure 2-6, note that the LDTR has a "visible" portion, which the operating system loads with a selector referring to the GDT; that is, the table index bit must always be reset in the LDTR. In addition, it has a 40-bit "hidden" portion consisting of the 24-bit base address of the LDT and the 16-bit LDT length. When the operating system loads the visible part, the processor automatically loads the hidden part from the GDT. Subsequent references to the LDT do not need to first access the GDT.

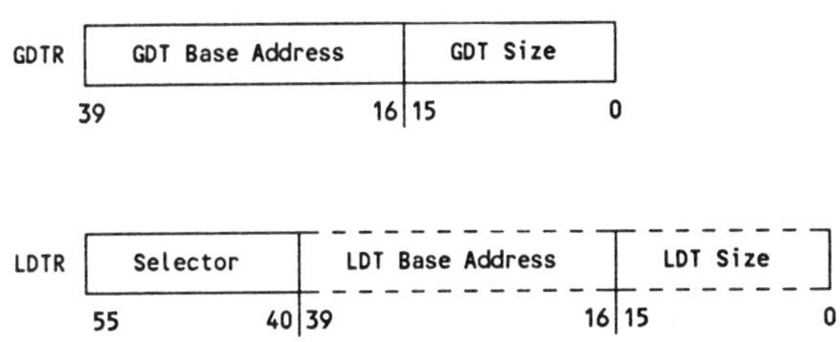

Figure 2-6. GDT and LDT Registers

It might seem strange that the LDTR must be translated through the GDT. Why not load it with a physical address and handle it just like the GDTR? Actually, this approach makes a lot of sense from the viewpoint of the operating system designer. Physical memory is a precious resource that OS/2 must manage very efficiently, and this requires frequent examination and changing of the LDTs. By having them all mapped into the GDT, OS/2 can handle this chore very efficiently. Also, the selector value that defines a process's LDT descriptor in the GDT can be used as a unique tag to identify that process.

2.3.2 Segment Descriptors

During the translation from logical to physical address, the 13-bit INDEX portion of the selector indicates which of the 8192 possible descriptors in the GDT or LDT is being selected. The processor then uses the descriptor information in the following way:

- Verify that the memory area defined by this descriptor can be accessed by the current process.
- For a normal segment, verify that the offset portion of the logical address is less than the size of the memory area as specified in the first 16 bits of the descriptor. For a stack segment, which expands downward, verify that the offset is equal to or greater than the complement of the size.
- Add the offset to the base address specified in the next 24 bits of the descriptor, producing the 24-bit target physical address.

If the processor had to actually fetch a descriptor from memory during each logical address conversion, performance would be terrible. To prevent this, each segment register has a 48-bit hidden portion, called the *segment descriptor cache*, shown in Figure 2-7. Whenever the contents of a segment register changes, its descriptor cache is automatically loaded with the first six bytes of the descriptor.

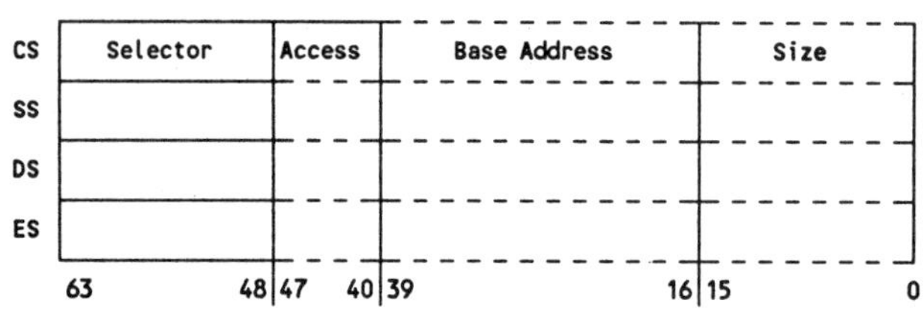

Figure 2-7. Segment Descriptor Cache

Of course, in order for this loading operation to succeed, the selector must specify a valid descriptor. And so, when the program attempts to place a new value in a segment register, the processor checks the GDTR or LDTR to verify that index portion of the selector, multiplied by 8, is less than the GDT or LDT size, whichever is appropriate. Several other access checks are also made at this time, as we'll see in the next section. If any of these fail, a *protection violation* interrupt occurs, and the operating system takes some corrective action, such as aborting the program. This is why you cannot use segment registers for temporary storage in protected mode; only valid selectors should be placed into segment registers.

The descriptor cache mechanism makes protected-mode address translation almost as fast as real mode. However, you must always remember that it is much more costly to load a segment register in protected mode, because the processor must copy six bytes of the descriptor from memory into the cache. That is why some DOS programs suffer serious performance loss when they are moved to OS/2 protected mode.

2.3.3 Access Control Information

The sixth byte of each segment descriptor contains information that controls the access to that segment. The format of this byte, shown in Figure 2-8, varies slightly, depending on whether the descriptor refers to a code segment or a data segment. First we'll describe the common information and then look at code and data segments separately.

Bit 7 - Present Flag
The *present flag* is set when the descriptor refers to a segment that is actually in physical memory. Unused descriptors must have this flag reset. Also, OS/2 resets bit 7 if the segment has been temporarily swapped out to a disk file. When a program loads a segment register with a selector for a segment that is not present, the processor generates an interrupt. OS/2 fields this interrupt and either brings the segment into memory if it was swapped out or aborts the program if the segment is not defined.

Bits 5 and 6 - Descriptor Privilege Level
The *descriptor privilege level* is a part of the 80286 *protection ring* mechanism that is presented in the next section.

Bit 4 - Segment Flag
The *segment flag* must be set to indicate that this descriptor is for a code or data segment and not for a *call gate*, which is a topic that we'll discuss later.

Bit 2 - Executable Flag
This bit is set for a code segment and reset for a data segment. Only code segment selectors can be loaded into the CS register. If you at-

tempt to load CS with a selector for a non-code segment, a protection violation occurs. This means that you cannot construct code in a data segment and then call it, as some DOS programs do. You must first ask the operating system to mark the segment as executable, thereby converting it from a data segment to a code segment. OS/2 provides a simple means to do this via the *DosCreateCSAlias* function.

Bit 0 - Accessed Flag
The processor sets the *accessed flag* in the memory copy of the descriptor whenever the descriptor has been successfully loaded into a segment register cache. This is the only bit in the descriptor that the processor can change automatically. OS/2 comes around periodically and checks this flag to determine which segments are being used. Those that aren't being accessed very often become candidates to be swapped out to disk when some memory must be freed up.

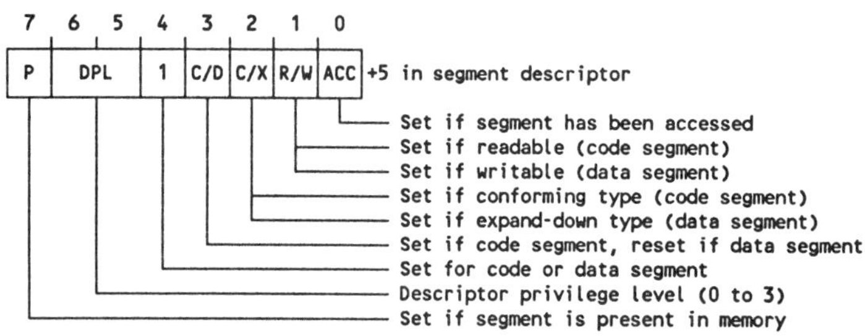

Figure 2-8. Segment Access Control Byte

Code Segments

Code segments are usually accessed via selectors placed in the CS register. Once loaded, CS only changes when a *far jump, far call, far return* instruction is executed or when an interrupt occurs. Explicit loading of CS by *MOV* and *POP* instructions is not allowed in protected mode, and so DOS programs using these techniques must be changed.

It is also possible to read code segments, if the descriptor access control byte is set up correctly. Bits 1 and 2 of the this byte have the following meanings for code segments:

Bit 2 - Conforming Flag
This flag, like the descriptor privilege level in bits 5 and 6, is part of the *protection ring* mechanism for code segments, discussed later.

Bit 1 - Readable Flag
The *readable flag* is set if the segment can be read. Otherwise, the code in the segment can only be executed, which is a nice feature for certain programs that should not be copied or "reverse-engineered". You cannot load a code segment selector into DS, ES, or SS unless the segment is defined as readable.

Notice that there is no flag to indicate that a code segment can be written. They cannot, because all code segments in protected mode are expected to remain "pure" so they can be used by several different processes at the same time. If you have any DOS programs that are self-modifying, they cannot be moved to OS/2 protected mode unless you eliminate the writes to the code segments.

Data Segments

Data segments are accessed via selectors placed in the DS, ES, and SS registers; a protection violation occurs if you attempt to place a data segment selector into CS. Bits 1 and 2 of the access control byte are used in the following way for data segments:

Bit 2 - Expand Down Flag
This flag is set if the segment expands downward instead of upward. Normally a segment is addressed from offset 0 through SIZE-1, where SIZE is the 16-bit segment size contained in the descriptor. However, if this flag is set, then the segment is addressed with offsets that begin at 65535 (i.e. hexadecimal FFFF) and continue downward through 65536-SIZE. This latter offset value is actually the 16-bit one's complement of SIZE.

Downward expansion is typically used for the stack segment, since the Intel processors all have register stacks that grow downward from offset FFFF. By starting the stack at the high-offset end of a segment, it is easy to add more space when the stack overflows.

Bit 1 - Writable Flag
The *writable flag* is set if the segment can be written. If this flag is reset, any attempt to write in the segment is treated as a protection violation.

2.3.4 Privilege Levels

The 80286 has four *privilege levels* numbered from 0 to 3, with level 0 being the most privileged. Sometimes these levels are called *protection rings* because they are shown as a set of concentric circles, with the innermost circle containing the most privileged programs.

"Privileges to do what?", you're probably asking. Well, the goal here is to give the operating system total control of the basic system resources: processor, memory, and I/O. We've already discussed how the GDT and LDT control an application's ability to access memory. Privilege levels, then, control its ability to do the following things:

- Block interrupts, which would enable the program to commandeer the processor and prevent other programs and/or the operating system from running;
- Change the GDT, LDT, or related processor control registers, which would enable the program to overide the memory access controls established by the operating system;
- Execute I/O instructions, which would enable the program to get around the operating system's management of peripheral devices.

OS/2 accomplishes this control by assigning code segments to privilege levels that are appropriate to their purpose, as follows:

Level 0 Code segments containing the fundamental OS/2 resource management routines, interrupt handlers, and I/O drivers. These segments are collectively known as the *OS/2 kernel.*

Level 1 Not used.

Level 2 Code segments for processes that must perform direct I/O operations. This is known as the *I/O privilege level,* or IOPL.

Level 3 Code segments for normal processes.

The typical OS/2 application programmer always works at level 3 and rarely needs to be concerned about the other privilege levels. If that's the case for you, then you don't need to know anything more about privilege levels. However, if you plan to design I/O drivers, or if your application needs to access I/O devices in a special way, you should be familiar with this fairly complex protection scheme.

Four distinct 2-bit items, plus a 1-bit item, come into play when the processor makes privilege level checks:

IOPL - I/O Privilege Level
This item is located in bits 12 and 13 of the processor's status flag register. It can only be changed by a program, usually the operating system, executing at privilege level 0. IOPL indicates the lowest privilege level that can block interrupts and execute I/O instructions. OS/2 usually sets this item to a value of 2, indicating that levels 0, 1, and 2 have I/O privileges.

DPL - Descriptor Privilege Level
The DPL is located in bits 5 and 6 of each segment descriptor access control byte, as discussed earlier. The operating system sets this item to an appropriate value when it constructs the descriptor.

CPL - Current Privilege Level
The CPL is the privilege level of the program that is currently executing. This item is located in bits 0 and 1 of the CS register. It is normally copied there from the DPL item in the code segment descriptor whenever CS changes.

RPL - Requested Privilege Level
The RPL is essentially bits 0 and 1 of any selector. The term "requested privilege" refers to the fact that when a program attempts to load a selector into a segment register, it is requesting the processor to grant it the privileges associated with the RPL value.

Conforming Flag
This flag is in bit 2 of the access control byte for a code segment descriptor. Its use is described later.

Now let's examine how these five items are used to protect the critical system resources.

Data Segment Accesses

The protection ring mechanism is pretty simple for data segments. Whenever you try to load a new selector into DS, ES, or SS, the processor checks if both CPL and RPL are numerically less than or equal to DPL. In other words the current privilege level and the requested privilege level must each be at least as high as the descriptor privilege level.

Note that since level 0 is the highest privilege level, the processor must use a "numerically less than or equal to" test. This can sometimes cause confusion. For instance, we say that the DPL is at a *higher* level than the CPL when it has a *lower* value.

The use of RPL might also be a bit confusing here. Actually this is a part of the protection scheme requiring some cooperation from programs that run at several levels and pass data pointers. RPL is intended to reflect the CPL of the routine that "owns" the data pointer. Suppose routine A is running at level 3 and calls routine B, running at level 2, to copy some data. But routine A, being sneaky, supplies B with a pointer whose RPL has a value of 2 and which refers to a segment whose DPL is also 2. Should B use that pointer to copy data? No, because A does not have the right to access a segment whose DPL is 2.

To prevent this *Trojan horse* problem, privileged routines should always examine, and possibly downgrade, the RPL in caller-supplied pointers. The 80286 designers thoughtfully provided the *adjust RPL* (ARPL) instruction to do this, as shown here:

```
FUNC    PROC    FAR
        PUSH    BP              ; save frame pointer
        MOV     BP,SP           ; load new frame pointer
        MOV     AX,[BP+4]       ; get caller's CS
        ARPL    [BP+8],AX       ; adjust RPL of pointer
```

In this example, the caller places a 32-bit pointer on the stack and then enters the function via a *far call*. Before using the pointer, *FUNC* first gets the caller's CS register, which was saved on the stack by the *far call*. Then it uses ARPL to make sure that the pointer's RPL is numerically equal to or greater than the caller's CPL, which is in bits 0 and 1 of the caller's CS. For instance, if the caller's CPL is 3, then the RPL will contain 3 after the ARPL instruction. If *FUNC* later passes the pointer on to another routine at level 1 or 0, the RPL will will still reflect the original caller's privilege level, not that of *FUNC*.

Code Segment Accesses

The protection ring mechanism is quite a bit more complex when applied to code segments, although it starts out with a simple rule: A program can only change its CS register by executing a *far jump*, a *far call*, or a *far return*. As long as the new code selector refers to a valid segment at the same privilege level, execution will proceed. This assumes, of course, that the instruction pointer is within the segment limit.

Only the *far call* and *far return* are allowed to change the current privilege level; an attempt to make a *far jump* to a different privilege level causes a protection violation. A *far call* can only be made to code segments at the current privilege level or above, while a *far return* can only go a code segment at the current level or lower.

Now here's where it gets complicated, but this next feature is one of the most important aspects of the 80286 in the OS/2 environment, for it facilitates the use of *dynamic link libraries*, which is the basis for the extendable *OS/2 Application Programmer Interface*, or API. These following rules apply to *non-conforming* code segments, that is, to those having bit 2 reset in their access control bytes. The rules for *conforming* code segments are slightly different, as we'll see later.

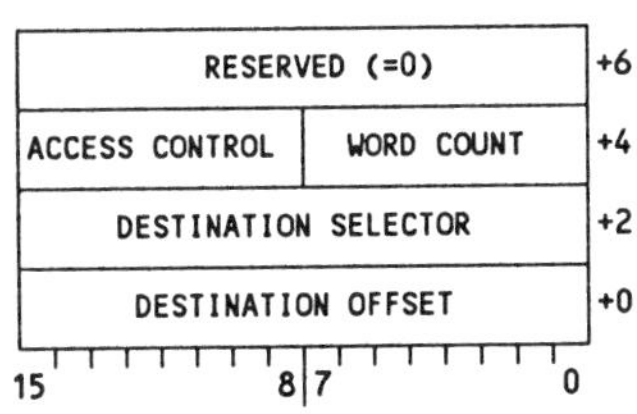

Figure 2-9. Call Gate Descriptor

You cannot make a direct *far call* into a code segment with a higher privilege level; control must must pass through a *call gate*, which is a *pseudo-address* whose segment descriptor has the form shown in Figure 2-9. From the caller's viewpoint, the call gate *is* the address of the function being called; and from the function's viewpoint, it just gets entered in the normal way. However, when the processor detects that a call gate has been reached, it performs a complicated series of operations:

- Verify that the caller's CPL and RPL are each numerically less than or equal to the DPL of the call gate. If either is greater, signal a protection violation.
- Load CS:IP with the *selector:offset* from the call gate descriptor. CS now refers to the *target code segment*.

- Perform the normal memory access checks on the target address. That is, make sure that the target code segment is present in memory and that the offset is within the segment size limit.
- If the caller is more privileged than the target code segment, signal a protection violation because call gates are only supposed to be used to enter code segments with the same or greater privileges.
- If the caller's privilege level is the same as that of the target code segment, proceed with the JMP or CALL instruction. This is known as an *intra-level control transfer.*
- If the caller is less privileged than the target code segment, switch to the stack specified in the *Task State Selector*, or TSS, for the target segment's privilege level. Then save the caller's SS:SP on the new stack, and copy the number of words specified in byte 4 of the call gate descriptor from the caller's stack to the new stack. Finally, push the return address onto the new stack, and enter the function at the new privilege level. Figure 2-10 shows the old and new stacks for a call gate function that accepts three words as parameters. Note that the processor cannot copy more than 31 words from the caller's stack. If more words are needed, the function must use the caller's SS:SP, stored on the function's stack, to get the rest of them.

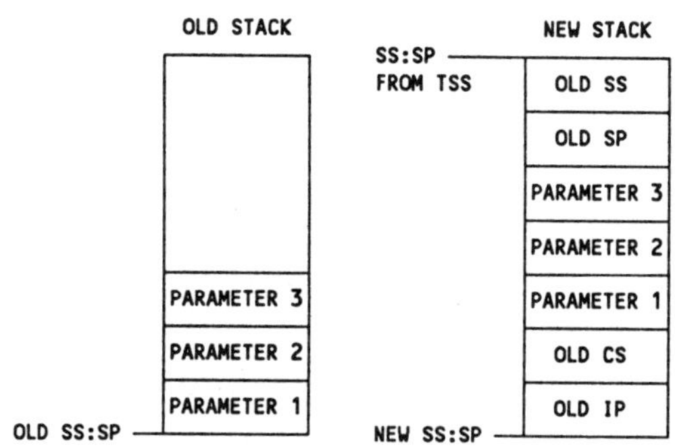

Figure 2-10. Call Gate Stack Switching

The Task State Selector is a memory area in which the operating system keeps information about the current process. Since the layout of this area is mainly of interest to operating system designers, it's not necessary to get into the details here. For our purposes, we need only note that the TSS defines a separate stack for each privilege level at which the current process can operate.

Eventually the function reached via the call gate will execute a *far return* instruction to pass control back to the caller. When the processor detects that the code segment being returned to is at a lower privilege level (i.e. its DPL is numerically greater than the function's CPL), it performs the following operations:

- Restore SS:SP from the next two words of the current stack.
- Adjust SP by the number of words specified in the *far return* instruction. Normally, this value matches the *word count* value in byte 4 of the call gate.
- Check DS and ES. If either refers to a segment whose DPL is numerically less than the new CPL, load it with a null selector, which contains a value of zero. A null selector in DS or ES invalidates that segment register's cache so that the less privileged code cannot continue to use data that were previously approved for access by the privileged function.
- If all of the previous checks pass, return to the caller at the lower privilege level.

So, call gates provide a controlled way for programs to elevate their privilege level, and they guarantee that the privileged code is entered only at valid points. Typically, this feature is used to call operating system service functions, such as I/O drivers, file managers, memory allocators, and so on. OS/2 refers to this collection of service routines as the Application Program Interface, or API. Because of call gates, an OS/2 application program, unlike its DOS counterpart, cannot cause a crash by accidentally jumping into the middle of the operating system.

Conforming Code Segments

If bit 2 is set in the access control byte for a code segment, then the segment is said to be *conforming*. In that case, the normal protection level rules previously described are changed in several important ways.

First of all, you are allowed to make a *far call* or a *far jump* directly into a conforming segment without passing through a call gate. The only requirement is that the CPL must be numerically greater than or equal to the DPL of the conforming segment; that is, you must not be executing at a higher privilege level. After the *far call* or *far jump*, the CPL remains the same. In other words, the privilege level *conforms* to that of the caller.

Next, if a conforming segment calls another segment, the intersegment return receives special handling. The new CPL is set to the RPL of the return address or to the DPL of the conforming segment, depending on which is numerically greater. So, the conforming segment will revert to the privilege level it had when it made the call.

Finally, if a conforming segment is marked as readable, it can be read from any privilege level.

Now what good is a conforming segment, since it seems to circumvent many of the privilege checks? This facility is most commonly used to store common subroutines and data tables that can be used from any privilege level. Such subroutines must not take on privileges greater than their callers, and so the call gate mechanism is inappropriate.

2.4 DOS-to-OS/2 Conversion Rules

The main purpose of this chapter has been to contrast the DOS and OS/2 processor environments. DOS is essentially an 8086 operating system, regardless of which Intel processor is actually being used. OS/2 is designed for the 80286, although it can be used on the 80386 and, presumably, future members of the Intel processor family.

If you plan to convert DOS real-mode programs to the OS/2 protected mode, you must observe some basic programming rules that arise from the fundamental differences between the 8086 and 80286:

Do not push the SP register.
On the 8086, SP is decremented by two before being pushed, while on the 80286 it is decremented after being pushed. This difference applies regardless of whether the 80286 is in real or protected mode, and so it can prevent some DOS programs from working in the DOS compatibility mode provided by OS/2.

Do not use privileged instructions.
The IN, OUT, CLI, and STI instructions will cause protection violations if used in normal OS/2 protected-mode programs. OS/2 provides a means to obtain I/O privileges if you really need to block interrupts or directly access I/O ports.

Do not rely on timing loops.
This is a bad practice in general, because the time delay will vary from one Intel processor type to another. In OS/2, the problem is compounded by multitasking. All timing should be derived via operating system calls except in some very special cases usually found only in I/O drivers.

Do not use the segment registers for temporary storage.
If you attempt to put anything other than a valid selector in a segment register, your OS/2 program will be aborted with a protection violation.

Do not attempt to "normalize" addresses.
Protected-mode selectors must be used in exactly the form that they are provided by the operating system, or else protection violations will occur. You must use methods other than normalization to avoid segment overruns in protected mode.

Do not attempt to directly load the CS register.
In protected mode, CS can only be changed by a *far jump*, *far call*, *far return*, or as the result of an interrupt.

Do not attempt to execute data.
Some DOS programs build instructions in a data segment and then call or jump to them. This will cause a protection violation in OS/2. You must first inform OS/2 that you want to execute a data segment by calling *DosCreateCSAlias*.

Note that you'll run into these situations only if you program in assembly language. If you use a high-level language such as C or Pascal, then the compiler should take care of these things automatically.

Of course, there are many other conversion rules that are due to the operating system differences. These will be mentioned in Chapter 5, where we discuss the techniques for converting DOS programs to OS/2, and in later chapters where we discuss the OS/2 programming features.

Chapter 3

OS/2 Features

OS/2 provides a single-user multitasking environment on Intel 80286 and 80386 processors. It is oriented towards integrated workstations like the IBM-AT and IBM Personal System/2, which contain at least two megabytes of main memory, a hard disk, a keyboard, a high-performance display, and, optionally, a mouse-like pointing device. The traditional PC peripherals are also supported, including printers, plotters, modems, and network adaptors. Like DOS, OS/2 allows I/O drivers to be installed during system initialization, which means that other devices can be supported if you install the appropriate drivers.

IBM produces two editions of OS/2. The Standard Edition (SE) contains the basic operating system and a sophisticated human interface package known as the Presentation Manager. These are shipped as two different versions: SE 1.0, which is just the basic operating system, and SE 1.1, which includes the Presentation Manager. The Extended Edition (EE) adds a Communication Manager and a Database Manager. EE is also available as EE 1.0 and EE 1.1, with the latter containing the Presentation Manager.

Microsoft also supplies a version of OS/2 similar to IBM's Standard Edition, and other software developers will undoubtedly offer many OS/2 enhancements such as network managers.

This book covers only the basic operating system, which IBM calls OS/2

Standard Edition 1.0. It concentrates on the more than 200 service functions that SE 1.0 provides to programmers – the so-called *Standard Application Program Interface*, or SAPI. As we'll see in the next chapter, OS/2 is designed in such a way that the SAPI can be extended to accommodate new subsystems like the Presentation Manager, Communication Manager, and Database Manager just mentioned. Furthermore, a subset of the SAPI has been defined to be compatible with DOS, the predecessor of OS/2. This subset is called the *Family Application Program Interface*, or FAPI.

IBM and Microsoft have guaranteed the software development community that they will keep the standard API identical in their respective versions of OS/2. Microsoft has also promised to keep their Presentation Manager API compatible with IBM's. Therefore, you can develop application software for the IBM Standard Edition with reasonable assurance that it will also run on most non-IBM computers that use Microsoft's OS/2.

This chapter takes a quick tour of the many OS/2 features. Subsequent chapters then get into more detail on topics of importance to OS/2 programmers.

3.1 Multitasking

A major goal of OS/2 is to handle more than one application at a time. For example, you should be able to initiate a long series of compilations in the background while you edit some other source code in the foreground. Then, if your boss stops by and asks for a quick project estimate, you should be able to temporarily suspend the text editor in order to run a project management program.

OS/2 supports this type of operation by treating each application as a *session* running in its own *virtual PC*. That is, each application can behave as if it has the entire PC to itself, including the keyboard, screen, and mouse. This architecture is shown in Figure 3-1.

OS/2 includes a *Session Manager* which serves as an umpire for these multiple applications, determining which one gets to use the real keyboard, screen, and mouse at any moment. The Session Manager monitors the keyboard and mouse in order to receive directions from the user, who can request that sessions be added or deleted and can also dictate which one should be visible.

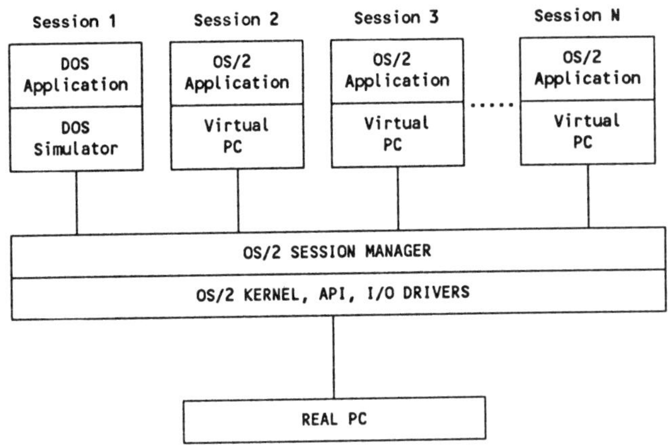

Figure 3-1. OS/2 Session Management

OS/2 can be configured to include a single session that runs in real mode and contains a DOS simulator. This allows many programs written for DOS Version 3 to run under OS/2 with no changes, and these DOS applications can share the system with other applications written specifically for OS/2 protected mode. Of course, since the 80286 allows only one real-mode session, only one DOS program can be running under OS/2 at any time.

As Figure 3-2 shows, each protected-mode session contains one or more *processes*, and each process contains one or more *threads*. The computing resources needed by the application (e.g. memory, I/O) are allocated to the processes in that session. The threads then consume processor time (i.e. CPU cycles) as the application goes about its business. Now let's look at sessions, processes, and threads in a little more detail.

3.1.1 Sessions

After system initialization, the Session Manager presents a menu like the one shown in Figure 3-3. The right side of the screen identifies the sessions that are currently active, while the left side lists the programs that you can choose to run in a new session. OS/2 typically begins with only the DOS session active.

To start a new session, you simply use the cursor and ENTER keys or the mouse to select an item from the left side. OS/2 then creates a new session and places it in the foreground, thereby giving that session control of the

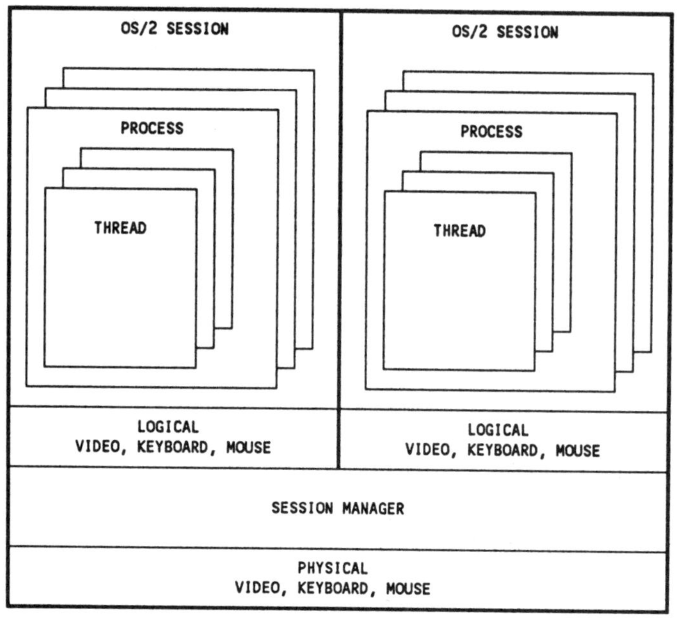

Figure 3-2. Protected-Mode Session Structure

keyboard, screen, and mouse. To get back to the Session Manager screen, hold down the CTRL key and press ESC. You can also use the ALT-ESC key combination to cycle through the active sessions without visiting the Session Manager screen. Figure 3-4 shows the Session Manager screen after several other sessions have been started.

The significance of this session scheme is that each application appears to have its own keyboard, screen, and mouse. While the foreground session is using the real devices, each background session can either continue to operate, using *virtual devices*, or else it can be suspended until it once again returns to the foreground.

Figure 3-2 hints at how this virtual device scheme works. Each session has its own *Keyboard Queue* (KBQ), *Logical Video Buffer* (LVB), and *Mouse Event Queue* (MEQ). These buffer the data for the real keyboard, screen, and mouse when the session is not running in the foreground. Of course, once a background session consumes all buffered keyboard and mouse data, it can

```
UPDATE                                                  F1=Help

                         Program Selector

     To select a program, use arrow keys and then press ENTER.
     To select UPDATE, press F10.   Then, press ENTER.

 Start a program                  Switch to a Running Program

 • Introducing OS/2               • DOS Command Processor
 • OS/2 Command Prompt
 • C Compiler
 • Assembler
 • Linker
 • Editor
 • Word Processor
 • Spreadsheet
```

Figure 3-3. Initial Session Manager Menu

```
UPDATE                                                  F1=Help

                         Program Selector

     To select a program, use arrow keys and then press ENTER.
     To select UPDATE, press F10.   Then, press ENTER.

 Start a program                  Switch to a Running Program

 • Introducing OS/2               • DOS Command Processor
 • OS/2 Command Prompt            • OS/2 Command Prompt 1
 • C Compiler                     • Editor 1
 • Assembler                      • C Compiler
 • Linker                         • Editor 2
 • Editor                         • OS/2 Command Prompt 2
 • Word Processor
 • Spreadsheet
```

Figure 3-4. Session Manager Menu With Several Active Sessions

normally receive no more input from those devices until it is once again in the foreground. If the background session attempts to read more data from the keyboard or mouse, OS/2 will suspend it. The session resumes execution after it once again gets the *keyboard focus* (which is a fancy way of saying that the session is in the foreground).

Since many existing DOS programs interact directly with the I/O devices, the concept of virtual devices cannot be applied to the DOS session. Therefore, this session is always suspended whenever it moves to the background. This, of course, means that OS/2 cannot multitask DOS programs; only protected-mode programs can run in the background.

It's also important to note that the only reason OS/2 cannot support more than one DOS session on the 80286 is because of the limitations of that processor. The 80386 has been designed to handle several DOS sessions, and this feature will probably be added to OS/2 (or perhaps OS/3?), although it was not present in the initial release.

3.1.2 Processes

OS/2 views each session as a collection of *processes*, called a *screen group*, for which it manages the available computing resources. The term *screen group*, of course, refers to the fact that all the processes in a session usually share the same logical video buffer, as shown in Figure 3-2.

A new screen group is created whenever the user selects a program to run from the left side of the Session Manager menu. This program becomes the *parent process* in that group, and it can create *child processes* as necessary to complete its work. Each child is automatically made a member of the parent's screen group, although a process can create a new group (i.e. a new session) if that is appropriate. The Session Manager, for instance, is itself a process whose primary purpose is to create new screen groups.

When OS/2 creates a process, it first examines the program file (i.e. the EXE file) and allocates the memory needed for the program, data, and stack. Next, it loads the EXE file into memory and schedules the process to begin execution at its main entry point. After that, OS/2 handles requests for I/O operations, additional memory, and other services. These requests are all made through the Application Program Interface (API), which is discussed in the next chapter.

The process creation procedure differs slightly if the EXE file has already been loaded into memory for another process. Since 80286 protected mode does not allow code segments to be changed (see Chapter 2), two or more processes can share the same in-memory copy of the EXE file. However, a separate copy of the data and stack segments must be allocated for each process.

This *shared code* feature can, in some cases, greatly reduce the amount of memory needed by an application. For example, an electronic bulletin board system (EBBS) could be implemented as a set of processes, each of which would service one phone line. These processes would all share the same program, which could be fairly simple since it would only have to deal with a single line. In an environment without multitasking, such as DOS, this application would have to be designed to handle all the phone lines itself, using its own form of task management. This would tend to make the program much larger and more complex.

Dynamic linking, another powerful OS/2 feature, is similar to code sharing. It enables you to share commonly-used functions among several processes, even though the processes may be running different programs. The shared functions must be gathered into a *dynamic link library*, or DLL, file that is created by the OS/2 linker and some other utility programs that we'll discuss later. These utilities also produce a LIB file which you mention to the linker when constructing EXE files for programs that use these shared functions. The linker tags all references to these shared functions but does not include the actual function code in the EXE files. Then when OS/2 loads the first of these executables, it detects the references to the shared library, loads the DLL file into memory, and completes the linkage to it. As the other EXE files are loaded, OS/2 simply completes the linkage to the shared library that is already in memory.

The technique of completing linkages while programs are being loaded into memory is what gives rise to the name *dynamic linking*; in other operating systems, this feature has been called *delayed linking*, *deferred linking*, and *run-time binding*. But no matter what you call it, it's an important part of OS/2. In fact, all communication between processes and the operating system – the Application Program Interface – is actually a collection of shared functions that you reference via a file named *doscalls.lib*. Similarly, OS/2 extensions such as the Presentation Manager, Communication Manager, Database Manager, and Network Manager all use dynamic link libraries.

3.1.3 Threads

The steps needed to create a new process are fairly time consuming, and so you should not spawn child processes frivolously. Nonetheless, when you design OS/2 applications, you'll often find it useful to introduce a bit of multitasking. Fortunately, OS/2 allows processes to create *threads*, thereby providing an efficient means to multitask without incurring the cost of setting up new processes.

When a process first starts, it has a single thread which contends with all other threads for use of the processor. If appropriate, this *parent thread* can initiate *child threads*. These share all of the process's resources, including program memory, data memory, and I/O facilities. However, each thread in a process has its own stack and is scheduled as an independent entity by OS/2. That is, when OS/2 has to decide who gets to use the processor next, it examines a list of threads that are ready to run and assigns the processor to the one with the highest priority.

You will find threads to be extremely useful in many applications. For example, a spreadsheet program could have one thread to receive input from the keyboard, another to handle the screen display, and a third to recompute the cell expressions. Since all three threads share the same data space, they can easily coordinate their activities, and by adjusting the thread priorities correctly, you can eliminate most of the user-perceived delays associated with recalculation and screen updating.

3.1.4 Scheduling

In OS/2, as in any multitasking operating system, you must always remember that the processor is a resource being shared by several applications as well as by the operating system itself. So, when the current thread reaches a point where it cannot proceed, such as during a lengthy I/O operation, OS/2 will pass control to another thread. Furthermore, OS/2 will periodically interrupt the current thread to see if a more important one is ready to execute.

Therefore, you must design your applications so that they can be interrupted for lengthy periods by other applications which the user considers to be more important. And even if your application is the most important one in the system, you should not design it in such a way that OS/2 cannot pre-empt it occasionally to do other important work. For instance, you must avoid traditional DOS programming techniques such as blocking interrupts and spinning in loops.

OS/2 employs a fairly sophisticated algorithm for scheduling threads to use the processor. Each thread resides in one of three *priority classes*. The *time-critical* class contains those threads which, when ready, must run as soon as possible. The *regular* class contains, as its name implies, typical application threads which don't have any special response requirements. Finally, the *idle-time* class contains threads that run only when there is no activity in the other two classes.

Each class has 32 *priority levels*, numbered from 0 to 31, with level 31 at the highest priority. OS/2 attempts to optimize the use of system resources (i.e. CPU, memory, and I/O devices) by monitoring all threads and adjusting their priority levels (but not their classes). Threads that are doing a lot of I/O work will gradually attain higher levels so that they will get short bursts of CPU time at the end of I/O operations. But those doing CPU-intensive work (i.e. much computation with little I/O) will drift down to the lower priorities. In this way, the CPU and I/O devices will usually stay as busy as possible.

You can tune your application for optimal performance by choosing the priority classes for its threads. Furthermore, you can specify each thread's initial priority level and can lock the thread at that level so that OS/2 will not automatically adjust it. You can even have your threads dynamically adjust their priority classes and levels as the processing load changes. This flexible scheduling mechanism is one feature of OS/2 that makes it well suited for complex real-time applications such as point-of-sale and factory automation systems.

3.1.5 Multitasking Jargon

So far, we've used the term *multitasking* to refer to the processor sharing technique employed by OS/2. Not surprisingly, the threads that share the processor are often called *tasks*. You'll sometimes hear other terms such as *multiprogramming* and *multithreading*, which are equivalent to *multitasking*. The term *multiprocessing*, however, is different; it refers to the scheduling technique used in a system that contains more than one processor.

Multitasking is one of the main reasons OS/2 was developed. Even though DOS can manage the memory space for several programs, it has no built-in support for sharing the CPU and I/O devices among those programs. DOS is inherently a single-task operating system.

Many clever designers have gotten around this limitation by hooking into the various hardware and software interrupt vectors and forcing DOS to support more than one active program. But this is something like balancing a pyramid on its point; the underlying DOS architecture and the real addressing mode are just not robust enough to support multitasking safely and efficiently. So, I'm not sure what to call these DOS techniques, but they are certainly not multitasking in the OS/2 sense.

3.2 Operating System Services

Even if OS/2 provided only simple multitasking, it would still be a major improvement over DOS. But, as we've seen, its multitasking feature is surprisingly sophisticated and includes some capabilities rarely found in much larger systems, such as shared code, threads, and dynamic linking. In addition, OS/2 offers a rich set of services to application programs running in protected mode. These include:

Interprocess Communication
Cooperating processes often have to communicate with each other in order to coordinate their actions. OS/2 provides a variety of interprocess communication (IPC) techniques, including:

- Signals
- Semaphores
- Message Queues
- Pipes
- Shared Memory

These are listed more or less in the order of increasing bandwidth. That is, if two processes need to exchange a lot of data, they should probably use pipes or shared memory. Occasional handshaking should be done with signals or semaphores. Transaction processing is usually best done via message queues.

Improved Memory Management
Like DOS, OS/2 allows an application to obtain additional memory in order to meet its processing requirements. However, memory management in the protected-mode multitasking environment is much more flexible. The process that owns a segment determines whether that segment is sharable, writable, swappable, and discardable. A sharable segment can be given a global name so that any process can access it, or it can be made available only to specific processes identified by the owner.

OS/2 also provides sub-allocation services for efficiently managing many small blocks within a segment. These services are similar to the heap management functions provided by most high-level languages.

Improved File Management
While the OS/2 file system is compatible with that provided by DOS Version 3, it includes these improvements:

- Fixed disk partitions can be larger than 32 megabytes, although the initial releases of OS/2 enforce the 32-megabyte limit in order to remain compatible with DOS.
- Processes can use *Asynchronous I/O*, which enables them to continue working while the operating system handles their I/O operations.
- File sharing and locking are an integral part of OS/2, as you would expect in a multitasking operating system.
- Each file has three date/time stamps: creation, most recent access, and most recent change. DOS files carry only a single stamp, which is updated whenever the file changes. In order to remain compatible with the DOS file system, the initial versions of OS/2 maintain only one of these stamps. However, a future version will introduce an improved File Manager that will maintain all three stamps.

High-Performance I/O Subsystems
In the DOS environment, interactive applications achieve snappy performance by directly accessing the keyboard, screen, and mouse. However, in the OS/2 multitasking environment, the user would become very confused if several applications tried to do this at the same time. So, OS/2 provides *I/O subsystems* which arbitrate the use of these basic human interface devices in conjunction with the Session Manager. These subsystems are designed so that protected-mode applications can achieve the same high performance that users have come to expect in DOS.

Improved National Language Support
The OS/2 National Language Support (NLS) feature enables you to design applications that can automatically adapt themselves to various countries. Although DOS contains some NLS capabilities, OS/2 does

a better job of handling character set differences in the keyboard, screen, and printer devices. Also, OS/2 includes a message facility with which you can totally separate your on-screen messages from the executable file. Then you can provide message files in several languages, and your application program can choose the appropriate file for the country in which it is executing.

Device Monitors
OS/2 allows you to easily design *monitor processes* which hook into the I/O data streams associated with character devices such as the keyboard and printer. By monitoring a device data stream, this type of process can serve as a *pop-up utility*, a *print spooler*, a *keyboard macro package*, or it can perform any of the other functions that are handled in DOS by so-called *Terminate and Stay Resident*, or TSR, programs. But unlike DOS TSR programs, OS/2 monitors are much less likely to interfere with each other and with the operating system.

Improved I/O Driver Architecture
Like DOS, OS/2 allows you to add or replace I/O drivers. However, OS/2 drivers are considerably more complex, since they must serve both real-mode and protected-mode processes. To simplify the chore of driver design, OS/2 includes an extensive collection of *device helper services*, which form a kind of API for drivers.

As an application programmer, most of your interactions with drivers are indirect, through the File Manager or one of the I/O subsystems. However, the OS/2 API contains a much improved version of the I/O control, or IOCTL, function, which provides direct communication between application processes and I/O drivers. For instance, OS/2 includes comprehensive I/O driver support for serial communication devices (i.e. modems) - a feature that was omitted from DOS. IOCTL is used to control the many parameters associated with these communication devices.

3.3 Command Processor and Standard Commands

In addition to the Session Manager, OS/2 also includes a protected-mode version of the familiar DOS command processor. This serves several important purposes:

- Some people are just more comfortable using a command-line interface, as in DOS, rather than having to choose applications from the Session Manager menu.

- The command processor supports a "programming language" which is quite simple to use, but can handle fairly sophisticated operations without the time and expense of "real programming."
- When you install an application in the Session Manager menu, you can specify the invocation of only a single program. If the application requires that several programs be called in succession, you can construct a *command file* containing those program commands. Then the Session Manager invokes the command processor to execute the command file.

The OS/2 command processor resembles the one from DOS Version 3.3, but it has a few more programming features. One interesting characteristic is that a protected-mode command file must have a CMD extension, while its DOS equivalent, called a *batch file*, has a BAT extension. If you have two files, say *abc.bat* and *abc.cmd* and then type the command

```
abc
```

the former will be executed in real mode, while the latter is executed in protected mode. Thus, the same command can do different things depending on which mode is active.

The OS/2 standard command repertoire is also similar to that of DOS and consists of the following command verbs:

```
+ANSI        *APPEND      *ASSIGN      ATTRIB
 BACKUP      *BREAK        CHCP        CHDIR
 CHKDSK       CLS         +CMD        *COMMAND
 COMP         COPY         CREATEDD    DATE
+DETACH       DIR          DISKCOMP    DISKCOPY
+DPATH        ERASE        EXIT        FDISK
 FIND         FORMAT       GRAFTABL   +HELP
*JOIN         KEYB         LABEL       MKDIR
 MODE         MORE         PATCH       PATH
 PRINT        PROMPT       RECOVER     RENAME
 REPLACE      RESTORE      RMDIR       SET
*SETCOM40     SORT        +SPOOL      +START
*SUBST        SYS          TIME       +TRACE
+TRACEFMT     TREE         TYPE        VER
 VERIFY       VOL          XCOPY
```

The commands marked with a plus sign (+) are new to OS/2 and can be used only in protected mode. Those marked with an asterisk (*) can only be used in real mode.

3.4 System Configuration

Like DOS, OS/2 reads a system configuration file called *config.sys* during initialization. This file contains special commands which establish the working characteristics of the operating system. For example, the RMSIZE command lets you specify the size of the DOS memory area. The configuration file also defines any nonstandard I/O drivers that are to be installed.

Most of the DOS configuration commands have been carried over to OS/2, and many new ones have been added, as shown here:

```
 BREAK            BUFFERS          CODEPAGE         COUNTRY
 DEVICE          +DEVINFO         +DISKCACHE        FCBS
+IOPL            +LIBPATH         +MAXWAIT         +MEMMAN
+PAUSEONERROR    +PRIORITY        +PROTECTONLY     +PROTSHELL
 REM             +RMSIZE          +RUN              SHELL
+SWAPPATH        +THREADS         +TIMESLICE       +TRACE
+TRACEBUF
```

The new OS/2 configuration commands are identified with plus signs.

The OS/2 installation program includes a handy editor for *config.sys*. It presents full-screen displays of the configuration data arranged in logical groups. Any changes that you make are translated back into the appropriate configuration statements, thereby producing an updated *config.sys* file.

3.5 Summary

From this quick tour of the many OS/2 features, you've probably surmised that the new operating system is considerably larger and more complex than DOS. However, with this complexity comes the ability to construct much more ambitious applications than were possible under DOS. In the remaining chapters, I'll highlight these features and show how they can be used to make complex applications more efficient.

Chapter 4

Application Program Interface

In any computing environment, application programs need to call upon the operating system for services such as disk I/O and memory management. The collection of such services, including the technique for calling them, has come to be known as the *Application Program Interface*, or API.

An extendable operating system like OS/2 can have several APIs, and the one provided with the minimal system is often called the *Standard API*, or SAPI. Since this book discusses only the standard API, I'll use terms API and SAPI interchangeably. Later on, we'll see that there is also a DOS-compatible subset of the OS/2 API known as the *Family API*, or FAPI.

In the broadest sense, the standard API includes all methods by which applications can interface with the operating system, not just the techniques for calling service functions. Specifically, both the DOS and OS/2 APIs define protocols for:

- Requesting operating system services such as I/O
- Receiving control from the operating system when the application starts
- Returning control to the operating system when the application finishes
- Connecting I/O drivers to the operating system

This chapter covers the first three of these, and Chapter 12 discusses I/O drivers.

It might seem strange to get into the OS/2 API, which is a programming detail, before delving more deeply into the OS/2 architecture. However, as a programmer I've found that much of my understanding of an operating system is based upon my understanding of its API. And so, in subsequent chapters I'll usually describe the OS/2 features by showing how you access them via the API.

4.1 Operating System Service Functions

Even though OS/2 is a successor to DOS, it uses a service function protocol that is markedly different.

In DOS, as in most other operating systems, the service functions can be conveniently accessed only by assembly language programmers. If you program in a high-level language such as C or Pascal, you must rely upon the compiler to provide the necessary access to the DOS API. Compilers usually provide this access to the mainstream API services through standard language or library features. For example, C programmers usually perform I/O operations via library functions such as *fread*, *fwrite*, and *printf*.

When you want to access a more unusual API service, you are often forced to write your own "glue" function in assembly language. To do this, you must not only learn the API protocol, but you must also know how your compiler interfaces with assembly-language functions. It's true that many DOS compilers provide general-purpose glue functions (e.g., *intdos* and *int86* in most C compiler libraries). But you still need to know the register requirements for the DOS API in order to use these functions, and their use is almost like embedding assembly language in your high-level program.

On the other hand, the OS/2 API functions can be called directly from higher level languages like C and Pascal. As a result, OS/2 application programmers can easily bypass the standard compiler libraries to obtain better performance or to handle special processing needs.

This is the essential difference between the DOS and OS/2 API. Now let's take a more detailed look at each system.

4.1.1 Accessing DOS Service Functions

When DOS was being designed, serious microcomputer applications were usually written in assembly language. It was quite natural, then, for the DOS designers to come up with an API that would appeal to assembly language programmers. What has finally evolved through three versions of DOS is an interface with about 100 services that are accessed with a four-point protocol:

- The application passes data via the machine registers, and DOS returns data in the same way.
- The application passes control to DOS via a software interrupt. The most common DOS services use interrupt 21H (where H means hexadecimal), but the API also includes many other interrupts, such as those which access the Basic I/O Services (BIOS).
- The API routines do not generally preserve the application's register contents.
- The API routines usually indicate errors by setting the carry flag (CF) when they return to the application. In most cases, an error code is also returned in the AX register.

For example, here is a DOS assembly-language function named *dread* which can be called from a C program to read a data block from a file.

```
;************************************************************
;
; name          dread -- Read a block from a file
;
; synopsis      count = dread(fh,buffer,length);
;
;               int count;       actual byte count or -1
;               int fh;          file handle
;               char *buffer;    buffer pointer
;               int length;      buffer length
;
; description   This function reads a block from the file
;               whose handle is given.  The file must be
;               opened for read access.  The data is read
;               into a buffer located in the current data
;               segment, whose address is assumed to be in
;               DS.
;
```

```
;*************************************************************
;
; Stack structure
;
STK    STRUC
       DW     ?                 ; BP save area
       DW     ?                 ; return address
FH     DW     ?                 ; file handle
BLKP   DW     ?                 ; block pointer (offset from DS)
BLKS   DW     ?                 ; block size in bytes
STK    ENDS
;
; Code Segment
;
_TEXT SEGMENT BYTE,PUBLIC,'CODE'
dread PROC
       PUSH     BP              ; save old stack frame pointer
       MOV      BP,SP           ; load new stack frame pointer
       MOV      AH,3FH          ; load type code for read
       MOV      BX,[BP].FH      ; load file handle
       MOV      CX,[BP].BLKS    ; load block size
       MOV      DX,[BP].BLKP    ; load block pointer
       INT      21H             ; call DOS via interrupt
       JNC      EXIT            ; jump if no error
       MOV      AX,-1           ; else return -1
EXIT:  POP      BP              ; restore old frame pointer
       RET
dread ENDP
_TEXT ENDS
       END
```

Notice how the function loads all parameters into registers, issues an interrupt, and then checks the carry flag for an error. Also note that if no error occurs, DOS returns in the AX register a count of the actual number of bytes that were read.

The DOS API is quite efficient, but it has some serious drawbacks. First, as I've mentioned several times already, it is well suited to assembly language, but it cannot be used at all from high-level languages because they do not generally allow direct manipulation of the machine registers and direct execution of interrupt instructions. Second, there are many exceptions to the four-point protocol described earlier. For instance, register usage varies widely, and some API functions don't use the carry flag to indicate errors.

The third point is not obvious from the previous example, but it is perhaps the most serious problem with the DOS API. Since DOS resides in the same memory space as its application programs, many programmers have discovered how to access "secret" data areas and functions within the operating system, and they treat these as part of the API. This can cause mysterious compatibility problems when you try to run the application program under a different but supposedly compatible version of DOS.

4.1.2 Accessing OS/2 Service Functions

The OS/2 designers set out to correct these problems by providing an API that could be called directly from popular high-level languages such as C and Pascal. Since these languages impose strict and consistent function calling protocols, and since high-level functions are fairly easy to document, this type of API is much more accessible to the average programmer. Furthermore, the risk of obscure errors caused by incorrect API calls is greatly reduced because the functions have easily remembered names instead of cryptic numbers and because the compiler can check for valid argument types.

One of the major problems that the OS/2 designers faced was how to link the API function names to the actual service functions in the operating system kernel, which is protected from access by application programs. Under DOS, this problem does not occur because the DOS API is defined in terms of software interrupts and function numbers instead of symbolic names, and because DOS itself resides in the same address space as its applications.

The problem was solved in OS/2 by *dynamic linking*, a technique in which the addresses of the API function names are resolved at execution time to *call gates*, as discussed earlier in Chapter 2. The code associated with these call gates is contained in *dynamic libraries* which are brought into memory as part of the dynamic linking procedure. Then, when the application program calls an API service function, the appropriate privilege-level change occurs because of the call gate, and the code in the dynamic library accesses the kernel in a valid manner.

The use of dynamic libraries for the OS/2 API makes it easy to accommodate operating system extensions such as the network manager and the presentation services, and these need not originate only from Microsoft or IBM. Since the libraries are *dynamic*, an OS/2 extension does not consume any system memory unless it is actually being used by one or more applications.

The standard OS/2 API consists of the several hundred functions listed in the Appendix, each of which is accessed via the following protocol:

- The application program places all parameters on its stack, and if the API function will return any information, the application must pass one or more pointers to the memory areas that will receive the data.
- Pointers (i.e. addresses) are always passed in the full 32-bit *selector:offset* form.
- The API function is accessed via a far call.
- The API function preserves all registers except AX and the status flags.
- As it returns, the API function removes all parameters from the user's stack and passes back an error code in the AX register. This code is 0 for success or non-zero if an error occurred. Note that most compilers use the AX register for return values from functions, and so the error code is available to the high-level-language programmer.

Most general-purpose OS/2 extensions, such as the Presentation Manager, conform to this protocol, although there is nothing in OS/2 that forces such conformance. You could, for example, design an API-like dynamic library whose functions do not return an error code in AX. However, it's difficult to imagine a good reason for deviating from the simple and effective protocol used by the standard API.

Note that the complete OS/2 standard API repertoire is available only to applications running in protected mode. DOS applications running in OS/2's real-mode partition can continue to use the DOS Version 3 API with a few restrictions. In addition, DOS programs can also use a fairly large number of OS/2 API services if they are constructed as *family applications*, which is described in Chapter 15.

Now to illustrate how the OS/2 API works, here is an OS/2 version of the *dread* function written in C:

```
extern far pascal DosRead(short, char far *,
  short, short far *);

dread(fh,buffer,length)
int fh,length;
char *buffer;
{
short actual;
```

```
int retcode;

retcode = DosRead(fh,(char far *)buffer,length,
  (short far *)(&actual));

if(retcode) return(-1);

return((int)actual);
}
```

DosRead is the OS/2 API function that performs the same operation as interrupt 21H, function 3FH, used in the DOS version of *dread*. In the C language, *DosRead* must be declared using the *far* and *pascal* keywords. The *far* keyword tells the compiler to use a far call (i.e. a full 32-bit address) to access the function. The *pascal* keyword indicates that the compiler should push the arguments onto the stack from left to right (C generally goes right to left) and that the function will pop the arguments.

Notice also that whenever you pass a pointer to an API function, it must be converted to a full 32-bit form. Since the *buffer* argument passed to *dread* may not be in that form, you can force the conversion by writing:

```
(char far *)buffer
```

C programmers refer to this as *casting a variable to a different type*. Similarly, the actual byte count word is declared on the stack, and to get a far pointer to it you should write:

```
(short far *)(&actual)
```

Casting of pointers is unnecessary in C programs that use the so-called *large memory model*, because in that case all pointers are in the full 32-bit form. Also, if your C compiler automatically casts arguments to the forms specified in function prototypes, then you do not need to explicitly cast these arguments. However, you must be sure to include the appropriate header files when you compile, or else the OS/2 API function prototypes will not be present, and so the casting will not occur.

I've omitted the casting operations from most of the examples in this book, just to make the API calls a little easier to read. The examples will work correctly if you compile them in the large memory model or if you use a compiler that performs implicit casting based on function prototypes in the OS/2 API header files.

Of course, the OS/2 API does not preclude assembly-language programming, because you can always hand-code in assembly language any instruction sequence generated by a compiler. However, it is definitely more complicated, more tedious, and probably more error prone to access OS/2 via assembly language, as shown by the following version of *dread*:

```
;
; Stack structure
;
STK     STRUC
        DW      ?               ; BP save area
        DW      ?               ; return address
FH      DW      ?               ; file handle
BLKP    DW      ?               ; block pointer
BLKS    DW      ?               ; block size in bytes
STK     ENDS
;
; Code segment
;
_TEXT SEGMENT BYTE,PUBLIC,'CODE'
        EXTRN   DosRead:FAR
        PUBLIC  dread
dread PROC
        PUSH    BP              ; save old stack frame pointer
        MOV     BP,SP           ; load new stack frame pointer
        PUSH    AX              ; reserve word for actual count
        MOV     AX,SP           ; save address of reserved word
        PUSH    [BP].FH         ; push file handle
        PUSH    DS              ; push buffer address
        PUSH    [BP].BLKP
        PUSH    [BP].BLKS       ; push buffer length
        PUSH    SS              ; push pointer to actual count
        PUSH    AX
        CALL    DosRead         ; call OS/2 function
        POP     BX              ; pop actual count
        OR      AX,AX
        JNZ     ERR             ; jump if error
        MOV     AX,BX           ; else return actual count
        POP     BP
        RET
ERR:    MOV     AX,-1           ; come here on error
```

```
        POP     BP
        RET
dread   ENDP
        END
```

If you carefully compare this version of *dread* with the one for DOS, you will see that the OS/2 API is less efficient than its predecessor. That is, it takes more instructions and machine cycles to push arguments onto the stack than to simply place them in registers, and the *far call* is larger and slightly slower than the INT instruction. But this is undoubtedly a reasonable trade-off, because in many cases the ability to directly access the API from a high-level language obviates the need for glue functions which, under DOS, simply pop the arguments right back off the stack and issue the appropriate software interrupt.

4.1.3 OS/2 API Function Names

The OS/2 API functions all have fairly long names which are intended to be easily remembered. I was originally skeptical about this, but after writing a few OS/2 programs, I concluded that the naming scheme is quite logical and should present no problem to an alert programmer, despite the fact that there are more than 200 names to remember.

However, the names seem much more meaningful when you write them in mixed case. For instance, I have an easier time with *DosRead* than with *DOSREAD*. Or how about *VioWrtCharAttr* versus *VIOWRTCHARATTR*? Doesn't the mixed case version make it much clearer that this is a video I/O function that writes a character and an attribute?

Unfortunately, the OS/2 API dynamic link library, *doscalls.lib*, contains all function names in full upper case, as do the C and assembly-language definition files provided in Version 1.0 of the IBM OS/2 Programmer's Toolkit. You can use mixed-case names, but somewhere in the program preparation procedure, these names must be converted to upper case. Most OS/2 assemblers and C compilers provide the means to convert all external symbols to upper case. Some of these also provide definition files that define the symbols in both mixed case and upper case. You can also instruct the OS/2 linker to convert all external symbols to upper case.

Because the pioneering OS/2 application programmers complained about the upper case names, IBM changed them to mixed case in the Version 1.1

Toolkit that works with the Presentation Manager. Therefore, after a false start with Version 1.0, the API naming standard is now mixed case instead of upper case.

As a final note on the OS/2 API function names, let me address a question that is often asked: *Why do most of the API function names begin with "DOS" instead of "OS2"*? There are several reasons. First, the operating system was not named OS/2 until just before its announcement. Previously it had been called ADOS, DOS Version 5, and several other names. So, the "DOS" prefix was pretty well established in the API when the name OS/2 was chosen. A second reason is that "OS2" is not the same as "OS/2", but most programming languages do not allow a slash within a function name. A third reason is that "OS2" is awkward to type, and some people might type a zero instead of the letter O. This mistake is less likely to occur when typing "DOS."

4.2 Program Initiation and Termination

The protocol used to initiate and terminate application programs is a part of the standard API with which few application programmers need to be familiar, because when you use a high-level language, the compiler takes care of this protocol for you.

For example, from a C programmer's viewpoint, execution begins at the function named *main*, which the operating system calls with two arguments. One of these, usually named *argv*, is an array of pointers to text strings which comprise the command line that the user typed to start the application. The other argument, usually named *argc*, is the number of strings in the array. The first string in the array is the name of the command program file. For example, in the command

```
revise file.1 file.2
```

the verb is "revise" and the residual command line is " file.1 file.2". The operating system searches through the disk directories for an executable file with the name *revise.exe*, which it then proceeds to load and execute.

So if the *revise* program were written in C and resided in the *c:\os2* directory, it would expect *argc* to have a value of 3 and *argv* to contain pointers to the following strings:

argv[0]	"c:\os2\revise.exe"
argv[1]	"file.1"
argv[2]	"file.2"

Now this is very convenient for the C programmer, but it's actually an illusion created by a *start-up routine* that the compiler provides. It is this start-up routine, not the *main* function, that accepts control from the operating system, parses the command line into substrings, constructs *argv* and *argc*, and then calls *main*. When *main* returns, this start-up routine passes control back to the operating system in the correct way. Most C compiler vendors supply the assembly-language source code for the start-up routine so you can examine or modify it if necessary.

So if you always program in a high-level language, don't bother to clutter your mind with the details of OS/2 initiation and termination. However, if you plan to write applications in assembly language, or if you are forced to do low-level debugging of a high-level program, or if you have to change your compiler's start-up routine, you'll need this information.

As with the API service functions, comparing the DOS initiation/termination protocol with that used by OS/2 can be quite illuminating.

It's not too surprising that the DOS initiation/termination protocol is suitable only for assembly language, since the entire DOS API is oriented towards assembly language. So, when DOS enters a program, the segment registers are not set up in such a way that compiler-generated code can run correctly. The compiler vendor must supply a start-up routine to examine the information that DOS provides in the registers and set things up correctly for the high-level code. Then, when the application program wants to terminate, it must drop back to assembly language in order to execute the appropriate DOS API interrupt. This is also done through a termination routine supplied by the compiler vendor.

What is surprising is that the OS/2 initiation protocol also requires an assembly-language start-up routine. However, OS/2 applications can terminate from within a high-level language routine by making a direct call to an OS/2 API function.

4.2.1 DOS Initiation/Termination Protocol

Before DOS enters an application, it initializes a memory block called the *Program Segment Prefix*, or PSP, with a lot of information about the application. I won't give a detailed description of the PSP here, since that is more appropriate in a book about DOS. Two PSP items, together with the contents of four registers, constitute the information that most applications need at start-up time:

DS Segment address of the PSP;

ES Same as DS;

SS Segment address of the default stack segment within the application;

SP Offset to the top of the default stack;

PSP+2CH Segment address of the environment area, which contains this application's copy of the environment strings, followed by the name of the executable file loaded for this application;

PSP+80H A 128-byte area containing the residual command line, preceded by a length byte.

After setting up these items, DOS executes a *far jump* into the application at the entry point specified in the EXE file, thereby setting up the CS register to point to the application's code segment. Note that this is a *jump*, not a *call*, so you cannot get back to DOS by executing a *RET* instruction.

Usually the start-up routine changes the DS register to point to the application's data segment. Often it will also move the residual command line into that data segment so the application can properly access it with normal data pointers. In the case of the C start-up routine, the residual command line is also broken down into its component parts and passed as the *argv* array.

As I mentioned earlier, C programs can terminate simply by returning from the *main* function. Alternatively, they can call the *exit* function, which is a standard feature of the C language. In either case, control gets back to DOS by means of an API service call using the interrupt 21H mechanism discussed earlier in this chapter.

Specifically, a *completion code* is placed into the AL register, the *terminate* function code 4CH is placed into the AH register, and interrupt 21H is triggered. A different API service function provides a means to "terminate and stay resident", which is a way of keeping the application program in memory so it can, perhaps, attempt some type of multitasking.

4.2.2 OS/2 Initiation/Termination Protocol

OS/2 does not set up a Program Segment Prefix for the application program, but it provides much more information than DOS in the registers at start-up time:

DS Segment selector for the default data segment, or 0 if there is no such segment;

ES A value of 0;

SS Segment selector for the default stack segment;

SP Offset to the top of the default stack;

AX Segment selector for the environment segment, which contains the environment strings, the application file name, the command verb, and the residual command line;

BX Offset to the command verb in the environment segment;

CX Length of default data segment, with a value of 0 indicating 64 kilobytes;

DX Stack size;

SI Heap size;

DI Module handle for the application executable;

BP A value of 0 which is normally pushed onto the stack to indicate the end of the stack frame chain.

After setting up the registers in this way, OS/2 jumps into the application program just like DOS. It's a shame that the OS/2 designers did not push all this information onto the stack and make a *far call* to the application program, because then the start-up routine could be written in a high-level language, which would make it much easier to understand and modify for special applications.

OS/2 applications, like those under DOS, terminate by returning from the *main* function or by calling an API service function with a completion code.

For OS/2, the function is named *DosExit*, and whereas DOS allows only an 8-bit code, OS/2 allows 16 bits. When calling *DosExit*, an OS/2 task which is part of a multitasking group can also specify that all associated tasks are to be terminated.

4.2.3 DOS and OS/2 Environment Areas

Both DOS and OS/2 maintain an *environment area* for each application program. This area contains an array of *environment variables* followed by some information about the command that was used to invoke the application.

Environment variables are a collection of symbols specified by the user and passed to application programs by the DOS or OS/2 command processor. The *set* command is typically used to create or change an environment variable. For example, the first three commands in this sequence:

```
set INCLUDE=c:\sysinc;c:\myinc
set LIB=c:\syslib;c:\mylib
set OBJ=c:\myobj
path c:\sysexe;c:\myexe
```

create three environment variables named *INCLUDE*, *LIB*, and *OBJ*. The value of each variable is the string of characters following the equal sign in its *set* command. In this example, these strings represent lists of disk directories that tell the various compilers and linkers where to find *include files*, *library files*, and *object files*, respectively.

The PATH command creates an environment variable named *PATH*, which is a list of the directories in which the command processor should search for programs to load. You can also use the SET command to create the PATH variable.

For DOS, the environment resides at offset 0 in the segment whose address is in location 2CH (i.e. bytes 44 and 45) of the Program Segment Prefix. It consists of an array of null-terminated environment variable strings, followed by a single null byte, followed by a word containing an argument count, followed by that number of null-terminated argument strings. For DOS Version 3, the first argument string gives the complete file name of the application program, including the directory path. No other arguments are supplied, and so the argument count word always contains a value of one. Figure 4-1 is a hexadecimal and ASCII dump of the DOS 3.2 environment

```
DOS ENVIRONMENT AREA...

18FA:0000 43 4f 4d 53 50 45 43 3d 43 3a 5c 43 4f 4d 4d 41 COMSPEC=C:\COMMA
18FA:0010 4e 44 2e 43 4f 4d 00 4c 49 42 3d 63 3a 5c 73 79 ND.COM.LIB=c:\sy
18FA:0020 73 6c 69 62 3b 63 3a 5c 6d 79 6c 69 62 00 4f 42 slib;c:\mylib.OB
18FA:0030 4a 3d 63 3a 5c 6d 79 6f 62 6a 00 50 41 54 48 3d J=c:\myobj.PATH=
18FA:0040 43 3a 5c 53 59 53 45 58 45 3b 43 3a 5c 4d 59 45 C:\SYSEXE;C:\MYE
18FA:0050 58 45 00 49 4e 43 4c 55 44 45 3d 63 3a 5c 73 79 XE.INCLUDE=c:\sy
18FA:0060 73 69 6e 63 3b 63 3a 5c 6d 79 69 6e 63 00 00 01 sinc;c:\myinc...
18FA:0070 00 43 3a 5c 4d 59 45 58 45 5c 41 42 43 2e 45 58 .C:\MYEXE\ABC.EX
18FA:0080 45 00                                           E.
```

Figure 4-1. DOS Environment Area

after the *INCLUDE, LIB, OBJ* and *PATH* variables have been defined as shown earlier and you have invoked the program named *c:\myexe\abc.exe* by typing the command:

```
abc def ghi jkl
```

Notice that the first environment variable, named COMSPEC, is created by DOS to indicate where the command processor resides on disk. If there is no SHELL command in *config.sys*, then COMSPEC defaults to the root directory of the disk from which the operating system was loaded. Otherwise, COMSPEC is set to the value you specify in the SHELL command.

```
OS/2 ENVIRONMENT AREA...

005F:0000 43 4f 4d 53 50 45 43 3d 43 3a 5c 43 4d 44 2e 45 COMSPEC=C:\CMD.E
005F:0010 58 45 00 44 50 41 54 48 3d 00 4c 49 42 3d 63 3a XE.DPATH=.LIB=c:
005F:0020 5c 73 79 73 6c 69 62 3b 63 3a 5c 6d 79 6c 69 62 \syslib;c:\mylib
005F:0030 00 4f 42 4a 3d 63 3a 5c 6d 79 6f 62 6a 00 49 4e .OBJ=c:\myobj.IN
005F:0040 43 4c 55 44 45 3d 63 3a 5c 73 79 73 69 6e 63 3b CLUDE=c:\sysinc;
005F:0050 63 3a 5c 6d 79 69 6e 63 00 50 41 54 48 3d 43 3a c:\myinc.PATH=C:
005F:0060 5c 53 59 53 45 58 45 3b 43 3a 5c 4d 59 45 58 45 \SYSEXE;C:\MYEXE
005F:0070 00 00 43 3a 5c 4d 59 45 58 45 5c 41 42 43 2e 45 ..C:\MYEXE\ABC.E
005F:0080 58 45 00 61 62 63 00 20 64 65 66 20 67 68 69 20 XE.abc. def ghi
005F:0090 6a 6b 6c 20 00 00                               jkl ..
```

Figure 4-2. OS/2 Environment Area

Figure 4-2 shows the OS/2 environment area after the same sequence of commands. As you can see, OS/2 does things a little differently than DOS. First, COMSPEC is followed by another system-supplied variable named *DPATH*, which is null because we did not type a DPATH command. This variable is similar to PATH, except that it tells the operating system where to find data files, while PATH indicates where to find program files.

The closest equivalent to this feature in DOS is the APPEND command, which does not place any information in the environment area. The DPATH feature is not as powerful as APPEND, because DOS searches the APPEND directories automatically when you open a file. If you want to use DPATH in OS/2, you must call the *DosSearchPath* function before opening the file.

Another difference in the OS/2 environment area is that the argument count word has been deleted, and the environment variables are followed by three null-terminated strings. The first is the program file name as in DOS. The second is the command verb, and the third is the residual command string. Remember that OS/2 passes the offset to the command verb in the BX register as part of the program initiation protocol. Also note that the residual command line usually begins with one or more blanks.

DOS does not provide the command verb, although it can usually be extracted from the program name. Furthermore, the older operating system places the residual command line in a 128-byte buffer at PSP+80H. This buffer looks sort of like a BASIC string variable; it is preceded by a count byte (at PSP+80H) which indicates how many bytes are in the line. The actual text then begins at PSP+81H and is terminated by a carriage return instead of a null byte.

4.3 Summary

The DOS and OS/2 Application Program Interfaces are markedly different. Nonetheless, experienced DOS programmers seem to have little trouble adapting to the OS/2 API, because it is a logical simplification of the older interface. And since the OS/2 API is easier to use, it presents no great learning barrier, which means that programmers can concentrate on employing the many new features of OS/2.

Chapter 5

Converting DOS Programs

A few lucky programmers will be able to forget about the old world of DOS and design new programs destined to run only under OS/2. Most of us, however, will get our initial OS/2 experience by converting DOS programs. You may ask why anyone would want to do this. After all, OS/2 provides a real-mode session in which you can run most existing DOS applications with no conversion effort.

The primary reason for undertaking a straightforward conversion of a DOS program is to give it more memory. Editors, compilers, spreadsheets, and database managers are just a few programs that are typically written in a high-level language like C and are capable of using whatever memory is available to them. That is, these programs usually obtain their working memory by calling standard C memory allocation routines such as *malloc*. So, if you convert one of these to run in OS/2 protected mode, it will automatically benefit from the greatly expanded memory space, assuming that the compiler is doing its job correctly.

This chapter presents some general guidelines that will help you convert DOS applications written in C and assembly language. These guidelines result from my experiences at Lattice, where we converted more than 100,000 lines of C and assembly-language code to OS/2 during late 1987 and early 1988. Although I'll focus on C, the rules are general enough that you should have no trouble adapting them to other high-level languages.

After summarizing the conversion process in this chapter, I'll present detailed information in Chapters 6 through 9 about the OS/2 programming features which are most important when converting DOS applications.

5.1 Programmer, Know Thy Code

The first few rules are so obvious that it's a little ridiculous to list them here. But I've seen several OS/2 conversion efforts get derailed because one of these "obvious" steps was not taken:

- Make sure you have all of the source modules that comprise your application. If you depend on somebody else's code and it's only available in object form, you'll probably be roadblocked. If the object code is a library product that you purchased without source code, you might be able to convince the publisher to give you the source if you agree to send back the changes that you make for OS/2. On the other hand, if the library is really complex, you might try waving green paper (i.e., $) at the publisher so he'll do the work.

- Make sure you know how to build the application. Some of the executables (i.e., EXE files) floating around have long grey beards, and the folks who originally built them may have disappeared without leaving any tracks.

- Go ahead and actually build the application under DOS to see if it still works. Use the latest version of the C compiler and assembler that you can, since old source code sometimes doesn't make it through the more recent language translators because of improved syntax checking. Undoubtedly, you'll have to face the latest versions of these language translators under OS/2, so you might as well get rid of any syntax problems immediately.

- If the source code you're using produces a flawed executable, debug it under DOS, since you're probably more efficient working in that environment.

- Once you have a clean version running under DOS, save the source and executable. You'll probably need to refer back to this *baseline* version when evaluating the converted program's performance under OS/2.

Remember that porting to OS/2 is a lot like painting a room: *If you take the time to do a good prep job, the actual work is much easier and usually turns out better.*

5.2 The Good, the Bad, and the Ugly

The next step is *triage*, classifying your application according to the likelihood that it will survive the operation. We've identified the following four classes (*quadrage*?):

- Well-behaved programs
- Highly interactive programs
- Terminate-and-stay-resident (TSR) programs
- I/O drivers

Let's examine each class in detail, explaining its characteristics and how they affect the conversion to OS/2.

5.2.1 Well-Behaved Programs

Well-behaved programs use few operating system services except for the File Manager, which they access through the C library via functions such as *fopen*, *getchar*, *read*, and so on. Since OS/2 has essentially the same file system as DOS, the OS/2 C library can provide exactly the same services, which makes well-behaved programs really easy to convert. In fact, most of the time you just run the source code through the OS/2 compiler or assembler and then build an executable with the OS/2 linker.

This sounds so simple, that you probably wonder if there are any significant programs in this category. Well, actually there are quite a few. At Lattice, we found that most of our DOS programming tools (e.g., compilers, assemblers, GREP, DIFF, and so on) were well-behaved and moved to OS/2 with few problems. Of course, the Lattice DOS C Compiler needed many changes in order to produce proper code for OS/2, but no changes were needed to make the original DOS compiler run under OS/2 and produce DOS code.

To be more specific, a well-behaved C program has the following characteristics:

1. All DOS interfaces are handled through the standard library.
2. The program does not use low-level DOS interface functions from the library, such as *int86*, *intdos*, *bdos*, or *bios*.

3. The program does not hook into any DOS hardware or software interrupts.

4. Keyboard and screen interactions use a simple command line protocol, or else the ANSI.SYS driver is used for any complex screen operations. In other words, the PC keyboard and screen are used just like a "dumb terminal" or "glass teletype".

5. The program always treats 32-bit pointers as atomic objects; that is, it does not manipulate the segment and offset portions separately.

These same rules apply to assembly language functions called by C programs, although it's usually more difficult to tell if such functions are well-behaved by just eyeballing them. So, in addition to the items already listed, you should also look out for these coding practices which will complicate the conversion:

1. INT instructions, which generate software interrupts;

2. IN and OUT instructions, which directly access the I/O ports;

3. CLI and STI instructions, which change the state of the interrupt enable flag;

4. Instruction sequences that change segment register contents, such as

```
        MOV     AX,ES    ; advance to next paragraph
        INC     AX
        MOV     ES,AX
```

   which is guaranteed to fail because segment register arithmetic is different in protected mode;

5. Timing loops, such as

```
        MOV     CX,1000  ; wait awhile
DELAY:  LOOP    DELAY
```

   which are risky even under DOS because they often become invalid when you upgrade to a faster computer.

The first three of these practices will cause protection violations because OS/2 does not allow normal processes to execute INT, IN, OUT, CLI, and

STI instructions. The fourth will usually cause addressing exceptions because the process will attempt to load in invalid selector into a segment register. The fifth just causes the program to behave erratically, since the time delay varies depending on how heavily OS/2 is loaded.

We discovered that much of our assembly-language code had none of these problems and was written at that level just to achieve the maximum speed and minimum size. The Lattice floating point library is an example; it moved to OS/2 with no changes at all.

However, if you find any of these transgressions, you'll have to do some redesigning. Fortunately, such functions are usually very simple, and you can often rewrite them in C, making direct calls to the OS/2 Application Program Interface (API). That is, many of these errant assembly-language routines were originally written just to get at the DOS API in some way not supported by the standard C libraries. But under OS/2, you can usually find an equivalent API function and call it directly from C.

So, if you're one of the lucky owners of only well-behaved programs, with just a few assembly-language changes to worry about, stop reading here and start converting. Of course, well-behaved programs, being typically command-line oriented, are often boring to use. So, you'll pay your OS/2 dues later if you decide to spiff them up by adapting them to the Presentation Manager, which is a nontrivial task.

5.2.2 Highly Interactive Programs

The DOS world is full of programs that do all sorts of magic with the keyboard, screen, and mouse. In fact, one of the things that has made DOS so popular is the ease with which such software can be written. Of course, this has less to do with DOS than with the *de facto* hardware standards caused by the IBM PC. The undeniable influence of IBM simplified many aspects of interactive programming that were quite chaotic in the earlier CP/M world, such as memory-mapped video techniques, keyboard scan codes, and extended character sets.

Nonetheless, DOS programs that interact heavily with their users generally present more OS/2 conversion difficulties than the well-behaved programs already discussed. This is because all interfaces with the BIOS and video RAM must be changed. However, if you've followed the recommended practice of isolating these into a few modules, you'll only be dealing with a small percentage of the code.

For example, the Lattice Unicalc Spreadsheet (about 25,000 C source lines) and the Lattice Screen Editor (about 15,000 C source lines) are both highly interactive, screen-oriented programs which write directly to the video buffers. Yet, each required less than one person-week to convert, mainly because the human interfaces were designed in a modular way. And surprisingly, there was no perceivable loss of performance relative to the DOS versions, as long as OS/2 was not running other tasks.

To convert an interactive program, you must replace all BIOS interrupts with calls to the corresponding OS/2 video (*Vio*), keyboard (*Kbd*), and mouse (*Mou*) functions that will be discussed in Chapters 7, 8, and 9. These interrupts are usually generated directly by assembly-language functions or indirectly from C programs via the *int86* function. Then you must modify all routines that directly address the video RAM.

Converting the Keyboard Interface

Adapting to the OS/2 keyboard interface is usually straightforward and has no noticeable effect on performance. For example, here's a piece of DOS-based C code that obtains a character and scan code via BIOS interrupt 16H, using *int86*:

```
union REGS r;         /* define register set */

r.h..ah = 0           /* set AH=0 to get next char */
int86(0x16,&r,&r);    /* generate INT 16H */
scancode = r.h.ah;    /* save scan code from AH */
charcode = r.h.al;    /* save character code from AL */
```

The same operation in OS/2 can be coded in the following way:

```
extern far pascal KbdCharIn();

struct CHARDATA       /* KbdCharIn return structure */
  {
  char acode;         /* ASCII character code */
  char scode;         /* scan code */
  char status;        /* device status */
  char nls;           /* National Language Support */
  short shift;        /* keyboard shift state */
  long time;          /* timestamp */
  } key;

int error;            /* error code */
```

```
error = KbdCharIn((far char *)(&key),0,0);

if(error == 0)
  {
  scancode = key.scode;         /* save scan code */
  charcode = key.acode;         /* save character code */
  }
else ...                        /* error handler goes here */
```

Although the OS/2 version looks more complicated, it's actually not. Most of the OS/2 statements are declarations that would normally be coded once and kept in header files. In fact, the OS/2 Programmer Toolkit includes such header files for both C and assembly language. Other OS/2 compiler packages, such as Microsoft Pascal, include the necessary declaration files for the OS/2 API.

KbdCharIn takes three arguments. The first one is a 32-bit pointer to the structure in which OS/2 will return information about the next keystroke. The second argument tells *KbdCharIn* what to do if no keystroke is ready. A value of 0 causes the function to wait until the user presses a key. The third argument is the *logical keyboard handle*, which should be 0 for the default keyboard. When OS/2 is managing several applications (called *sessions*) at the same time, it gives each one its own keyboard buffer, called *logical keyboard 0*, which will receive input characters when that application is in the foreground (i.e., is visible to the user). In some cases an application can request additional logical keyboards, which will have handles greater than 0.

Just in case you turned immediately to this chapter without reading the earlier sections of the book, let me point out once again that the OS/2 API requires all addresses to be passed in full 32-bit form, and so you must make sure that your C code expands 16-bit pointers to that form. The *cast* operation

```
(char far *)(&key)
```

does exactly that to the address of the *key* structure, if it is not already in the 32-bit form. Another way to guarantee that pointers are in this form is to use only the *large memory model* when you compile for OS/2. If you do that, then no casts are required in the OS/2 API functions.

However, if the DOS version does not use the large model, then you may open a can of worms by recompiling with that option. Some DOS programs are written with the assumption that pointers are only 16 bits wide, and mysterious problems occur when you challenge that assumption by compiling in the large model. The rule of thumb is: *Use the same memory model for the OS/2 version as was used in the DOS version.*

Converting the Mouse Interface

If you access the mouse under DOS via software interrupt 33H, the OS/2 conversion is similar to the keyboard work previously described.

However, if you rely upon a special mouse interface provided by a DOS driver or pseudo-driver, you're in for some redesign. Most DOS mice on the market today include the necessary software to handle the interrupt 33H protocols, and I'd suggest that you change your DOS code to use that approach. Then it should be a straightforward job to convert that code to OS/2 using the *Mou* functions.

Converting Video BIOS Calls

If your DOS program accesses the video subsystem through BIOS interrupts, then the conversion to OS/2 is, once again, similar to the keyboard work already described. For example, here's a DOS code snippet that clears the screen and moves the cursor to the upper left corner:

```
union REGS r;          /* define register set */

r.x.ax = 0x0619;       /* AH=6 for scroll up,
                          AL=25 for entire screen */
r.h.bh = 7;            /* BH=7 for white-on-black */
r.x.cx = 0;            /* (CH,CL) is upper left */
r.x.dx = 0x184F;       /* (DH,DL) is lower right */
int86(16,&r,&r);       /* generate video interrupt */

r.h.ah = 2;            /* AH=2 to set cursor position */
r.h.bh = 0;            /* BH=0 for page 0 */
r.x.dx = 0;            /* (DH,DL) is (row,col) */
int86(16,&r,&r);       /* generate video interrupt */
```

The same operation in OS/2 can be accomplished by this sequence:

```
extern far pascal VioScrollUp();
extern far pascal VioSetCurPos();
```

```
int error;

error = VioScrollUp(0,0,24,79,25,0x0720,0);
if(error) ...

error = VioSetCurPos(0,0,0);
if(error) ...
```

VioScrollUp accepts seven arguments. The first four define the scrolling area, that is, the upper left and lower right corners of the block being scrolled. Here we're dealing with the entire screen of 25 rows and 80 columns, and so the upper left and lower right corners are (0,0) and (24,79), respectively. The fifth argument specifies the number of lines to scroll, 25 in this case. The sixth argument is the attribute and character used to fill the new lines on the screen. The attribute value here is 7 for white-on-black, and the character value is 0x20, which is a blank.

The final argument to *VioScrollUp* and most other *Vio* calls is the *logical screen handle.* As with the keyboard, the OS/2 session manager provides a separate video buffer for each active session. The handle for this default buffer is 0. The initial versions of OS/2 only support the default buffer, but additional buffers might be allowed in future versions or in alternative video subsystems.

The *VioSetCurPos* argument list is much simpler. This function positions the cursor to the row and column specified by the first two arguments. The third argument is the logical screen handle.

Converting Video RAM Accesses

If your program paints the screen by writing directly into the video RAM, you must deal with the fact that OS/2 severely restricts your access to this special area of memory. When you run in protected mode, the video RAM doesn't even appear in your memory map, and so if you try something like writing into the monochrome video buffer at *segment:offset* B000:0000, OS/2 will abort your process with an addressing exception. Here's an example of some nonportable DOS C code for clearing the monochrome screen:

```
int i;
union                          /* makes video RAM pointer */
  {
  unsigned short x[2];
  unsigned short far *p;
```

```
  } q;

q.x[0] = 0;                /* form segment:offset */
q.x.[1] = 0xb000;          /* pointer to video RAM */

for(i = 0; i < 2000; q.p[i++] = 0x0720);
```

The strange-looking *union* is used to form a valid *segment:offset* pointer to the video buffer, and then the loop simply resets that area to blanks with white-on-black attributes.

Now, if you try to run this code in OS/2 protected mode, you'll see a fine example of an OS/2 abort message. But text-mode programs like this one can be easily converted to OS/2:

You just write into the logical video buffer and let OS/2 update the physical buffer. This technique is really nothing new; it's exactly what you have to do in DOS-based multitasking systems such as IBM Topview and Microsoft Windows. For example, the following code is a Topview-compatible version of the previous example:

```
int i;
union REGSS r;          /* register set with segments */
union                   /* makes video RAM pointer */
  {
  unsigned short x[2];
  unsigned short far *p;
  } q;

r.x.di = 0;             /* set ES:DI to video buffer */
r.x.es = 0xb000;
r.h.ah = 0xfe;          /* use BIOS function 254 to */
int86s(16,&r,&r);       /* get logical buffer pointer */

q.x[0] = r.x.di;        /* form far pointer */
q.x.[1] = r.x.es;

for(i = 0; i < 2000; /* clear the buffer */
  q.p[i++] = 0x0720);

r.x.di = q.x[0];        /* set ES;DI to logical buffer */
r.x.es = q.x[1];
r.x.cx = 4000;          /* set size to 25 rows, 80 cols */
r.h.ah = 255;           /* use BIOS function 255 */
int86s(16,&r,&r);       /* to update screen */
```

Here we use video BIOS function 254, which leaves ES:DI intact if Topview or some other session management system is not installed. Otherwise, ES:DI is loaded with the *segment:offset* pointer to the logical video buffer. Then, after the buffer is cleared, we use video BIOS function 255 to update the screen. If no session manager is active, function 255 does nothing, since we've actually been writing to the physical buffer.

The equivalent OS/2 code looks quite similar, except that the BIOS interrupts are replaced with *Vio* calls:

```
extern far pascal VioGetBuf();
extern far pascal VioShowBuf();

int i,error;
short far *p;
short size;

error =                      /* get logical buffer ptr */
  VioGetBuf((long far *)(&p),(short far *)(&size),0);
if(error) ...

for(i = 0; i < (size/2); /* clear the buffer */
  p[i++] = 0x0720);

error = VioShowBuf(0,size,0); /* update the screen */
if(error) ...
```

VioGetBuf returns a pointer to the logical video buffer. The pointer is stored into the 32-bit area whose 32-bit address is given by the first argument. That's the reason for the *(long far *)* cast in that argument position. The second argument is a 32-bit pointer to a short integer where the buffer length (in bytes) will be returned, and again, a cast operation is needed. The logical video handle completes the argument list, as we've already discussed.

After clearing the logical buffer, you must use *VioShowBuf* to get the physical screen updated, which will actually occur only if your program is running as the foreground session. The first argument is the offset into the logical buffer, and the second is the number of bytes being updated.

So, if you were prudent enough to incorporate this Topview type of logic into your screen-oriented programs over the past few years, you'll have an easy time moving to OS/2. However, if you scattered absolute addresses of video buffers throughout your code, you'll have some cleanup to do. I'm ashamed to admit that we had a few programs like that, and we found it worthwhile to first clean them up under DOS using the techniques previously described. Then the move to OS/2 was painless, and we also wound up with the improved DOS versions.

Converting Graphical Programs

So far we've only discussed text-oriented programs, that is, those programs which use the nongraphical video display modes. While OS/2 Standard Edition 1.0 provides excellent support for such applications, it has little to offer if your programs generate graphical displays.

However, the situation is not completely hopeless. Contrary to what some would have you believe, you can write graphical programs under OS/2 without the Presentation Manager. In other words, OS/2 Standard Edition 1.0 does provide the means to gain direct access to the physical video buffer and the display adaptor's I/O ports, both of which are necessary for generating graphical displays. This is not too surprising, since the Presentation Manager is itself an application on top of the OS/2 base, and it needs these capabilities to do its thing.

A detailed discussion of low-level graphics programming is presented later when we discuss the video subsystem and the multitasking feature. Here's a small example of how you can directly access the physical video buffer.

```
extern far pascal VioGetPhysBuf();
extern far pascal VioScrLock();
extern far pascal VioScrUnlock();

int i,error;
struct physdata
  {
  unsigned long real;       /* physical buffer address */
  unsigned long length;     /* buffer length */
  unsigned short prots;     /* buffer selector */
  } x;

union                       /* makes video RAM pointer */
  {
  unsigned short x[2];
  unsigned short far *p;
  } q;
```

```
x.real = 0xb0000;              /* load physical address */
x.length = 4000;               /* load length */
error = VioGetPhysBuf(         /* map the buffer */
  (struct physdata far *)(&x),0);
if(error) ...

q.x[0] = 0;                    /* form far pointer */
q.x[1] = x.prots;

error = VioScrLock(1,          /* lock the screen */
  (char far *)(&i),0);
if(error) ...

for(i = 0; i < 2000;            /* clear the buffer */
  q.p[i++] = 0x0720);

error = VioScrUnlock(0);        /* unlock the screen */
if(error) ...
```

VioGetPhysBuf maps the specified video buffer into your address space, if possible, and returns one or more selectors that you can use to form 32-bit pointers for protected-mode access. One selector is returned for each 64 kilobytes of video buffer area. The mapping, however, is only valid when your program is executing in the foreground, that is, when it has control of the actual display screen. So, you must call *VioScrLock* before accessing the buffer and *VioScrUnlock* when you are finished. The former, as used in this example, does not return until the user brings the program to the foreground via the session manager. Then it locks the screen so that the user cannot switch to another session until the current program unlocks the screen via *VioScrUnlock*.

Now even though the preceding example writes to the physical video buffer in text mode, you can use this same technique to draw graphical images. The general approach is:

- Use *VioGetConfig* to determine the type of display adaptor equipped. *VioGetMode* and *VioGetState* might also be needed to determine the current display mode and state.
- Use *VioSetMode* and, if necessary, *VioSetState* to establish the appropriate graphical mode.

- Create separate execution threads using *VioModeWait* and *VioSavRedrawWait* to re-establish the display mode and save or restore the display data when a session switch occurs.
- Use *VioGetPhysBuf*, *VioScrLock*, and *VioScrUnlock* as described to gain access to the physical video buffer in order to draw the graphical images.

If you need to access the display adaptor's I/O registers, as is often the case with EGA displays, then you'll also have to create a function with I/O privileges that you can then call from your program. This is necessary because normal OS/2 processes are not allowed to execute I/O instructions.

As I said, graphical programming can be done in OS/2 without relying upon the Presentation Manager. It isn't as easy as displaying text only, and it requires that you get involved with some new OS/2 features, such as multitasking and I/O privilege levels. These will be discussed in more detail in Chapter 7.

5.2.3 Terminate-Stay-Resident (TSR) Programs

TSR programs are a special category of highly interactive DOS applications. The typical TSR, such as Borland SideKick or Lotus Metro, is dormant until the user activates it via a *hot key*. Then it opens a window on the screen and enters into a dialogue with the user to accomplish some task such as updating an appointment calendar. When this dialogue is finished, the TSR restores the original screen contents and goes back to sleep.

So, TSR programs typically have the same OS/2 conversion problems as the interactive programs discussed earlier. That is, their keyboard, mouse, and screen access techniques must be changed to meet the OS/2 requirements.

In addition, you need to decide if you want the TSR to become a normal OS/2 process or a *monitor* process. If the TSR is providing a data management service, such as an appointment calendar, you could simply load it as an OS/2 session and then use the session manager hot keys to activate it.

However, if the TSR has to continuously monitor the keyboard input, as a keyboard macro package like Prokey must do, then you need to hook it into the keyboard I/O driver as a monitor process. Fortunately, OS/2 provides an elegant way that eliminates the TSR contention problems that often occur under DOS. Figure 5-1 shows how this works.

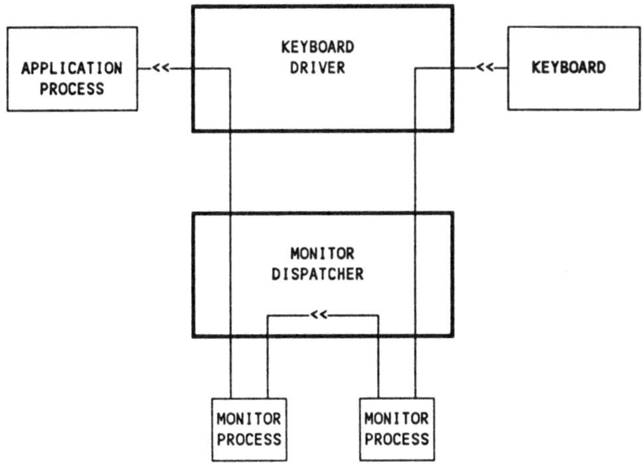

Figure 5-1. OS/2 Monitors

The monitor process calls *DosMonOpen* and *DosMonReg* to open a monitor chain in the device driver and register itself as a monitor. Then each time the device driver receives a keystroke, it sends a *keystroke data packet* out to the first monitor in the chain. That monitor reads the packet via *DosMonRead* and chooses to absorb the keystroke, pass it on, or substitute one or more pseudo-keystrokes. These latter two operations are done via *DosMonWrite*, which sends the keystroke packet on to the next monitor in the chain.

Unless everything gets absorbed in the chain, the original or substitute keystrokes eventually reach the end of the chain and are returned to the device driver, which passes them on to the application program that is waiting for keyboard data.

As with graphical techniques discussed earlier, there are many subtleties you must keep in mind when designing a monitor process, and so I'll defer this discussion until Chapter 8, when we discuss the keyboard subsystem. The main thing to keep in mind here is that you can provide pop-up utilities under OS/2 via monitors. However, these monitors must be very fast or else the system will appear to be sluggish. Also note that you can hook monitors into some of the other standard character drivers. For example, the OS/2 print spooler is implemented as a monitor process hooked into the printer driver.

5.2.4 I/O Drivers

I/O drivers present the toughest conversion challenges, if only because they connect into the messy guts of DOS and typically require a large amount of assembly language programming. Furthermore, as with DOS TSR programs, the rules for creating drivers have not been well documented, and so designers have had to use *ad hoc* techniques learned by experimentation.

Unfortunately, OS/2 drivers tend to be much more complicated than their DOS counterparts because they must operate in a multitasking environment supporting both real-mode and protected-mode processes. Because of these significant environmental differences, the typical DOS driver doesn't survive the conversion, except for small sequences of code that deal directly with the I/O devices. In other words, if you write drivers for a living, roll up your sleeves because you've got a lot of work ahead of you.

At Lattice, we were initially concerned that the techniques for creating OS/2 drivers would remain mysterious and that we could not obtain the knowledge experimentally because OS/2 is so well protected. But IBM's documentation was a pleasant surprise, because it explains this arcane topic in great detail and includes a fairly complete example. Microsoft has also been providing a driver development kit, including an OS/2 kernel debugger, to attendees of its driver design course.

The basic rule for converting DOS drivers to OS/2 is: *Don't*. The operating systems are so different in this area that it's best to start anew, using the DOS driver only as a general guide.

5.3 Family Mode Considerations

The final topic you must consider when converting a DOS program to OS/2 is whether you want the result to be a *family-mode application*. This means that the program will be put together in such a way that its executable (i.e., the EXE file) will run correctly in OS/2 protected mode, OS/2 real mode, or under DOS 3.x. The OS/2 Programmer Toolkit includes the *BIND* utility program and a special library named *API.LIB* to construct family-mode applications.

Chapter 14 contains a detailed discussion of the Family API, or FAPI. For now, here are four simple rules you must remember in order to achieve family compatibilty:

- Don't use any OS/2 API calls that are not part of the family-mode repertoire, described in Chapter 14, unless your program first tests that it is running in protected mode.
- Don't do any DOS-specific things, such as generate software interrupts, unless you first verify that the program is running in real mode.
- Don't do any internal manipulation of 32-bit pointers unless you first check whether your program is in real or protected mode and choose the appropriate algorithm.
- Stick to the common 8086 instruction set, and avoid oddball instruction sequences unless you first verify that your program is running on the correct processor.

Note that the first rule requires that you know which functions in the C compiler library, and possibly other libraries, call API functions that are not allowed in family mode. When we converted the Lattice C Compiler, we were able to make most of the mainstream functions fully compatible with family mode. The same thing is true of the Microsoft and IBM C compilers. Other language and library vendors should be able to tell you how their products are structured relative to family mode.

5.4 Summary

Our experiences at Lattice converting DOS applications to OS/2 protected mode were much happier than we originally expected. While OS/2 was designed with an eye to the future, it remains very compatible with the past. Because of this, you should consider moving your application programs to OS/2 in three steps:

- First, do a straight conversion using the techniques presented in this chapter. This will get you a version that works in protected mode and, in many cases, takes advantage of OS/2's expanded memory space.
- Second, consider ways to improve the application by using new OS/2 features such as multitasking. For example, if your application is a text editor, why not create a separate task (i.e., a *thread*) that wakes up every few minutes and automatically saves the user's work to a disk file, thereby safeguarding against catastrophes such as power failures.
- Third, convert your application's human interface to the Presentation

Manager in order to gain the benefits of a fully graphical interface. Of course, you might need to maintain a separate version for those users who do not have the hardware that the Presentation Manager needs.

In the next four chapters, we'll examine OS/2's techniques for accessing disk files, the display screen, the keyboard, and the mouse. With that information well understood, you should have no trouble with the first step. Then, beginning with Chapter 10, we'll get into the new OS/2 features that you can employ selectively in family-mode programs or use freely in programs that run only under OS/2. These features are the means by which you can accomplish the second step, tailoring your applications for OS/2. This book does not discuss the Presentation Manager and therefore provides no help with the third step.

Chapter 6

The File Manager

The File Manager, one of the most commonly used parts of DOS and OS/2, enables application programs to read from and write to *block devices,* such as disk and CD-ROM units. In addition, it allows you to access *character devices* such as the keyboard and display screen as if they were disk files.

OS/2 Version 1.0 uses exactly the same file formats as DOS, so you can freely exchange disks between the two operating systems. This has definite advantages while you are making the transition to OS/2. For instance, my desktop computer has OS/2 installed on its fixed disk, but that same disk also contains some network software that will only run under DOS. So, when I want to use the network, I just boot DOS from a floppy diskette, and I can access my fixed disk with no problems. Similarly, any fixed-disk files that I create while running under DOS are also accessible when I'm using OS/2. Kudos to IBM and Microsoft for keeping DOS and OS/2 compatible in this area!

Future versions of OS/2 may achieve increased performance by changing the fixed disk format such that it is no longer compatible with DOS. However, I think it's a safe bet that the floppy diskette format will remain the same because so many low-end machines will continue to use DOS. This book, for example, consists of text files that I created on my DOS-based lap-held computer and typeset on my OS/2 machine. During the book's gestation period, I kept the active files on 3.5-inch diskettes, which could be read and written by both computers.

Both DOS and OS/2 contain a fairly large number of API functions related to the file system. This chapter explains how the basic OS/2 file manager services relate to their DOS counterparts. Then, after covering some other important topics, we'll get into the more advanced file system features in Chapter 12.

6.1 File Names and Directories

DOS and OS/2 use the same file naming conventions. Each disk file is identified by three components: *drive code*, *directory path*, and *node*. The file manager maintains all names in upper case, and the DOS and OS/2 API functions convert lower case to upper case for you. This is convenient, because it's easier to type names in lower case.

6.1.1 Drive Code

The drive code is a single letter identifying the physical device on which the file resides. When you write a file name, the drive code must be followed by a colon (:). If you do not specify a this part, then the operating system assumes that the file resides on the *current drive*. The OS/2 command processor allows the user to specify the current drive for a session by just typing the drive letter followed by a colon. For example, the simple command

```
a:
```

makes drive A the current drive for this session.

A process can override the current drive setting for its session via the *DosSelectDisk* function. DOS, of course, has only one current drive indicator, which can also be overridden by API function 0EH.

6.1.2 Directory Path

The directory path tells the operating system how to find the *file descriptor* for the target file, and it consists of directory names separated by backslashes (\). These directory names have the same format as nodes, which are described in the next section.

If the path begins with a backslash, then it is said to be *absolute*; otherwise, it is *relative*. An absolute path begins in the *root directory*, which is a directory that the operating system can find when it is given only the drive code. A relative path begins in the *current directory* which, like the current drive, is a per-session parameter in OS/2. For example, *mystuff**main.c* is an absolute path, while *mystuff**main.c* is a relative path.

The user can specify the current directory via the CD command, and an OS/2 process can override this setting by calling *DosChDir*. DOS programs use function 3BH to change the current directory. Both operating systems maintain a current directory setting for each drive. For example,

```
c:
cd \mystuff
cd d:\extras
```

sets the current drive to C. Then the first CD command makes *mystuff* the current directory on drive C, and the second CD command makes *extras* the current directory on drive D.

6.1.3 Node Name

The node contains a *base name* of up to eight characters and an optional *extension* of up to three characters. If the extension is present, it must be separated from the base name by a period.

You can use any printable character in the base name and extension except the following, which are punctuation characters:

<table>
<tr><td>.</td><td>"</td><td>/</td><td>\</td><td>[</td><td>]</td><td>:</td><td>?</td></tr>
<tr><td>*</td><td>|</td><td><</td><td>></td><td>+</td><td>=</td><td>;</td><td>,</td></tr>
<tr><td>&</td><td>^</td><td></td><td></td><td></td><td></td><td></td><td></td></tr>
</table>

I generally avoid the { and } characters also, even though they are not prohibited in file names. As we'll see at the end of this chapter, there are also some names, such as CON and PRN, which you cannot use for disk files because they are device names.

6.1.4 Hierarchical Directory Structure

People often use the term file name when they are actually referring to the node. Strictly speaking, this is incorrect. In order to properly identify a DOS or OS/2 file, you must specify its drive, directory, and node; all of these together are actually the file name. Figure 6-1 shows why this is necessary.

This is an example of a simple directory structure for disk drive C. There are

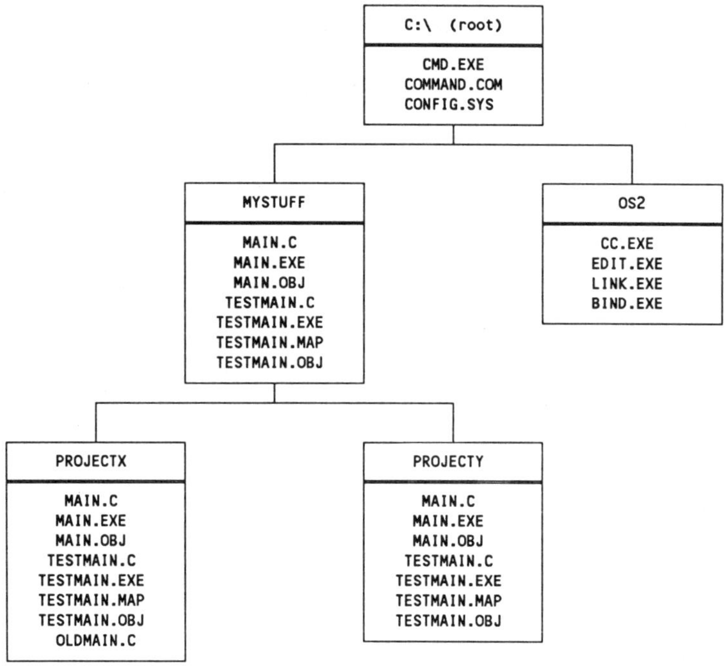

Figure 6-1. Hierarchical Directory Structure

two directories attached to the root: *mystuff* and *os2.* The former also has two child directories: *projectx* and *projecty*. Notice that these two, as well as *mystuff*, contain several identical nodes. So, you can't just refer to *main.c* without specifying the directory that contains it. The proper names are:

```
c:\mystuff\main.c
c:\mystuff\projectx\main.c
c:\mystuff\projecty\main.c
```

The file organization scheme shown in Figure 6-1 is known as a *hierarchical directory structure* because the directories form a hierarchy, that is, a number of levels. This feature was added to the DOS file manager when fixed disk support became available in Version 2. At that time, the typical fixed disk held 10 or 20 megabytes, and only "power users" had them. Today, most PCs have this type of storage and, in fact, a fixed disk is required for many DOS applications and for OS/2. Power users now often need drives holding more than 50 megabytes; network servers and electronic bulletin board systems often require several hundred megabytes. CD-ROM drives are also becoming popular, with capacities of 500 megabytes and more.

The hierarchical directory structure, which originated in UNIX, provides a means to manage the thousands of files that can reside on a large disk. The user typically needs to access only a few of these during a session. For example, when I'm working on this book, I'm only interested in the files that comprise its chapters, but when I'm doing my taxes, my attention is focused on an entirely different set of files. So, I might keep my book in a directory named *os2book*, while my tax data would be in another directory named *tax1988*. If both of these reside on disk drive C, then before working on my book, I could type:

```
c:
cd \os2book
```

which would restrict my view of the file system to those files in the *os2book* directory. In order to switch to some tax work, I would type

```
cd \tax1988
```

assuming that the drive C is already the current drive.

You'll often here the term *view path* as a way of referring to the user's perspective on the file system, which is established via the current drive and current directory commands as previously shown.

One last comment on directory names: Most people do not use extensions when they name a directory. However, both DOS and OS/2 allow you to do this, and it sometimes comes in handy. For example, suppose you wanted to keep an older version of the files that are in the *mystuff* directory shown in Figure 6-1. You could create a directory named *mystuff.old* to hold these older copies. This directory would also contain subdirectories named *projectx* and *projecty*. So, the old copy of *main.c* from *projectx* would be obtained via the name *c:\mystuff.old\projectx\main.c*.

6.2 Basic File Operations

DOS and OS/2 both provide six basic API functions for creating, removing, opening, closing, reading, and writing files. The DOS interrupt 21H codes and the corresponding OS/2 function names are:

Operation	OS/2 API	DOS API
Create a file	DosOpen	3CH,5BH
Remove a file	DosDelete	41H
Open a file	DosOpen	3DH
Close a file	DosClose	3EH
Read a file	DosRead	3FH
Write a file	DosWrite	40H

Chapter 3 already gave you a taste of these API services in the *dread* function. Let's now take a look at a function that uses more of the OS/2 File System API services. It accepts two file names and copies the first file to the second, creating the second if necessary.

```
copy(from,to)
char *from,*to;
{
int error,cerror;       /* error code */
unsigned ifile;         /* input file handle */
unsigned ofile;         /* output file handle */
unsigned action         /* action code from DosOpen */
unsigned arsize;        /* actual size from DosRead */
unsigned awsize;        /* actual size from DosWrite */
char buffer[4096];      /* data transfer buffer */

error = DosOpen((char far *)from,(unsigned far *)(&ifile),
  (unsigned far *)(&action),(long)0,0,1,0x20,(long)0);
if(error) return(error);

error = DosOpen((char far *)to,(unsigned far *)(&ofile),
  (unsigned far *)(&action),(long)0,0,0x12,0x11,(long)0);
if(error)
  {
  DosClose(ifile);
  return(error);
  }

while(1)
```

```
    {
    error = DosRead(ifile,(char far *)buffer,sizeof(buffer),
      (unsigned far *)(&arsize));
    if(error) break;
    if(arsize == 0) break;
    error = DosWrite(ofile,(char far *)buffer,arsize,
      (unsigned far *)(&awsize));
    if(error) break;
    if(awsize != arsize)
      {
      error = -1;
      break;
      }
    }

  DosClose(ifile);
  cerror = DosClose(ofile);
  if(error | cerror) DosDelete((char far *)to,(long)0);
  if(error) return(error);
  return(cerror);
  }
```

If you step back and look at the basic flow, you'll see that this example is pretty straightforward. First *DosOpen* is called to open the input and output files. Then *DosRead* and *DosWrite* are called repetitively to copy the input file to the output. Finally, both files are closed with *DosClose*. If an error occurs during any of these operations, the appropriate files are closed, and the OS/2 error code is returned to whoever called the *copy* function. If the input file is successfully copied to the output, the function returns a value of zero.

When examined more closely, the *copy* function does contain a few mysteries, especially those "magic numbers" passed as arguments to *DosOpen*. So let's walk through it a little more slowly, concentrating on the API calls.

First of all, the function is declared with two arguments, which are pointers to the input and output file names. These are named *from* and *to* respectively. Then come a few local storage declarations. Since OS/2 programs refer to files by *handles*, just like DOS, we must reserve two words, *ifile* and *ofile*, to hold the handles for the input and output file. Also, we reserve two words named *error* and *action* to receive status information from *DosOpen* and two words named *arsize* and *arwsize* to receive the actual block size read and written, respectively.

The data buffer is creatively called *buffer*, and it is arbitrarily sized at 4096 bytes. We could have used any size, but its best to go with a multiple of 512 bytes, since that is the standard disk block size for both OS/2 and DOS. Any size that is not a multiple of 512 will cause a lot of inefficient buffer manipulation in the operating system.

Also, performance improves as the buffer size increases. The buffer could be made as large as 65,535 bytes, or 64 kilobytes minus one, because *DosRead* and *DosWrite* accept a 16-bit word containing the buffer size. In this example the buffer actually resides in the stack, which can have a maximum size of 64 kilobytes, but is often much smaller in C programs (e.g., in the neighborhood of 10 kilobytes). Therefore, we chose a buffer size of 4096 bytes as a good compromise between I/O performance and stack utilization.

Another reason 4096 bytes is a good choice is that OS/2 and DOS usually allocate disk space in *clusters* containing several blocks. Floppy diskettes often use 1024-byte (i.e., 2-block) clusters, while hard disks typically use clusters of 4096 bytes. The most efficient copy operation will occur if at least one cluster is transferred on each read/write cycle.

6.2.1 Opening the Input File

Now comes the hard stuff. The first call to *DosOpen* is supposed to find the input file and assign a handle to it. So, the first *DosOpen* argument is a pointer to the input file name, and the second is a pointer to the word that will receive the handle. Note that both of these must be converted to far pointers, as discussed in Chapter 4.

The third argument is also a far pointer, and it refers to an *action word* into which *DosOpen* places some information about the action it took. The possible codes that can be returned here are:

CODE	MEANING
1	File already exists
2	File was created
3	File was replaced

In DOS, the API function that opens files does not return an action code; if you need this information, be prepared to go through some programming gymnastics. This is an example of something you'll find throughout the OS/2 API: Many clever improvements have been made over DOS, and so OS/2 API programming tends to be easier and more straightforward.

The fourth and fifth arguments to *DosOpen* are used only when a new file is being created, and so we'll ignore them for now.

Bits 0 to 3 of the sixth argument specify the action to be taken if the file exists. Similarly, bits 4 to 7 tell *DosOpen* what to do if the file does not exist. This word is encoded in the following way:

ACTION FLAGS	MEANING
xxxx xxxx xxxx 0000	Fail if file exists
xxxx xxxx xxxx 0001	Open file if it exists
xxxx xxxx xxxx 0010	Replace file if it exists
xxxx xxxx 0000 xxxx	Fail if file doesn't exist
xxxx xxxx 0001 xxxx	Create file if it doesn't exist

The x's indicate "don't care" bits, whose settings are not significant. We want the first *DosOpen* to fail if the file does not exist and to open the file if it does exist. Therefore, this argument has a value of 1.

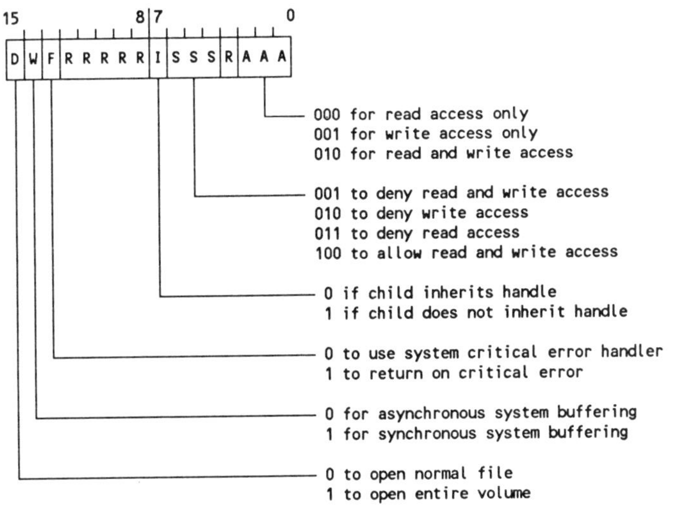

Figure 6-2. DosOpen Processing Mode

The seventh argument specifies the processing mode for the file. This is a complex, bit-encoded value that is, nonetheless, nearly identical to the processing mode used by the DOS open function. Figure 6-2 summarizes its contents. In simple programs like this example, you need only be concerned about the *access mode* in bits 0 through 2 and the *sharing mode* in bits 4 through 6. The former indicates whether you will be reading from the file, writing to it, or doing both. The latter indicates what operations you will allow other processes to perform on the file while you have it open. In our first call to *DosOpen*, we want to read the file, we don't care if another process reads it at the same time. Therefore, the access mode is 000, and the sharing mode is 010. The seventh argument is then 0x20.

The eighth argument is used internally by OS/2 and must always be a double word containing zero.

DosOpen, like all functions in the OS/2 API, returns a non-zero value if an error occurs. In that case, our copy function immediately aborts, passing the OS/2 error code back to its caller.

6.2.2 Opening the Output File

The second call to *DosOpen*

```
error = DosOpen((char far *)to,(unsigned far *)(&ofile),
  (unsigned far *)(&action),(long)0,0,0x12,0x11,(long)0);
```

creates the output file if it doesn't already exist. If there is already a file with that name, it is replaced. Let's compare this call to the previous one, which opens the input file.

The first three arguments are, once again, pointers to the file name, file handle word, and action word, respectively. The fifth argument, which specifies the file attributes, is also zero because this is just an ordinary file. If we did want to create a special file, this argument would be bit-encoded just like the DOS file attribute byte:

ATTRIBUTE	MEANING
0000 0000 00xx 0xx1	Read-only file
0000 0000 00xx 0x1x	Hidden file
0000 0000 00xx 01xx	System file
0000 0000 00x1 0xxx	Subdirectory
0000 0000 001x 0xxx	Archive flag

Bit positions shown as 0 are reserved and must be reset. The x's indicate bits that can be set in combination; for example, 0021H indicates a read-only file which should be archived.

The fourth argument, which specifies the file size, is also zero, as in the first *DosOpen* call. This may seem surprising, since we are creating a new file. Don't we have to specify its size? No, because as in DOS, OS/2 automatically expands an output file when you write to it. However, this may cause the file to have its blocks scattered all over the disk, which can have negative affects on performance in certain applications. For example, the blocks comprising a database index file should really be as close together as possible.

The DOS designers overlooked this need and provided no way to request contiguous space allocation. In OS/2, when the file size argument is not zero, *DosOpen* attempts to allocate a contiguous area of that size. If such an area cannot be found, *DosOpen* fails. You can then repeat the request with a file size of 0, thereby accepting a possible loss of performance because of the scattered allocation. In this example, we don't care if the new file is scattered around on the disk, and so the file size is specified as zero.

The sixth and seventh arguments have the values 0x12 and 0x11, respectively. The 0x12 indicates that the file should be replaced if it exists and created if it does not exist. The 0x11 indicates that the file should be opened for output only and that no other process is allowed to access it.

As with the first *DosOpen* call, the *copy* function aborts if it gets a non-zero error code when it attempts to open the output file. Before terminating, however, it calls *DosClose* to close the input file, an important step that is sometimes overlooked in functions of this type. When bailing out through an error exit, programmers often forget to close all the files that they have opened, which can cause the program to run out of file handles. This is the type of bug that often slips through system testing and only shows up after the program has been released into the hands of "real users."

Notice that we don't bother to check the error code from *DosClose* in this case, because we already have an error code from *DosOpen* to pass back to our caller.

6.2.3 The Copy Loop

The copy loop is very simple. First, *DosRead* is called to get a block from the input file, and then *DosWrite* is called to write the block to the output file. The loop is broken if either function fails, or if the entire input file has been read.

Both functions accept four arguments: a file handle, a far pointer to the data buffer, the data size in bytes, and a far pointer to a word that will receive a actual size of the block transferred. A nonzero return from either function means that an error has occurred, and the loop is immediately broken, with the OS/2 error code in the local variable named *error*.

In *DosRead* we specify the full buffer size (4096 bytes), hoping that the file contains that much data. If it does not, *DosRead* returns an actual size that is less than what we requested. The actual size is zero when there is no more data to be read, in which case we break out of the loop. Since this is the normal way that the operation terminates, the error code is zero.

DosWrite should never return an actual size that is different than its buffer size. If this happens, then there is no more space on the disk. In this case we break out of the loop with the error code set to -1, a value not used for OS/2 API errors. In other words, our *copy* function returns a value of -1 to indicate that there is not enough space for the new file.

6.2.4 Cleaning Up

When the copy loop finishes, *DosClose* is called to close the input file. As in the earlier abort leg, there is no need to inspect the error code after this call. It's extremely unlikely that OS/2 would encounter a problem here, and there's no chance of file mutilation, since we opened the file for read-only access. And besides, what can a poor application program do if the operating system gets so screwed up that it can't even close an input file?

Next we close the output file. Since OS/2 may actually write the last block during this close operation, we must check for a nonzero error code. If a failure occurs here, or if the copy loop was aborted because *DosRead* or *Doswrite* failed, *DosDelete* is called to remove the output file.

The *copy* function finishes its work by returning the first nonzero error code that occurred. If there were no errors, then a value of zero is returned.

6.2.5 File Positioning

File positioning is one basic file operation not covered in the previous example. OS/2 files, as in DOS and UNIX, consist of individually addressable bytes, starting with byte number 0. The *current file position* is the byte number at which the next read or write operation will occur. This position can be read via *DosGetFilePtr* and changed via *DosChgFilePtr*.

Let's see how file positioning works by examining a modified version of the *copy* function, which we'll call *snip*:

```
snip(from,to,pos,len)
char *from,*to;
long pos;
int len;
{
int error,cerror;      /* error code */
unsigned ifile;        /* input file handle */
unsigned ofile;        /* output file handle */
unsigned action        /* action code from DosOpen */
unsigned arsize;       /* actual size from DosRead */
unsigned awsize;       /* actual size from DosWrite */
long newpos;           /* new position from DosChgFilePtr */
unsigned rsize;        /* read size */
char buffer[4096];     /* data transfer buffer */

error = DosOpen((char far *)from,(unsigned far *)(&ifile),
  (unsigned far *)(&action),(long)0,0,1,0x20,(long)0);
if(error) return(error);

error = DosOpen((char far *)to,(unsigned far *)(&ofile),
  (unsigned far *)(&action),(long)0,0,0x12,0x11,(long)0);
if(error)
  {
  DosClose(ifile);
  return(error);
  }

error = DosChgFilePtr(ifile,pos,0,(long *)(&newpos));
if(error) break;

while(len > 0)
  {
  if(len > sizeof(buffer) rsize = sizeof(buffer);
  else rsize = len;
  error = DosRead(ifile,(char far *)buffer,rsize,
    (unsigned far *)(&arsize));
  if(error) break;
  if(arsize == 0) break;
  error = DosWrite(ofile,(char far *)buffer,arsize,
    (unsigned far *)(&awsize));
  if(error) break;
  if(awsize != arsize)
    {
    error = -1;
    break;
    }
```

```
        len -= arsize;
        }

    DosClose(ifile);
    cerror = DosClose(ofile);
    if(error | cerror) DosDelete((char far *)to,(long)0);
    if(error) return(error);
    return(cerror);
    }
```

This example accepts four arguments: the names of the input and output files, a file position, and a length. The job of the *snip* function is to copy the piece of the input file specified by the position and length arguments.

The process of opening and closing the files is unchanged from the *copy* function, but the copy loop is a bit different. First of all, the loop is preceded by a call to *DosChgFilePtr* to position the input file at the desired spot. This OS/2 API function accepts four arguments: a file handle, a long integer specifying the desired position, a code specifying the type of positioning desired, and a pointer to a long integer that will receive the new file position. The codes associated with the third argument, known as the *seek mode,* are the same as in the equivalent DOS API service:

0 Relative to the beginning of the file. The position argument specifies an absolute location in the file and cannot be negative.

1 Relative to the current position. The position argument is added to the current file position. The argument may be positive, negative, or zero.

2 Relative to the end of file. The position argument is added to the file size (i.e. the end of file position). The argument may be zero or negative.

In this case, our caller is passing us an absolute file position, and so we use 0 for the seek mode. Incidentally, when you call *DosChgFilePtr* using mode 0, the long integer to which the fourth argument refers should wind up containing the same value as the second argument. We don't bother to check that here, for the same reason that we don't check the error code when closing the input file. Sometimes you just gotta have faith!

The copy loop is actually a loop only if more than 4096 bytes is being snipped from the input file. Otherwise, there will be only a single read and write.

Notice that the call to *DosRead* uses a computed variable named *rsize* instead of just moving full buffers as we did before. The read/write error checking is unchanged from the previous example.

As an exercise, you might want to modify the *snip* function so that it appends the input block to the output file if the output file already exists. To do this, you'll need to change the second *DosOpen* call and introduce another call to *DosChgFilePtr*.

Notice also that if you call *DosChgFilePtr* specifying 0 for the position and 2 for the seek mode, the new file position is the same as the file size in bytes. We'll use this capability in a later example which checks if the disk has enough space for the new file before starting the copy loop.

6.2.6 Manipulating File Handles

When you call *DosOpen*, OS/2 assigns a file handle in a way that appears to be entirely arbitrary. What if you want to access a file via a handle having a specific value? For example, in Chapter 12 we'll see a very common situation in which you will want to associate handles 0 and 1 with the primary input and output file, respectively. This can be accomplished with *DosDupHandle*. As we'll see in Chapter 12, it is sometimes necessary to duplicate a file handle, which can be used in two ways, as follows:

```
int old;                     /* old handle */
int new1 = 0;                /* new handle, fixed at 0 */
int new2 = -1;               /* new handle, arbitrary */

DosDupHandle(old,&new1);     /* duplicate to handle 0 */
DosDupHandle(old,&new2);     /* duplicate to any handle */
```

If you specify the new handle as -1, then OS/2 will assign a valid one. Otherwise, it will use the one you specify, as long as it is positive or zero. If the duplicate handle refers to an open file, that file is closed.

When several handles refer to the same file as a result of one or more calls to *DosDupHandle*, all handles share the same file positioning information. However, when one of the handles is closed, the others remain open.

DosSetMaxFH is another useful API service which provides the means to increase the maximum number of handles for the current process. The typical OS/2 default for this maximum is 20. For example, you could increase it to 32 via the following call:

```
error = DosSetMaxFH(32);
```

Usually it's best to call this function at the very beginning of your program and to only increase, never decrease, the maximum.

6.2.7 File Locking

OS/2 provides a file locking mechanism similar to the one introduced with DOS Version 3 as a means of supporting local area networks. This feature takes on much more importance in OS/2, because not only can a file be accessed by other users via a network, but other processes within the same system can contend for the same file.

DosFileLocks provides the means to lock and/or unlock a contiguous range within a file. For instance, suppose you want to lock 50 bytes beginning at file position 1000. Then, at some later time you want to unlock that range and lock 200 bytes at position 150. Here are the API calls:

```
int fh;                           /* file handle */
long range1[2] = {1000,50};     /* 1st lock range */
long range2[2] = {150,200};     /* 2nd lock range */

DosFileLocks(fh,NULL,range1);     /* lock 1st range */

/*** Do other work here ***/

DosFileLocks(fh,range1,range2); /* unlock 1st, lock 2nd */
```

Notice that *DosFileLocks* accepts two range pointers. The first specifies the area to be unlocked, and the second is the area to be locked. If only locking or unlocking is being done, as in the first API call, then the other range pointer must be NULL. If you do specify both operations, the unlock occurs first.

It is an error to overlap locked ranges, but you are allowed to specify a range that extends beyond the end of the file. Any active locks are removed when you close the file and when your program terminates. Since duplicate handles share in their file's locks, active locks are not removed until all duplicate handles are closed.

6.3 Directory Operations

In many applications it is quite common to search a directory for all files matching a certain pattern. For example, a menu-oriented "front end" for a C compiler could present you with a list of all files having ".C" extensions. You would then use a mouse or the arrow keys to select the source files that you want to compile. To achieve snappy performance in this type of application, the operating system must provide an efficient set of API functions for searching directories.

The DOS API was usable, but skimpy, in this area, and so some programmers bypassed it in order to deal more efficiently with large disks. Of course, this practice of bypassing the DOS API made it difficult for IBM and Microsoft to introduce a new, high-performance DOS file manager with a substantially different directory structure.

The OS/2 designers wanted to avoid this trap, and so they crafted a more robust set of directory services with the hope that programmers would then not get too involved with the inner details of the file manager. As if to underscore this point, Microsoft announced, shortly after the introduction of OS/2 Version 1, that a new file manager was under development and would be included in a future release. I took this as a gentle warning to programmers: *Even though OS/2 directories are now compatible with DOS and can therefore be accessed as normal "flat files," avoid the temptation to do so. In the future, the directories could well be stored in a more sophisticated database that cannot be processed in this way.*

The following table shows the OS/2 directory functions and the related DOS interrupt 21H services. Unlike the basic operations discussed in the preceding section, the OS/2 directory functions do not correspond exactly to their DOS counterparts, but there are still enough similarities to make the conversion pretty easy.

OPERATION	OS/2 API	DOS API
Create a directory	DosMkDir	39H
Remove a directory	DosRmDir	3AH
Find first matching file	DosFindFirst	4EH
Find next matching file	DosFindNext	4FH
Close directory handle	DosFindClose	

There are two primary differences between DOS and OS/2 in this area: what directories contain and how you search them.

6.3.1 Directory Contents

Each directory contains one or more *file descriptors* which, as you might expect, are records that describe the files and indicate where their data can be found on the disk. Note that the data for these files do not actually reside in the directory; they can be scattered all over the place. However, we generally say that a file is *in* the directory which contains its descriptor.

In DOS, and also in the initial versions of OS/2, a directory is simply a "flat file" in which file descriptors appear one after another with no index or other information that could be used to speed up the searching procedure. In fact, very large directories can become a real performance bottleneck, and so it's generally best to limit each directory to about 50 files or so. However, if you really need to keep a lot of files together, there is no inherent directory size limit.

When the operating system finds a matching file during a directory search, it gives you a portion of the file descriptor in a standard format. As I mentioned earlier, it's probably best that you not know exactly how a descriptor is actually stored or, for that matter, how a directory is actually organized. If you work only with the standard information returned by the API, then you'll be immune from future changes in the directory structure.

DOS returns 43 bytes of descriptor information in the Data Transfer Area, as discussed previously. This has the following format:

OFFSET	SIZE	INFORMATION
00	21	Reserved for "find next"
21	01	File attribute
22	02	File time
24	02	File date
26	04	File size
30	13	File name, null-terminated

The OS/2 descriptor is returned in a buffer that you provide, and it has a format that is considerably different than that of DOS:

OFFSET	SIZE	INFORMATION
00	02	Creation date
02	02	Creation time
04	02	Last access date
06	02	Last access time
08	02	Last write date
10	02	Last write time
12	04	End-of-file position
16	04	File size
20	02	File attribute
22	01	Length of name (nn)
23	nn	File name, null-terminated

You're probably wondering how the file descriptors can be so different if DOS and OS/2 use the same file structure. Actually, the OS/2 descriptor is a superset of the one used by DOS. OS/2 is able to determine if a disk is using the DOS format and, if so, translate to and from the DOS directory structure.

Now let's look at these descriptors in more detail.

Dates and Times

Both DOS and OS/2 use the same format for file dates and times. Dates are encoded as follows:

BITS	INFORMATION
00:04	Day (1 to 31)
05:08	Month (1 to 12)
09:15	Year-1980 (0 to 119)

Similarly, the encoding for time values is:

BITS	INFORMATION
00:04	Two-seconds (0 to 29)
05:10	Minutes (0 to 59)
10:15	Hours (0 to 23)

Notice that dates and times will compare correctly as unsigned integers, because the most significant portions are in the high-order bits. In other words, if the encoded form of date A is less than that of date B, then A preceeds B chronologically.

If you are interested in the utmost programming efficiency, you've probably noticed that the OS/2 designers screwed up by putting the dates and times in the wrong order. Under DOS, the time value came first, followed by the date. You could then declare these two items as a single unsigned long integer and perform chronological comparisons in a single step. For example, here's how you might write some DOS code to check if file A is older than file B:

```
struct FILEDESC             /* DOS file descriptor format */
  {
  char resv[21];            /* Reserved */
  char fattr;               /* File attribute */
  unsigned long ftime;      /* File date and time */
  unsigned long fsize;      /* File size */
  };

struct FILEDESC fa,fb;      /* Two file descriptors */

if(fa.ftime < fb.ftime)     /* Check if A preceeds B */
```

In OS/2, this test is a little more difficult:

```
struct FILEDESC             /* OS/2 file descriptor format */
  {
  unsigned short cdate;     /* Creation date */
  unsigned short ctime;     /* Creation time */
  unsigned short adate;     /* Access date */
  unsigned short atime;     /* Access time */
  unsigned short wdate;     /* Write date */
  unsigned short wtime;     /* Write time */
  unsigned long eof;        /* End-of-file position */
  unsigned long fsize;      /* File size */
  unsigned short fattr;     /* File attribute */
  unsigned char nsize;      /* File name size */
  unsigned char name[17];   /* File name */
  };

struct FILEDESC fa,fb;      /* Two file descriptors */

if((fa.wdate < fb.wdate) ||
```

```
((fa.wdate == fb.wdate) && (fa.wtime < fb.wtime)))
```

The complicated *if* statement checks first if date A is less than date B. If not, it checks if date A is equal to date B and time A is less than time B. This is certainly more difficult to read and it also generates more code than the DOS approach. Why did the OS/2 designers do this?

Another difference between DOS and OS/2 is that the former maintains only one timestamp for each file, while the latter has three. DOS sets the initial timestamp when you create the file and updates it whenever you write to the file. With this approach, it's impossible to tell when the file was created or when it was used but not changed.

OS/2 has a DOS-compatible timestamp that keeps track of when the file was written last, but it also preserves the creation timestamp and notes whenever the file is accessed in a third timestamp. Unfortunately, these latter two are not supported in the initial version of OS/2, which stores zeroes there. So, before using the creation and/or access timestamps, check if they are zero, which means that the file was created under an early version of OS/2.

File Size and End of File

In DOS, the end-of-file position and the file size are one and the same because DOS allocates file space only as you need it. OS/2 file descriptors have distinct values for these two items because you can preallocate space when the file is created with *DosOpen*. There is also an API function named *DosNewSize* which allows you to increase the space allocated to an existing file.

Of course, an application can establish its own end of file convention using some special data pattern, but OS/2 will not detect this. As far as the operating system is concerned, the end-of-file is the highest position that you have written, the so-called "high-water mark."

6.3.2 Searching Directories

When searching a directory, you must supply a *file name pattern* and a *file attribute*. DOS and OS/2 use exactly the same format for these patterns and attributes, although the OS/2 API has been designed to allow for patterns that are longer than the 64 characters permitted by DOS.

File Name Patterns

A file name pattern can simply be a file name, as described earlier in this chapter. In that case, the directory search succeeds if an exact match for that name is found.

In order to find all files in a certain class, you use the asterisk (*) and question mark (?) as *wild card characters* in the node portion of the pattern. An asterisk can appear at the end of the base name or the extension, and it matches 0 or more trailing characters in that portion of the file name. A question mark can appear anywhere in the node, and it matches any single character. All other characters in the pattern must exactly match the corresponding positions in the directory entries. Here are some examples of valid patterns:

***.c** Matches all file names in the current directory on the current drive having the letter C as their extension. Remember, directory searches are insensitive to case, and so *.c and *.C are equivalent.

abc*.def Matches all file names in the current directory on the current drive that begin with ABC and have extensions of DEF.

a:abc*.def Same as above, except the search occurs in the current directory of drive A.

\abc*.def Same as above, except the search occurs in the root directory of the current drive.

a:\abc*.def Same as above, except the search occurs in the root directory of drive A.

\mystuff\?bc*.* Matches all file names in the directory *\mystuff* which have BC as the second and third letters in the base name, followed by 0 or more additional letters and any extension.

\mystuff\?bc Matches all file names in the directory *\mystuff* which have base names of exactly three characters, with BC in the second and third characters, and no extension.

Notice that the * and ? can be used only in the node portion of the pattern. If the pattern specifies a drive or directory, they cannot contain wild cards. So, a pattern such as *my***abc* is not valid.

File Attributes

The file attribute for directory searches is the same as the attribute you can specify when creating a file, which was discussed earlier in this chapter. When you supply an attribute of 0, both DOS and OS/2 search for normal files.

Directory Search Procedure

When you want to search a directory under DOS, you call function 4EH, and it returns directory information about the first matching file in the *Data Transfer Area*, or DTA. This is a buffer that DOS uses for a variety of purposes; you can change the default DTA to a different buffer via API function 1AH. To find additional files matching the search pattern, you call function 4FH. However, you must be very careful not to disturb the DTA while searching a DOS directory, because it contains information that DOS needs to continue the search.

In OS/2, you begin by calling *DosFindFirst*. If a matching file is found, this function returns its descriptor and also assigns a *directory handle*. To find additional matching files in that directory, you call *DosFindNext*, specifying that handle. When you are finished with the directory, call *DosFindClose* to release the handle.

OS/2 performs some special tricks with directory handles in order to make the conversion from DOS a little easier. *DosFindFirst* assigns a new directory handle only if you call it with a value of -1 in the handle argument. For any other value, this API function assumes that you want to close the directory to which the handle is currently attached and then attach it to a new directory. If the handle is unassigned, and if you did not specify handle #1, then *DosFindFirst* fails. Handle #1 is always available. Therefore, when you convert a DOS program to OS/2, you simply translate the 4EH and 4FH from the DOS API into their OS/2 equivalents, *DosFindFirst* and *DosFindNext*, using handle #1.

The following example shows how you can use the OS/2 API to get a list of all the file names matching a certain pattern and attribute. The list consists of null-terminated file names packed into the buffer supplied by the caller.

The last name is followed by a null string, that is, by a string consisting of a single null byte.

```
getnames(name,attr,buff,buffsize,count)
char *name;             /* file name pattern */
unsigned attr;          /* file attribute mask */
char *buff;             /* file name buffer */
unsigned buffsize;      /* size of buffer */
int *count;             /* number of matching files */
{
struct FILEDESC fd;     /* file descriptor area */
int i = 0;              /* number of matching files */
int j = 0;              /* buffer index */
int error;              /* error code */
int dh = -1;            /* directory handle */
int mc = 1;             /* matching file count */

*count = 0;             /* reset file count */
*buffer = 0;            /* terminate the buffer */
if(--buffsize <= 0) return(-1);

error = DosFindFirst(name,&dh,attr,&fd,
  sizeof(fd),&mc,0L);

while(1)
  {
  if(error)
    {
    DosFindClose(dh);
    return(error);
    }
  if(mc != 1) break;
  if(fd.nsize > buffsize)
    {
    DosFindClose(dh);
    return(-1);
    }
  strcpy(buffer,fd.name);
  buffer += fd.nsize;
  *buffer = 0;
  buffsize -= fd.nsize;
  *count++;
  error = DosFindNext(dh,&fd,sizeof(fd),&mc);
  }
```

```
    DosFindClose(dh);
    return(0);
```

The caller supplies five arguments to *getnames*: the file name pattern, the file attribute, the buffer address, the buffer length, and the address of a word that will receive the matching file count. The function returns a value of 0 if it is successful. A positive return code indicates that an OS/2 error occurred, and the return value is the OS/2 error code. A value of -1 is returned if the buffer cannot hold all of the matching names.

The function begins by resetting the matching file count and terminating the buffer with a null byte. The buffer size is reduced by one to allow for the terminating null, and if it becomes 0 or negative, the function aborts immediately.

Then *getnames* calls *DosFindFirst* to begin the search. This API routine accepts a file name pattern, a directory handle pointer, an attribute, a file descriptor pointer, a file descriptor size, a pointer to a match count word, and 32-bit value of 0 which is used internally by the API.

The file descriptor area is defined via the OS/2 *FILEDESC* structure that was presented earlier. *DosFindFirst* and *DosFindNext* allow you to specify an array of these structures if you want to grab more than one file descriptor at a time. That's why you need to also tell the API the size of the descriptor area and also specify the number of descriptors that you want to retrieve in each call. This may seem redundant, but it's not unusual for the OS/2 API to do things this way. At some future time, there may be several different descriptor formats. So, by providing both the buffer length and the number of descriptors, OS/2 can figure out what type of information you want.

After calling *DosFindFirst*, this example enters a loop to process the descriptors. First, the OS/2 error code is checked, and the function aborts if an error occurred. Then if the match count is not 1, the loop is broken and a successful return is made. Next, if the file name will not fit into the buffer, the function returns a value of -1. In all of these termination cases, *DosFindClose* is called to close the directory.

If the loop continues, it moves the file name to the caller's buffer, bumps the caller's file name counter, and adjusts the buffer pointer and size. Then *DosFindNext* is called to find the next matching file name in the directory.

6.3.3 Creating and Removing Directories

The DOS and OS/2 command processors correspond exactly when it comes to creating and removing directories. Both use the MD and MKDIR commands to create directories and the RD and RMDIR commands to remove them. The longer command verbs, MKDIR and RMDIR, were provided for the convenience of users who are familiar with UNIX.

The DOS and OS/2 API functions are also very similar in this area. To create a directory, you use interrupt 21H, function 39H, in DOS and the *DosMkDir* function in OS/2. For example, the following OS/2 code fragment creates a subdirectory named *mystuff* in the current directory:

```
int error;

error = DosMkDir("mystuff",0L);
if(error) ...
```

Note that this function, like many others in the OS/2 API, needs a long integer with a value of 0 as its last argument.

The procedure to remove a directory is also quite simple. The following example gets rid of the directory created by the previous example:

```
int error;

error = DosRmDir("mystuff",0L);
```

Again, note that the last argument must be a long integer set to 0.

6.4 File Names Revisited

Before leaving this chapter, I want to touch on an important, but somewhat peculiar, feature of the DOS and OS/2 File Managers, namely, their ability to access nondisk devices as if they were disk files. As we'll see in the next two chapters, this feature provides one means for you to utilize the keyboard and screen, and it is also a good way to write very flexible and portable programs.

When you ask the file manager to open a file, it first checks the name to see if it matches one of the nondisk devices attached to the computer. If not, the file manager proceeds to deal with the appropriate disk drive as we've already discussed. Otherwise, a connection is established to that device for subsequent data transfer operations. Here is a list of device names that you'll normally find in DOS and OS/2:

NAME	DESCRIPTION	DOS	OS/2
AUX	Auxiliary port	X	
CLOCK$	System clock	X	X
COM1	Communication port #1	X	X
COM2	Communication port #2	X	X
CON	System console	X	X
KBD$	Keyboard		X
LPT1	Line printer #1	X	X
LPT2	Line printer #2	X	X
LPT3	Line printer #3	X	X
MOUSE$	Mouse device		X
NUL	Null device	X	X
POINTER$	Pointer device		X
PRN	System printer	X	X
SCREEN$	System screen		X

The X's in the DOS and OS/2 columns indicate whether a device is supported in that operating system. The names ending with dollar signs ($) are special devices not normally accessed by application programs. All other names represent devices that you can open via the File Manager.

The NUL device is one which returns an end-of-file condition when you read from it and discards any data that you write to it. This is most often used when you want to suppress a large printout while testing a program. If you connect the program's output to NUL instead of PRN, no output will be printed, but the program will not know the difference.

The CON device refers to the keyboard for input and the video display (i.e. the screen) for output. These two devices together are called the *system console*.

The LPT devices are usually *parallel ports* to which printers are attached. However, other devices can attach to these ports, but the operating system will still know them by the LPT names. LPT1 can also be referred to by the name PRN. This is called the *system printer*.

Similarly, the COM devices are usually *serial ports* using the RS-232 protocol to which communication devices (i.e. modems) are attached. However, many other devices can connect to RS-232 channels, including printers, scanners, mice, and video terminals. Regardless of what is attached, however, the operating system still refers to these channels via their COM names.

When you attach a printer to a COM port on a DOS computer, you can reroute any of the line printers to that port via the MODE command. For example, the following command routes LPT1 to COM1.

```
mode lpt1=com1
```

After this command, PRN also refers to COM1. In OS/2 this type of redirection is not allowed. OS/2 includes a *print spooler* as a standard feature which can be activated via the SPOOL command. To accomplish the redirection of LPT1 to COM1, you would type this command:

```
spool c:\spool /d:lpt1 /o:com1
```

The first argument is a disk directory where the spooled data will be saved. The second argument specifies the device that will be rerouted to this disk area, and the third argument indicates where the actual printer is located. It is unfortunate that the second and third arguments use colons as punctuation, since it makes the "d:" and "o:" look like disk drive letters. Actually, "/d:" and "/o:" are command options; the letter "d" indicates that this option specifies the *spooled device*, and the letter "o" means that this is the *output device*. The colons, then, just separate the option letters from the device names.

While the names just listed are standard, both DOS and OS/2 support user-installed device drivers. These are specified via the DEVICE command in the *config.sys* configuration file. Whenever you install device drivers in addition to the standard ones, new device names are defined.

6.5 Summary

In the initial versions of OS/2, the File Manager remains compatible with DOS, although the new operating system offers better control of space allocation and file sharing. Despite these improvements, the OS/2 File Manager is still pretty simple and needs further evolution.

For instance, more sophisticated allocation and access algorithms are needed in order to meet the performance requirements of file servers having large numbers of high-capacity disks. Similarly, the inevitable multi-user version of OS/2 will require the File Manager to provide better file sharing mechanisms. Each file needs to have a "user ID" associated with it, and disk space rations must be established for each user.

Shortly after OS/2 was announced, Microsoft indicated that the File Manager was being redesigned to address these needs in a future release.

Chapter 7

Video Interface

Despite OS/2's sophisticated set of *big system* features, it is nonetheless an operating system tailored for personal computers. PCs are generally used for highly interactive applications in which it is extremely important to have efficient access to the basic human interface devices, namely the video screen, the keyboard, and the pointing device (i.e., the mouse).

This chapter explains how OS/2 accomplishes what many believed was an impossible feat: *Providing high-performance video in a protected, multitasking environment.* In fact, OS/2's approach to the video interface is one of its most innovative features, and after this discussion, Chapters 8 and 9 describe OS/2's equally innovative handling of the keyboard and mouse.

7.1 Video Access Methods

Both DOS and OS/2 provide four methods to access the video display device:

- Via the File Manager, without translation;
- Via the File Manager, with translation;
- Via the ROM BIOS in DOS or the video I/O subsystem in OS/2;
- Via direct interfaces to the logical and physical video buffers and registers;

Each method has its own advantages, disadvantages, and performance characteristics. The first two are preferred for plain vanilla applications which use the display screen as a "glass teletype" or a "dumb terminal" like you might find attached to a minicomputer. In fact, the C library employs these techniques for the the standard C output functions such as *putchar*, *puts*, and *printf*.

The latter two methods are generally employed in full-screen applications, whether textual or graphical, including spreadsheets, word processors, drawing programs, and CAD systems. Most C compilers provide some library support for these techniques, but since ANSI has not sanctioned any high-speed screen functions for the C language, compiler vendors have diverged quite a bit in this area. The closest thing to a standard is the *curses* library which was invented for the UNIX environment and has been adapted to DOS by several software vendors. OS/2 versions of *curses* will probably also be available from these or other vendors.

7.2 Video Access Via File Manager

In Chapter 6 we saw how the File Manager allows you not only to access disk files but also connect to various non-disk devices. For instance, if you request the File Manager to open a file named "CON", then you will be reading from the keyboard and writing to the display screen. This combination of devices is often called the *console*.

To see how this works, we could write a simple program that displays the contents of a file on the screen, using the *copy* function which was presented in Chapter 6:

```
main(argc,argv)
int argc;
char *argv[];
{
if(argc < 2)             /* abort if no file name */
  return(1);
if(copy(argv[1],"con"))  /* copy file to console screen */
  return(1);             /* return 1 for error */
return(0);               /* return 0 for success */
}
```

We'll call this source module *list.c*. When we compile and link it together with *copy.c* from the preceding chapter, the result is a new program file named *list.exe*. Then you can use the *list* command to display the contents of a file, say *copy.c*, via the following command:

```
list copy.c
```

This command is basically the same as the *type* command that is provided with DOS and OS/2. Neither of these commands is very useful for browsing through files that contain more than a few lines of text, because the lines move by on the screen so fast. In the next chapter, we'll modify this program to pause when the screen is full.

7.2.1 Standard I/O Handles

While the *list* program is a simple and effective way to display files on the screen, it is limited by the fact that the CON device is "hard coded" as the output file name. It would be nice if we could use this same program to copy files to the printer, a serial port, or another disk file. One way to accomplish this would be to let the user specify the output device or file as the first command line argument. The second argument would then be the input file name. But an easier way is to use the standard I/O handles provided by DOS and OS/2. These standard handles are, in fact, the way most programs access the keyboard and screen through the file manager.

You'll recall that open files are identified by *handles*, which are simply positive numbers assigned by the file manager. The DOS and OS/2 command processors automatically assign several file handles to an application program before it begins to execute. These assignments are:

HANDLE	USAGE	DEFAULT	MODE
0	Standard input file	Keyboard	Read
1	Standard output file	Screen	Write
2	Standard error file	Screen	Write

DOS also assigns handle 3 to the the first serial port (COM1) and handle 4 to the printer (PRN). OS/2 does not make these assignments.

Handles 0, 1, and 2 make it easy to write programs that read from the keyboard and/or write to the screen as if they were "byte stream" files. For example, here is a program named *xfer* which transfers data from standard input to standard output.

```
main()                    /* main routine for "xfer" */
{
char buffer[1024];        /* data buffer */
int rsize;                /* DosRead actual size */
int wsize;                /* DosWrite actual size */

while(DosRead(0,buffer,sizeof(buffer),&rsize) == 0)
   {
   if(DosWrite(1,buffer,rsize,&wsize)) return(1);
   if(rsize != wsize) return(1);
   }
return(0)
}
```

If you build this program and run it with no command line arguments, it will simply echo each line that you type. When you enter a CTRL-Z character, which is the "keyboard end-of-file", the program will terminate.

A more interesting use of the *xfer* program is to display the contents of a file on the screen as we did with the *list* program earlier. This can be done using the < character on the command line to switch the standard input away from the keyboard. For example, to display the file *xfer.c*, which is the source file for the *xfer* program, you would type:

```
xfer <xfer.c
```

Both the DOS and OS/2 command processors also allow you to connect the standard output handle to something other than the screen, via the > character. For instance, you can copy *xfer.c* to *xfer.bak* by typing:

```
xfer <xfer.c >xfer.bak
```

So by just using the standard input and output handles, you can write very general programs that work with the keyboard, screen, or any other input and output devices that can be read and written sequentially.

The OS/2 command processor is considerably more advanced than its DOS counterpart in this area of file handle assignment. Its additional features are:

Append to standard output
If you specify the standard output file with >> instead of >, then the

output data are appended to the file if it exists. If the file does not exist, it is created, just as with normal redirection via >.

Assign specific handles
If you place a handle number in front of the <, >, or >> redirection codes, then that handle is connected to the specified file for input, output, or appending, respectively. Here are some examples of how this feature is used:

2>error.log — Connects handle 2 (the standard error file) to *error.log*.

2>>error.log — Connects handle 2 to *error.log* in such a way that new data are appended to the file.

2>&1 — Connects handle 2 to the file or device that is associated with handle 1.

The most common use for this feature is to redirect the standard error file, as shown in the previous examples. However, its use is not restricted to handle 2; any valid handle number can be assigned in this way.

7.2.2 Translated Screen Output

The IBM PC is essentially an ASCII system. Accordingly, the PC video subsystem converts decimal codes ranging from 32 through 126 into readable characters using the ASCII coding conventions. In addition, if you access the video subsystem in "TTY mode," which is what happens when you go through the file system, several ASCII *control codes* are recognized. These codes all have values below 32, as follows:

7 — Generates a beep (not really a screen operation).

10 — Moves the cursor to the same position on the next line. This character is called the *line feed*, or LF.

13 — Moves the cursor to the leftmost position of the current line. This character is call the *carriage return*, or CR.

What happens to the other codes from 0 to 31 and from 128 to 255? Well, when IBM introduced the PC, they extended the ASCII standard by assigning useful display characters to all 256 codes. Chapter 13 shows these display characters for the standard *code page* that is normally used in the USA, and it also shows several other coding schemes that are more appropriate in other countries.

So, when you send information to the screen via the file manager, you can not only display text information, but you can also use IBM's extended character set to draw horizontal and vertical lines, create boxes, and generate many other visual effects that go well beyond original ASCII, which was defined in an era when teletype machines were the predominant computer output device. However, you cannot easily move the cursor around the screen or control display attributes such as flashing, intensity, and colors. This is where *translated video* comes into play.

Translated video is provided in DOS and in the OS/2 DOS session by the *ansi.sys* driver, which you activate by placing the following command in *config.sys*:

```
device=ansi.sys
```

You can deactivate video translation in an OS/2 session via the ANSI command:

```
ansi off
```

You can also activate translation for a session by specifying "on" instead of "off".

When video translation is on, the data stream sent to the screen via the file manager is examined for the following ANSI terminal control sequences, each of which must be preceded by an escape character (decimal value 27):

[#;#H Moves cursor to the position specified by the #'s. Replace the first # with the row number as one or more ASCII digits. Replace the second # with the column number. Row 1 is the top row, and column 1 is the left column. If you omit the #'s and the semicolon, the cursor moves to row 1, column 1, which is the upper left corner of the screen.

[#A Moves cursor up # rows. If # is omitted, it defaults to 1.

[#B Moves cursor down # rows. If # is omitted, it defaults to 1.

[#C Moves cursor forward (right) # columns. If # is omitted, it defaults to 1.

[#D Moves cursor backward (left) # columns. If # is omitted, it defaults to 1.

[s Saves the current cursor position.

[u Restores the cursor to the position that was previously saved.

[2J Erases entire screen and moves cursor to the home position at row 1, column 1.

[K Erases from the cursor position to the end of the current row.

[6n Causes console device to issue a cursor position report as if it came from the keyboard. The position report has the form

```
ESC [#;#R
```

where the first # is the current row number and the second # is the current column number.

[#m Sets a display attribute to the code specified by #. If several attributes are being set at the same time, specify several #'s separated by semicolons. The display attributes are:

0	Normal. All attributes are turned off.
1	Bold or high-intensity.
4	Underline (monochrome displays only).
5	Blink.
7	Reverse video.
8	Invisible.
30 or 40	Black foreground or background.
31 or 41	Red foreground or background.
32 or 42	Green foreground or background.
33 or 43	Yellow foreground or background

34 or 44	Blue foreground or background.
35 or 45	Magenta foreground or background.
36 or 46	Cyan foreground or background.
37 or 47	White foreground or background.

[=#h Sets the video mode to the code specified by #, which must be one of the following:

- **0** Black and white text, 25 rows by 40 columns.
- **1** Color text, 25 rows by 40 columns.
- **2** Black and white text, 25 rows by 80 columns.
- **3** Color text, 25 rows by 80 columns.
- **4** Color graphics, 200 rows by 320 columns.
- **5** Black and white graphics, 200 rows by 320 columns.
- **6** Black and white graphics, 200 rows by 640 columns.
- **7** Automatic wrap at end of line; that is, the cursor automatically advances to column 1 of the next line.

To see how ANSI control sequences work, consider the following example:

```
int i;

for(i = 25; i > 0; i--)
  printf("\x1b[%d;0HRow %d",i,i-1);
```

This prints the phrase "Row x" on every row of the screen, beginning with bottom row and working upwards. The row number displayed goes from 24 to 0, although the ANSI translator requires that you refer to this range as 25 to 1.

The ANSI terminal control sequences enable you to control the display screen through the file manager in a way that is quite portable. That is, by using these control sequences, your program won't care if it is dealing with an IBM PC screen or with a DEC VT100 terminal on a UNIX system. Now let's look at two other ways to use the PC screen which are not so portable.

7.3 Video I/O Subsystem

The major disadvantage of the two video techniques presented earlier, in which the File Manager routes data to the video device, is that the performance is not adequate for highly-interactive full-screen applications.

When DOS programmers discovered this problem, they had an easy solution: *They simply bypassed the operating system*. One way to do this is to call the video BIOS routines directly via software interrupt 10H. An even faster method is to write directly into the video display buffers and the video controller registers.

Both techniques are now widely used and are a primary reason why the PC has become the dominant platform for applications such as spreadsheets and business graphics. The lack of such methods in other operating systems, most notably UNIX and XENIX, has inhibited the development of this type of application in those environments.

These thoughts undoubtedly caused many sleepless nights for the OS/2 designers. They had to wrestle with the thorny problem of providing the traditional PC high-bandwidth screen access methods to several sessions in such a way that the sessions would not interfere with one another. Happily, they solved the problem with a video subsystem that is truly one of the most innovative features of OS/2.

In this section we'll see how OS/2 provides an equivalent to the BIOS technique, and then the next section describes how you access the video buffers and registers in OS/2's protected environment.

7.3.1 Logical Video Buffers

The OS/2 video subsystem is a portion of the standard API which provides efficient access to the screen driver and the underlying display hardware. As with the rest of the OS/2 API, the features of the video subsystem are accessed via function calls. In this case, the functions all begin with *Vio*.

If you recall from Chapter 3, each OS/2 session has a *logical video buffer* which holds that session's screen contents when it is in the background. When the session returns to the foreground, this buffer is copied to the *physical video buffer*, and when the session returns once again to the background, the physical buffer is saved in the logical buffer.

And so, the primary duty of the video subsystem is to route the screen output from the various sessions to the appropriate buffers. However, in versions of OS/2 that do not include the Presentation Manager, no buffer management is provided for graphical display modes. Only the text modes are fully supported.

Most processes are happy with the single logical video buffer that is provided automatically. However, the video subsystem was designed in such a way that additional buffers could be provided. This is why most *Vio* calls include a *video handle* argument. The handle for the default buffer is 0, and that is the only value supported by the IBM and Microsoft editions. Alternative video subsystems could be developed to support multiple buffers. For instance, you could implement a text-mode windowing system in this way for environments that do not need the expensive graphical capabilities of the Presentation Manager.

To facilitate installation of the Presentation Manager or some other enhanced display manager as an OS/2 option, the basic video subsystem allows most of its API services to be redirected. In other words, the Presentation Manager calls the *VioRegister* function to replace some of the text-oriented services in the basic video subsystem with the graphically-oriented services appropriate to the more advanced environment. Then any sessions created under the Presentation Manager will operate correctly in that graphical environment even though they are calling the text-oriented *Vio* functions.

7.3.2 Basic Video Functions

The following table lists the *Vio* functions that are equivalent to the video BIOS services accessed under DOS via interrupt 10H.

BIOS 10H	OS/2 API	DESCRIPTION
03H	VioGetCurPos	Get cursor position
0FH	VioGetMode	Get display mode
08H	VioReadCellStr	Read cell string
	VioReadCharStr	Read character string
07H	VioScrollDn	Scroll down
	VioScrollLf	Scroll left
	VioScrollRt	Scroll right
06H	VioScrollUp	Scroll up
02H	VioSetCurPos	Set cursor position
01H	VioSetCurType	Set cursor type

00H	VioSetMode	Set display mode
0BH	VioSetState	Set video state
09H	VioWrtCellStr	Write cell string
0AH	VioWrtCharStr	Write character string
	VioWrtCharStrAttr	Write character string with attribute
	VioWrtNAttr	Write N attributes
	VioWrtNCell	Write N cells
	VioWrtNChar	Write N characters
0EH	VioWrtTTY	Write a TTY string

Note that OS/2 extends the BIOS repertoire by adding functions to scroll the screen horizontally and by providing more flexible functions for writing multiple characters.

Now let's look at an example. The following function draws an empty box on the screen at the coordinates specified by the caller:

```
static short vhorz = 0x07c4;     /* horizontal line */
static short vvert = 0x07b3;     /* vertical line */
static short vulc = 0x07da;      /* upper left corner */
static short vllc = 0x07c0;      /* lower left corner */
static short vurc = 0x07bf;      /* upper right corner */
static short vlrc = 0x07d9;      /* lower right corner */
static short vfill = 0x0720;     /* fill value */

box(d)
short *d;
{
int i,rows,cols;

rows = d[2] - d[0] - 1;     /* compute rows within box */
if(rows <= 0) return(-1);   /* fail if no rows */

cols = d[3] - d[1] - 1;     /* compute cols within box */
if(cols <= 0) return(-1);   /* fail if no cols */

VioScrollUp(d[0],d[1],d[2],d[3],  /* clear the box */
     -1,&vfill,0);

VioWrtNCell(&vulc,1,d[0],d[1],0); /* upper left corner */
VioWrtNCell(&vurc,1,d[0],d[3],0); /* upper right corner */
VioWrtNCell(&vllc,1,d[2],d[1],0); /* lower left corner */
```

```
VioWrtNCell(&vlrc,1,d[2],d[3],0); /* lower right corner */
VioWrtNCell(&vhorz,cols,d[0],d[1]+1,0); /* upper border */
VioWrtNCell(&vhorz,cols,d[2],d[1]+1,0); /* lower border */

for(i = 0; i < rows; i++)          /* left/right borders */
  {
  VioWrtNCell(&vvert,1,d[0]+i+1,d[1],0);
  VioWrtNCell(&vvert,1,d[0]+i+1,d[3],0);
  }

return(0);                         /* success return */
}
```

The caller supplies an array containing four short integers, as in the following statements:

```
short rect[4] = {10,0,20,79};

box(rect);
```

The first two integers (10 and 0) are the upper left row and column, while the last two (20 and 79) are the lower right row and column. The *Vio* functions use the coordinate (0,0) as the home position in the upper left corner of the screen. In other words, the rows are numbered from 0, beginning at the top of the screen, and the columns are numbered from 0 beginning at the left side.

The *box* example begins with some data declarations that are used for clearing the box and drawing its border. While these may look like "magic numbers", they are just the standard IBM PC line-drawing characters that we mentioned earlier as extensions to the ASCII character set.

Notice that we declare these as two-byte constants called *cells*. This is because when the video display is operating in text mode, each character position on the screen is actually driven by a 16-bit value. The low-order byte is the character code, while the high byte is the attribute, which contains the following fields:

BITS	ATTRIBUTE
00:02	Foreground color
03	Intensity
04:06	Background color
07	Blink

For monochrome displays, the normal color codes are 0 for black and 7 for white. In other words, attribute 7 produces the normal white on black display, while attribute 0x70 produces black on white, which is often called reverse video. The intensity and blink bits can be used with either combination. Most monochrome display adaptors also generate an underline if the foreground color code has the value 1.

For color displays, the intensity bit works in conjunction with the foreground color code to produce the following 16 hues:

CODE	INTENSITY=0	INTENSITY=1
0	Black	Gray
1	Blue	Light blue
2	Green	Light green
3	Cyan	Light cyan
4	Red	Light red
5	Magenta	Light magenta
6	Brown	Yellow
7	White	Bright white

Advanced displays, such as the Enhanced Graphics Adaptor (EGA), allow these codes to be mapped to different colors, but most existing DOS programs were designed to produce good results with the standard color arrangement shown in this table.

In this example, we are drawing blank boxes with simple white borders. So, the attributes are all set to 7, which is the code for white foreground and black background. Since this code works correctly on both monochrome and color displays, the function does not need to check the display type. The right portion of each cell constant is one of the PC line drawing characters shown in Chapter 13. For example, *vhorz* is defined as the hexadecimal value 07C4. The high-order byte (07) is the attribute portion of the cell, indicating white on black. The low-order byte (C4) is the value for the horizontal line character.

Next we get to the *box* function itself. It is called with one argument, a pointer to a four-word array that defines the rectangle. The first step is to verify that this array defines a valid box. Note, however, that we don't check if the box really fits on the screen. This could (and probably should) be done via another API function named *VioGetMode*, which we will introduce in the next example.

Next we call *VioScrollUp* to clear the box. This API function scrolls a rectangular area of the screen upward by the specified number of rows, filling the vacated rows with the specified cell data. The first four arguments give the upper left and lower right corners of the rectangular area. The fifth argument specifies the number of rows to scroll upward, leaving that many empty rows at the bottom of the area. If you supply a value of -1 for this argument as we did here, then the entire area is scrolled, which clears the block. The sixth argument is a pointer to the cell data that will be used to fill this empty area. A cell is simply a 16-bit item with the display attribute in its high-order byte and the display character in its low-order byte. The seventh argument is the video device handle, which should be 0 for the default logical screen.

We could have cleared the area in much the same way with any of the other scrolling functions: *VioScrollDn*, *VioScrollLf*, *VioScrollRt*.

After clearing the rectangular area, we call *VioWrtNCell* several times to draw the border. This function sets a number of display cells to the same value. The first argument points to the value, and the second gives the number of display positions that are to be changed. The third and fourth arguments specify the starting row and column, respectively. Finally, the fifth argument is the video device handle, which should once again be 0 for the default logical screen.

If you are familiar with the standard IBM PC ROM BIOS, you should recognize *VioScrollUp* as interrupt 10H, function 6. *VioWrtNCell* is, in effect, one or more calls to interrupt 10H, functions 2 and 9.

7.4 Direct Access to Video Buffers

In the DOS environment, the highest video performance is achieved by programs which directly access the video buffers. This is quite easy under DOS, since these buffers can be read and written by any programmer who is clever enough to discover their locations. And even that doesn't require a lot of cleverness; you just have to consult *IBM PC Technical Reference* or one of the many books about the PC and DOS.

In a multitasking environment, the video buffers must be more tightly controlled by the operating system. Imagine what the user would see if several unrelated processes were writing to directly to the screen at the same time! As I mentioned earlier, this presented a tough challenge to the OS/2 designers. They had to provide direct screen access if OS/2 were to support the popular DOS applications, but they had to do it in such a way that the important protection and multitasking features were not compromised.

As a result of their efforts, OS/2 offers two ways for you to access the video buffers. The preferred method is to use the logical video buffer in a way reminiscent of IBM's Topview and similar DOS extenders. Another way is to use the physical video buffer, which is slightly faster but makes the program much more complicated. Without the Presentation Manager or an equivalent graphical session manager, the latter method is the only way you can use the screen in a graphical mode, because the basic video subsystem only supports logical buffers for text-mode applications.

7.4.1 Accessing the Logical Video Buffer

The *box* function in the preceding example does not need to know where the logical buffer is located, since all information is written there indirectly via the video API functions. Now let's examine a different version that writes directly to the logical video buffer.

As I mentioned earlier, one of these buffers is allocated for each screen group, and you can write to it even when executing in the background. Then when the session manager flips your screen group into the foreground, the logical video buffer is copied to the *physical video buffer*, causing the screen display to change. You may recognize this as essentially the same approach used by IBM's Topview and other DOS multitasking packages. In other words, if you trigger BIOS interrupt 10H, function 255, under Topview, you'll receive back the address of Topview's logical buffer. Then, after updating the buffer, you trigger interrupt 10H, function 254, to flush the buffer to the screen. This is basically what the revised *box* function does, using *Vio* functions instead of BIOS interrupts.

```
struct ModeData         /* data area for VioGetMode */
  {
  short length;         /* length of structure */
  char type;            /* display type */
  char colors;          /* number of colors */
  short cols;           /* number of text columns */
  short rows;           /* number of text rows */
```

```
   short pcols;        /* number of pixel columns */
   short prows;        /* number of pixel rows */
   };

static short vhorz = 0x07c4;      /* horizontal line */
static short vvert = 0x07b3;      /* vertical line */
static short vulc = 0x07da;       /* upper left corner */
static short vllc = 0x07c0;       /* lower left corner */
static short vurc = 0x07bf;       /* upper right corner */
static short vlrc = 0x07d9;       /* lower right corner */
static short vfill = 0x0720;      /* fill character */

box(d)
short *d;
{
int i,j,rows,cols;      /* miscellaneous */
int trx,brx;            /* index to top and bottom rows */
short far *b;           /* logical video buffer pointer */
short s;                /* size of video buffer */
struct ModeData mode; /* data area for VioGetMode */

rows = d[2] - d[0] - 1;    /* compute rows within box */
if(rows <= 0) return(-1); /* fail if no rows */

cols = d[3] - d[1] - 1;    /* compute columns within box */
if(cols <= 0) return(-1); /* fail if no columns */

mode.length = sizeof(struct ModeData); /* get video mode */
if(VioGetMode(&mode,0)) return(-1);

if(d[2] >= mode.rows) return(-1); /* fail if off screen */
if(d[3] >= mode.cols) return(-1); /* ditto */

trx = d[0] * mode.cols + d[1];  /* get top row index */
brx = d[2] * mode.cols + d[1];  /* get bottom row index */

if(VioGetBuf(&b,&s,0)) return(-1); /* get buffer address */

b[trx] = vulc;               /* upper left corner */
b[brx] = vllc;               /* lower left corner */
for(i = 1; i <= cols; i++) /* top and bottom borders */
  {
  b[trx+i] = vhorz;
  b[brx+i] = vhorz;
  }
b[trx+i] = vurc;             /* upper right corner */
```

```
b[brx+i] = vlrc;           /* lower right corner */
for(j = 1; j <= rows; j++) /* left and right borders */
  {
  trx += mode.cols;
  b[trx] = vvert;
  for(i = 1; i <= cols; i++) /* erase interior of box */
    b[trx+i] = vfill;
  b[trx+i] = vvert;
  }

VioShowBuf(0,s,0);  /* update the screen if foreground */

return(0);          /* success return */
}
```

Three additional API functions are used here. *VioGetBuf* gets the address of the logical video buffer, and *VioGetMode* gets information about the current display mode, which enables us to transform row-column coordinates into buffer indices. *VioShowBuf* directs the operating system to copy the screen image from the logical to the physical buffer if the process is running in the foreground.

Notice that *VioGetMode* returns information in a structure that we define as *ModeData*. This is generally true of the OS/2 API: Complex information is returned in structures allocated by the application. Most of these structure formats are defined in the header files provided with the compiler or with the OS/2 Programmer's Toolkit. The structure is declared explicitly here so you can see what it contains.

This version of the *box* function begins by checking for a valid rectangle just as in the previous example. Then, it calls *VioGetMode* and verifies that the box actually fits on the screen in the current display mode.

Next the buffer address and length is obtained via *VioGetBuf*. Then the program uses several *for-loops* to clear the box and draw the border. Finally, *VioShowBuf* is called to update the actual display, if necessary.

7.4.2 Accessing the Physical Video Buffer

The preceding video techniques are useful only if you are working strictly in text mode, that is, if you are just sending IBM's extended ASCII character codes to the screen. The display hardware is responsible for translating these codes into clusters of dots which the user perceives to be letters, digits, and so on. Typical cluster sizes range from 8-by-8 to 9-by-16, depending on the display hardware. Obviously, it's better to have more dots in each cluster, since the characters will appear to be smoother and better formed.

But what if you need to display information that cannot be represented via the extended ASCII character set? For example, suppose you need to draw a pie chart or a map of the United States? In that case, you must access the screen down at the dot level, which requires that you put the display hardware into a *graphics mode*, thereby disabling its automatic translation of character codes into dot clusters.

The base version of OS/2 doesn't provide much support for processes that operate in graphics mode, and some pundits claim that you must have the Presentation Manager in order to produce graphical displays under OS/2. But that's not entirely true, as long as you're willing to do some extra work. Let's take a look at two examples to see how it's done.

Using the Physical Buffer in Text Mode

First, we'll make some minor changes to the *box* function so that it will use the real video buffer. However, we'll continue to operate in text mode.

```
struct BufData                  /* area for VioGetPhysBuf */
  {
  unsigned long real;           /* real address of screen */
  unsigned long length;         /* length of screen buffer */
  unsigned short prots[2];      /* protected-mode selector(s) */
  };

struct ModeData                 /* area for VioGetMode */
  {
  short length;                 /* length of structure */
  char type;                    /* display type */
  char colors;                  /* number of colors */
  short cols;                   /* number of text columns */
  short rows;                   /* number of text rows */
  short pcols;                  /* number of pixel columns */
  short prows;                  /* number of pixel rows */
  };

static short vhorz = 0x07c4;        /* horizontal line */
static short vvert = 0x07b3;        /* vertical line */
static short vulc = 0x07da;         /* upper left corner */
static short vllc = 0x07c0;         /* lower left corner */
static short vurc = 0x07bf;         /* upper right corner */
```

```
static short vlrc = 0x07d9;      /* lower right corner */
static short vfill = 0x0720;     /* fill character */

box(d)
short *d;
{
int i,j,rows,cols;     /* miscellaneous */
char status;           /* VioScrLock status byte */
int trx,brx;           /* index to top and bottom rows */
union {               /* physical video buffer pointer */
  short far *x;
  short y[2];
  } b;
struct BufData buf;    /* storage area for buffer data */
struct ModeData mode; /* storage area for mode data */

rows = d[2] - d[0] - 1;    /* compute rows within box */
if(rows <= 0) return(-1); /* fail if no rows */

cols = d[3] - d[1] - 1;    /* compute columns within box */
if(cols <= 0) return(-1); /* fail if no columns */

mode.length = sizeof(struct ModeData); /* get video mode */
VioGetMode(&mode,0);
if(mode.type & 2) return(-1);      /* fail if graphics mode
*/

if(d[2] >= mode.rows) return(-1); /* fail if off screen */
if(d[3] >= mode.cols) return(-1); /* ditto */

trx = d[0] * mode.cols + d[1];     /* get top row index */
brx = d[2] * mode.cols + d[1];     /* get bottom row index */

if(mode.type & 1)  /* use CGA address if type bit 0 set */
  buf.real = 0xb8000;
else buf.real = 0xb0000;     /* else use MDA address */
buf.length = 25 * 80 * 2;    /* 25 rows, 80 columns */
VioGetPhysBuf(&buf,0);       /* get physical buffer */
b.y[0] = 0;                  /* form a valid pointer */
b.y[1] = buf.prots[0];

VioScrLock(1,&status,0);     /* wait for foreground */

b.x[trx] = vulc;             /* upper left corner */
b.x[brx] = vllc;             /* lower left corner */
for(i = 1; i <= cols; i++) /* top and bottom borders */
```

```
        {
        b.x[trx+i] = vhorz;
        b.x[brx+i] = vhorz;
        }
    b.x[trx+i] = vurc;          /* upper right corner */
    b.x[brx+i] = vlrc;          /* lower right corner */
    for(j = 1; j <= rows; j++) /* left and right borders */
        {
        trx += mode.cols;
        b.x[trx] = vvert;
        for(i = 1; i <= cols; i++) /* erase interior of box */
            b.x[trx+i] = vfill;
        b.x[trx+i] = vvert;
        }

    VioScrUnlock(0);             /* unlock the screen */
    return(0);                   /* success return */
    }
```

Notice that everything is pretty much the same as in the preceding example using the logical video buffer, except for the calls to *VioScrLock*, *VioGetPhysBuf*, and *VioScrUnlock*. These provide access to the real video buffer.

Also, we use some additional information from *VioGetMode* to determine which of the various possible physical video buffers is in use. This information is returned in the display type code, which is the element named *type* in the *ModeData* structure.

If bit 1 of this code is set, then the video adaptor is in a graphical mode and cannot correctly interpret the text characters that we'll be placing in the buffer. In that case, we immediately abort, returning -1 as an error indicator.

If bit 0 of the display type code is reset, then the Monochrome Display Adaptor (MDA) is in use; otherwise, it's some other hardware such as the Color Graphic Adaptor (CGA), Enhanced Graphics Adaptor (EGA), or Video Graphics Array (VGA). The EGA and VGA can operate in modes that are compatible with CGA. The CGA modes use a real-memory buffer at *segment:offset* address B800:0000, while the MDA buffer is at B000:0000. You must pass the appropriate real-mode address to *VioGetPhysBuf* in order to identify the particular video buffer that you want to access.

VioGetPhysBuf maps a physical video buffer into your virtual address space so that you can read and write it directly. These physical buffers are located in real memory between the 640-kilobyte and the 1-megabyte boundaries. The mapping operation performed by *VioGetPhysBuf* is necessary because you can only use virtual addresses (also called *logical addresses*) while running in protected mode. For example, the CGA buffer at *segment:offset* B800:0000 might wind up being mapped into your virtual address space at 06FF:0000, using the protected-mode *selector:offset* format.

It is very important that you do not try to access the physical buffer via its real-memory address when your process is running in protected mode. If you make this mistake, OS/2 will most likely abort your process for a memory protection violation. However, it is possible that some of your data might be mapped into those virtual addresses, in which case you would not get a protection violation and would probably mutilate the data.

If you're new to IBM PC graphics, you're probably wondering where we got these physical buffer addresses. They, plus a lot of other important programming information, can be found in the technical reference manuals for the various display adaptors. Familiarity with these manuals is a prerequisite to successful graphics programming under DOS or OS/2, unless you use a thick layer of insulation such as Microsoft Windows or the Presentation Manager.

Continuing with the example, we come to *VioScrLock*. This function informs OS/2 that you want direct access to the physical video buffer. Such access is possible only when your process is in the foreground session. The first argument determines what the function should do if you are in the background:

0 Return with a value of 1 in the *status* byte, whose pointer is passed as the second argument.

1 Wait until the calling process returns to the foreground, and then return with the *status* byte cleared.

In this case, we call *VioScrLock* with the first argument set to 1, and so it doesn't return until we are running in the foreground. When it does return, we have complete control of the screen, and the user cannot direct the session manager to flip to another screen group. *VioScrUnlock* relinquishes this control.

Using the Physical Buffer in Graphics Mode

Now, the preceding version of the *box* function just scratches the surface of this whole topic of protected-mode access to the physical video buffer. Specifically, it's a text-mode example, even though you only really need to use this approach when you want to put up graphical displays. So let's undertake a major overhaul of the function to draw a graphical box instead of one that is formed with extended ASCII characters.

```
struct BufData                  /* area for VioGetPhysBuf */
  {
  unsigned long real;           /* real address of screen */
  unsigned long length;         /* length of screen buffer */
  unsigned short prots[2];      /* protected-mode selector(s) */
  };

struct ModeData                  /* area for VioGetMode */
  {
  short length;                  /* length of structure */
  char type;                     /* display type */
  char colors;                   /* number of colors */
  short cols;                    /* number of text columns */
  short rows;                    /* number of text rows */
  short pcols;                   /* number of pixel columns */
  short prows;                   /* number of pixel rows */
  };

char lmask[8] =                 /* left masks */
  {0,0x80,0xc0,0xe0,0xf0,0xf8,0xfc,0xfe};

char linsert[8] =               /* left inserts */
  {0x80,0x40,0x20,0x10,8,4,2,1};

char rmask[8] =                 /* right masks */
  {0x7f,0x3f,0x1f,0xf,7,3,1,0};

char rinsert[8] =               /* right inserts */
  {0x80,0x40,0x20,0x10,8,4,2,1};

box(d)
unsigned short *d;
{
int i,j,rows,cols;               /* miscellaneous */
char c;                          /* miscellaneous */
char status;                     /* VioScrLock status byte */
```

```
char mask = 255;                /* clearing mask */
int trx;                        /* byte index to top row */
int lcx;                        /* left column byte index */
int lcm;                        /* left column mask */
int lcb;                        /* left column bit position */
int lci;                        /* left column insertion */
int rcx;                        /* right column byte index */
int rcm;                        /* right column mask */
int rcb;                        /* right column bit position */
int rci;                        /* right column insertion */
union {                         /* physical screen pointer */
  char far *x;
  unsigned short y[2];
  } b;
struct BufData buf;             /* storage for buffer data */
struct ModeData mode;           /* storage for mode data */
char far *p;                    /* miscellaneous */
rows = d[2] - d[0];             /* compute rows in box */
if(rows <= 0) return(-1);       /* fail if no rows */

cols = d[3] - d[1];             /* compute columns in box */
if(cols <= 0) return(-1);       /* fail if no columns */

mode.length =
  sizeof(struct ModeData);      /* set buffer length */
mode.type = 3;                  /* CGA hi-res graphics */
mode.colors = 1;                /* Black-and-white */
mode.cols = 80;                 /* 80 text columns */
mode.rows = 25;                 /* 25 text rows */
mode.pcols = 640;               /* 640 pixel columns */
mode.prows = 200;               /* 200 pixed rows */
if(VioSetMode(&mode,0))         /* change to CGA mode 6 */
  return(-1);

if(d[2] >= mode.prows)          /* fail if off screen */
  return(-1);
if(d[3] >= mode.pcols)          /* ditto */
  return(-1);

trx = (d[0] / 2) * (640/8);   /* compute top row index */
lcx = d[1] / 8;             /* compute left column index */
lcb = d[1] % 8;             /* compute left bit position */
lcm = lmask[lcb];           /* compute left column mask */
lci = linsert[lcb];         /* compute left column insert */
rcx = d[3] / 8;             /* compute right column index */
rcb = d[3] % 8;             /* compute right bit position */
```

```
rcm = rmask[rcb];            /* compute right column mask */
rci = rinsert[rcb];          /* compute right column insert */

buf.real = 0xb8000;          /* use CGA address */
buf.length = (640 / 8) * 200;  /* length for 640 x 200 */
VioGetPhysBuf(&buf,0);       /* get physical buffer */
b.y[0] = 0;                  /* form a valid pointer */
b.y[1] = buf.prots[0];

VioScrLock(1,&status,0); /* wait for foreground */

for(i = 0; i < buf.length; i++)  /* clear the screen */
  b.x[i] = 0;

for(i = d[0]; i <= d[2]; i++)  /* draw the box */
  {
  if(i == d[2]) mask = 255;
  if(i & 1) b.y[0] = 0x2000;
  else b.y[0] = 0;
  b.y[0] += trx+lcx;
  p = b.x;
  if(lcx != rcx)
    {
    c = (*p & lcm) | (mask & ~lcm) | lci;
    *p++ = c;
    for(j = lcx+1; j < rcx; j++) *p++ = mask;
    *p = (*p & rcm) | (mask & ~rcm) | rci;
    }
  else *p = (*p & lcm) | (*p & rcm) |
    (mask & ~(lcm | rcm)) | lci | rci;
  mask = 0;
  if(i & 1) trx += 640/8;
  }

VioScrUnlock(0);             /* unlock the screen */
return(0);                   /* success return */
}
```

The first thing different here is that we use *VioSetMode* to force the video subsystem into a graphics mode, instead of just passively accepting whatever mode happens to be in effect. *VioSetMode* uses a *ModeData* structure just like *VioGetMode*, but before calling the former, you must load the structure with information describing the video mode that you want to establish.

OS/2 has gotten away from the simple video mode numbers used in DOS, because the OS/2 designers felt that the DOS approach was too confining. As new video adaptors like EGA and VGA become available, DOS requires that new codes be assigned. Meanwhile, the older adaptors, such as CGA, are disappearing, and yet their video codes must still be reserved for historic compatibility. So, in order to clean up this accumulating detritus of old video codes, the OS/2 designers introduced a method whereby you describe the mode in more general terms.

In our example, we want to use the high-resolution CGA mode, which the DOS BIOS knows as video mode 6. This mode can be handled by all of the color graphics adaptors. In fact, the EGA supports all CGA modes, and the VGA supports all CGA and EGA modes. The characteristics of this and the other BIOS modes are shown in the following table:

BIOS MODE	TYPE	HUES	TEXT COLS	TEXT ROWS	PEL COLS	PEL ROWS
00	CGA Text	2	40	25	N/A	N/A
01	CGA Text	8	40	25	N/A	N/A
02	CGA Text	2	80	25	N/A	N/A
03	CGA Text	8	80	25	N/A	N/A
04	CGA Graphics	8	40	25	320	200
05	CGA Graphics	2	40	25	320	200
06	CGA Graphics	2	80	25	640	200
07	MDA Text	2	80	25	N/A	N/A
13	EGA Graphics	16	40	25	320	200
14	EGA Graphics	16	80	25	640	200
15	EGA Graphics	2	80	25	640	350
16	EGA Graphics	16	80	25	640	350
17	VGA Graphics	2	80	25	640	480
18	VGA Graphics	16	80	25	640	480
19	VGA Graphics	256	80	25	320	200

Note that you cannot perform operations at the pixel, or pel, level when using a text mode; you must switch to a graphics mode. This is done by calling *VioSetMode* with the appropriate type and color information, together with the row and column dimensions.

On the other hand, the basic video subsystem does not support the display of text characters while in a graphics mode. IBM and Microsoft decided to omit this feature in order to keep the *Vio* system small and because most graphical DOS programs include their own font management routines for displaying text. If you want to add graphical text support to the basic video subsystem, you can use *VioRegister* as described later to supply alternative routines.

Continuing with the example, notice that the call to *VioGetPhysBuf* is slightly different because of the graphics mode. Specifically, the buffer length must be declared to be 16,000 bytes, which is what CGA mode 6 requires for a 640-by-200 dot display. In this mode, there are eight dots per byte, which gives rise to the expression:

```
buf.length = (640 / 8) * 200;
```

Since 16,000 bytes is less than a 64-kilobyte segment, *VioGetPhysBuf* will return a single selector to address the buffer. For other modes the buffer is larger than a segment, in which case OS/2 returns several selectors. You must make sure that the *prots* element in the *BufData* structure is large enough to hold these selectors.

The remainder of this example locks the screen, clears it, draws the box, and then unlocks the screen again. We clear the screen here because when you switch into a graphics mode, the physical buffer is likely to contain garbage, resulting in a messy display. Also, the code to draw the box is considerably different in graphics mode than in text mode. In fact, each graphics mode requires a different technique because the dots on the screen have different representations in memory. I won't go into details on this topic here, since a thorough treatment would require a complete book by itself.

Unfinished Business

If you run the preceding example in the foreground session, everything will work fine until you switch to a different session and then switch back. At that point, the box will disappear from the screen, and garbage may appear in its place. Why? Because the standard OS/2 video I/O system does not guarantee proper saving and restoring of the physical video buffer when in a graphics mode.

However, OS/2 does provide the means for you to manage graphical displays correctly during session switches by using the multitasking feature. First you must create two threads which will run independently of your main thread. In the first of these, you call *VioModeWait*, which will not return until the Session Manager signals that you need to save or restore the video mode and state information. In the second thread, you call *VioSavRedrawWait*, which will not return until it is time for you to save or restore the physical video buffer. *VioModeUndo* and *VioSavRedrawUndo* can be used by the main thread to cancel these waits, if necessary. After introducing the multitasking services in Chapter 10, I'll revisit this example and show how these four API functions are used.

Another potential problem you face when doing graphical programming under OS/2 is how to access the I/O registers on the video adaptor. This is sometimes necessary when you want to set up a display mode other than the standard ones previously listed or when you want to manipulate the adaptor's bit planes in some special way.

Again, the base video subsystem does not provide much support for this type of programming, but there is a solution. You must create a code segment that has I/O privileges and then call it at the appropriate time to manipulate the video registers. These so-called *IOPL routines* are tricky to write and debug, and they can crash the system in much the same way as user-designed I/O drivers. However, for those who like excitement, I'll cover this topic in Chapter 12 when we discuss OS/2's advanced I/O features.

7.5 Pop-Up Screens

By now your head is probably spinning with all these different video techniques. However, none of the preceding methods takes care of a very important requirement in the OS/2 multitasking environment: *Background processes must be able to alert the user when a condition arises requiring immediate attention.* For instance, suppose you are running a background process that backs up a database to diskettes and that you want to notify the user whenever a new diskette should be inserted.

The OS/2 video subsystem provides two handy functions for accomplishing this. *VioPopUp* saves the current contents of the physical video buffer and gives you immediate access to the screen, even if your process is not in the foreground. In effect, you move into a "super foreground" mode and have exclusive access to the keyboard and screen until you call *VioEndPopUp*. Options on *VioPopUp* enable you to clear the screen or to leave the current contents displayed. The latter, called *transparent mode*, is used by pop-up utilities such as on-line help systems which are sensitive to the current screen contents. We'll see an example of this in the next chapter.

But as the preceding example indicated, the most common use for the pop-up screen feature is probably to notify the user of some error and request keyboard instructions concerning which error recovery option to use. OS/2 employs *VioPopUp* to implement a fancy pop-up version of the dreaded "Abort, Retry, Ignore" prompter from DOS.

7.6 Font Management

Some video adaptors, most notably the EGA and VGA, have several fonts available for displaying characters. These fonts are either in ROM or else they are downloaded into the adaptor's RAM space.

VioGetFont is used to obtain information about the current font, and *VioSetFont* changes to a different font. To use these calls properly, you must have fairly detailed knowledge about the video adaptor, which can be obtained from the technical references mentioned earlier.

The video subsystem also contains two related calls, *VioGetCP* and *VioSetCP*, which manipulate the current *code page*. Code pages are used to translate the 256 extended ANSI character codes into font table indices. This translation varies from one country to another, and is discussed more thoroughly in Chapter 13.

7.7 Replacing the Video Subsystem

Before you invest a lot of effort writing programs for OS/2 using the basic video subsystem, it's wise to consider what will happen to these programs if you try to run them under the Presentation Manager. Happily, the answer is that most of them will work just fine, because the Presentation Manager replaces the basic video subsystem with an advanced version suited to the the graphical window environment. The only *Vio*-based programs not compatible with the Presentation Manager are those that write directly to the physical video buffers and I/O registers. However, such programs can continue to run independently in their own sessions.

The need to replace the basic video subsystem for the Presentation Manager and other alternate screen managers gave the OS/2 designers yet another interesting challenge. They could not simply replace the dynamic library containing the *Vio* calls, because then all sessions would be forced to use the replacement subsystem. This would conflict with an important OS/2 goal, namely to allow the system to simultaneously host sessions that use the Presentation Manager and sessions that use other screen managers or none at all.

The solution to this problem was to provide a means for the basic video subsystem to steer certain *Vio* calls to an alternate screen manager for each session. The screen manager sets this up by calling *VioRegister* with a list of the *Vio* functions that it wants to replace. From that point on, whenever a process in that session calls one of the registered *Vio* functions, control passes to the screen manager with the appropriate information about the call. The screen manager can perform the appropriate actions using its own windowing system, or it can pass the call on to the basic video subsystem if no special action is needed.

The screen manager can call *VioDeRegister* to remove the *Vio* steering, or else OS/2 will automatically remove it when the screen manager terminates.

7.8 Summary

The OS/2 designers have done a masterful job of preserving the snappy screen performance required of a personal computer while offering the large memory and multitasking features so long desired by DOS programmers. Even without the Presentation Manager, you'll find that that OS/2 allows you to design screen-intensive applications with only a little more work than DOS required.

Chapter 8

Keyboard Interface

The OS/2 keyboard interface is much easier to understand than the video subsystem presented in Chapter 7, but efficient keyboard access is just as important in highly interactive applications. For instance, when you hold down one of the arrow keys while running a spreadsheet program, you want to see the cursor move crisply from one cell to another. This performance level can only be achieved if the bandwidth between the keyboard and the spreadsheet program is fairly high.

As with the video subsystem, it is difficult to achieve this high bandwidth in a multitasking environment, which is the reason why spreadsheets and similar applications often seem sluggish under environments such as UNIX. But once again, the OS/2 designers came up with an innovative solution that allows OS/2 applications to achieve the same level of keyboard performance as their DOS counterparts.

In this chapter we'll discuss the OS/2 approach to keyboard input and compare it to that used by DOS. Both operating systems provide the following three keyboard access methods:

- Via the File Manager, without translation
- Via the File Manager, with translation
- Via the ROM BIOS in DOS or the keyboard I/O subsystem in OS/2

In addition, DOS allows you to directly address the keyboard I/O registers, bypassing both the operating system and the ROM BIOS routines. OS/2 does not provide an easy means to do this, since few DOS programmers have found it necessary to use this direct access method with the standard PC keyboards. Special keyboards, such as those used in banking or factory automation, almost always require their own I/O drivers, which puts them outside the scope of the OS/2 keyboard subsystem.

Reading the keyboard through the File Manager is the slowest but most general technique. In fact, this method is used by the standard C input functions *getchar*, *gets*, *scanf*, and so on. Most DOS C compilers also have library functions that support the ROM BIOS access method, although specific function names vary from one compiler manufacturer to another. Equivalent OS/2 versions of these functions are usually provided in the OS/2 C compilers.

In addition to discussing basic keyboard I/O in this chapter, we'll cover another important keyboard requirement imposed on OS/2 by the DOS programming environment, namely, the ability for a program to monitor the keyboard data stream as it is being passed to another program. This capability is needed in order to implement the *pop-up utilities* that have become a mainstay of the DOS environment.

8.1 Keyboard Access Via File Manager

Just as you can write to the screen through the File Manager, you can also read from the keyboard. One way to do this is to open the device named CON via *DosOpen* and then read from the keyboard via *DosRead*. Another approach is to simply call *DosRead* using file handle 0, which is the standard input file and defaults to the keyboard.

Both of these techniques were covered pretty well in Chapter 7. As an exercise, you could play around with the two example programs in section 7.2 named *copy.c* and *xfer.c*, observing what happens when the keyboard is the input file.

One thing you'll notice when using *DosRead* on the keyboard is that each keystroke is automatically displayed on the screen, and that OS/2 returns when you press the ENTER key even if you have not typed the number of bytes requested. For most applications, this is considered "natural behavior", because the user typically expects to see each character as it is typed and wants something to happen when he or she presses the ENTER key. In other words, the ENTER key usually terminates a *command line*.

This natural behavior occurs only when the keyboard subsystem is operating in its normal *ASCII mode*. The behavior is quite different in *binary mode*, as we'll see next.

8.1.1 ASCII Translation

The basic keyboard translation is from *scan codes* to extended ASCII characters. That is, for each keystroke, the keyboard driver receives an 8-bit scan code and some additional information about which shift keys are pressed. The driver examines these items and, if possible, produces an 8-bit extended ASCII code which is then passed to the application program.

This translation is based upon the *keyboard code page* that is currently active. OS/2 defaults to the PC keyboard translation most frequently used in the USA. However, you can activate a different code page via the KEYB command in *config.sys*, and you can also call *KbdSetCP* in your program to change the keyboard code page. Chapter 14 has more information on this subject.

If the keyboard data cannot be converted into an extended ASCII code, the driver passes two characters to the application. The first has a value of either 0 or 0xE0, and the second is the original scan code. Some examples of keys that have no extended ASCII codes are the arrow keys, function keys, HOME, END, INS, DEL, PGUP, and PGDN.

A prefix of 0 indicates that the next byte is a "universal scan code" that can be produced by any PC keyboard. The 0xE0 prefix indicates that the scan code is from the extended PC keyboard, which is always used on the IBM PS/2 and optional on other machines. For example, on the standard keyboard, the HOME key is actually key 7 in the numeric keypad. If you press that key, the two-byte sequence is 0x00-0x47. The extended keyboard has two HOME keys: one in the numeric keypad and one that stands alone. The former produces the 0x00-0x47 combination, while the latter produces 0xE0-0x47.

Note that these two-byte sequences do not contain any information about the shift keys, although the OS/2 API includes some *Kbd* calls to get that data, as we'll see later in the chapter.

When you access the keyboard via the File Manager, the two-character scan code sequences are usually discarded before they reach you. This is known as *ASCII mode* because the only keystrokes your application will see are those which have valid ASCII codes. Furthermore, in ASCII mode the keyboard driver allows the user to do some rudimentary editing of the input line before pressing the ENTER key. Specifically, he or she can use the backspace or back-arrow key to erase and retype characters in the line. As soon as the ENTER key is pressed, the entire line is sent to the application calling *DosRead*, with the ENTER key replaced by a carriage return and line feed sequence (CR-LF).

If you want to receive the two-character scan code sequences, then you must first place the keyboard into *binary mode* via the *KbdSetStatus* function that will be described later. However, in that mode, characters are not echoed as you type them, the ENTER key does not terminate the input operation, and none of the editing functions are available.

This can be confusing to the typist, and to minimize the confusion you usually have to call *DosRead* requesting only a few characters at a time so that your application program has frequent opportunities to see what the user is doing. However, this increases the overhead of the File Manager and can cause some keyboard data to be lost. Because of these problems, most programmers who need to see all the keystrokes rather than just the ASCII ones prefer to use the more efficient lower level method (i.e., ROM BIOS calls under DOS or VIO calls under OS/2).

8.1.2 ANSI Translation

Chapter 7 showed how to activate the ANSI mode, which causes both the keyboard and the screen to take on some of the characteristics of ANSI terminals typically used with minicomputers.

The basic difference between the normal PC keyboard and an ANSI keyboard is that the latter reports non-ASCII keystrokes, such as the HOME key, via sequences of ASCII characters which can get quite lengthy. For instance, the PC scan code sequence for the up-arrow key is 0x00 followed by 0x48. An ANSI keyboard generates the following three-character sequence, which is fifty percent longer than the information sent by the PC keyboard:

```
ESC [ A
```

Most PC programmers prefer the more efficient keyboard method when processing non-ASCII keys, and so neither the DOS nor the OS/2 ANSI translation automatically produces ANSI sequences. All it does is activate a keyboard mapping facility that enables you to construct some or all of the ANSI translator if you so desire.

For example, you can cause the up arrow key to generate the preceding ANSI sequence by sending the following character string to the screen when in ANSI mode:

```
ESC [ 0;72;27;"[A"p
```

The ESC and [character introduce the ANSI control sequence. The next two numbers (0 and 72), separated by a semicolon, specify the scan code that is being mapped. These numbers are decimal; 72 is the decimal equivalent of the hexadecimal value 0x48, which is the up-arrow scan code. The remainder of the control sequence defines the characters that will be produced whenever the up-arrow key is pressed. The first value, 27, is the decimal equivalent for the ESC character. The quoted string specifies the [and A, which follow the ESC in the ANSI up-arrow sequence. The lower-case p terminates the remapping sequence.

This keyboard mapping feature is not restricted to producing ANSI control sequences. Consider the following remap commands:

```
ESC [ 0;68;"dir";13p
ESC [ 31;"one";13p
```

The first causes function key 10 (F10) to produce a DIR command. F10 has the scan code of decimal 68, and the DIR command consists of the letters *dir* followed by a carriage return (decimal code 13). The second sequence causes the 1 key (decimal code 31) to produce a line containing the word *one*. Notice that when you remap a normal ASCII character instead of a scan code, you do not precede the decimal value with 0.

8.2 Keyboard I/O Subsystem

The keyboard I/O subsystem contains API functions which enable you to exert much more control over the keyboard than when you access it through the File Manager. Of course, using this API results in programs that are more difficult to convert to systems other than OS/2.

In this section, we'll examine the keyboard subsystem, beginning with the API functions most similar to the ROM BIOS routines that DOS programmers use for high-performance keyboard operations.

8.2.1 Basic Keyboard API Functions

Highly interactive DOS applications typically access the keyboard via ROM BIOS interrupt 16H. OS/2 provides an equivalent set of services, as follows:

BIOS 16H	OS/2 API	DESCRIPTION
00H	KbdCharIn	Read character and scan code
01H	KbdGetStatus	Get keyboard status
02H	KbdPeek	Peek at character and scan code
	KbdSetStatus	Set keyboard status

KbdCharIn is the basic keyboard input function. It returns a 10-byte data record for each keystroke, in the following format:

OFFSET	SIZE	INFORMATION
00	01	ASCII code
01	01	Scan code
02	01	Status
03	01	Reserved
04	02	Shift state
06	04	Time stamp

The ASCII code and scan code were discussed earlier. The status byte defines the type of character being returned, including information about special keyboards used outside of the USA. Bit 6 of the status byte is set when a keyboard character is being returned, and bit 0 is set if only the shift state is being returned. This latter condition can occur if you use *KbdSetStatus* to request the keyboard subsystem to report all shift key operations.

The shift state word summarizes the condition of the shift keys. Each bit in this word corresponds to a shift key, as follows:

BIT	MEANING (when set)
00	Right shift key down
01	Left shift key down
02	Either CTRL key down
03	Either ALT key down

04	ScrollLock on
05	NumLock on
06	CapsLock on
07	Insert on
08	Left CTRL key down
09	Left ALT key down
10	Right CTRL key down
11	Right ALT key down
12	ScrollLock key down
13	NumLock key down
14	CapsLock key down
15	SysReq key down

The time stamp is a 32-bit value specified as the number of milliseconds since the system was started. This item is provided to "age" keystrokes, so you don't take action on an old data record that was laying around in the buffer.

KbdCharIn returns the next keyboard data record if one is available. When you call this function, you specify whether it should wait or return immediately if no key has been pressed. *KbdPeek*, on the other hand, always returns immediately. If a keyboard data record is available, it is copied to the caller's area but is not removed from the system buffer. If no key has been pressed, *KbdPeek* returns with bit 6 of the status byte reset.

The remaining two BIOS-like keyboard routines are *KbdGetStatus* and *KbdSetStatus*. Notice that the ROM BIOS uses function code 1 to get the status, but it has no function code to set the status. DOS programmers have to do this by writing directly into the BIOS work area.

Both of the OS/2 keyboard status routines accept a structure that has the following format:

OFFSET	SIZE	INFORMATION
00	02	Record length (10 bytes)
02	02	Keyboard function mask
04	02	Turnaround character
06	02	Interim character flags
08	02	Shift state

The keyboard function mask contains some important flags that define how the subsystem operates:

BIT	MEANING (when set)
00	Echo on
01	Echo off
02	Binary mode on
03	ASCII mode on
04	Modify shift state
05	Modify interim flags
06	Modify turnaround character
07	2-byte turnaround character
08	Shift report on

Notice that bits 0 and 1 are mutually exclusive; that is, only one of them can be set. If you do not want to change the echo mode when calling *KbdSetStatus*, leave both of these bits reset. Bits 2 and 3 behave similarly. Also, bits 1 and 2 are usually set together, because echo must be turned off when in binary mode.

If bit 5 is set when you call *KbdSetStatus*, then the shift states are set according to word 4 (offset 8) of the structure. This word has the same format as the shift state word in the keyboard data record described earlier. When you change the shift state, OS/2 automatically adjusts the lighted indicators on the keyboard.

If bit 6 is set, then the turnaround character is modified. This is the character that keyboard subsystem detects as the end of each input line when in ASCII mode. It is called a "turnaround character" because, from the user's perspective, pressing this key turns the system around from input mode to output mode.

The turnaround character is either a one-byte ASCII code or a two-byte scan code in word 2 (offset 4) of the status structure. Bit 7 of the function mask is set to indicate the latter case, and the scan code prefix (0 or 0xE0) is in byte 4 followed by the scan code itself in byte 5. Otherwise, the single ASCII code is in byte 4, and byte 5 is unused. The default turnaround is an ASCII carriage return character, which has a value of 13 and is generated by the ENTER key.

Bit 6 of the function mask and word 3 of the status structure are used primarily in international applications, where special keyboards are employed.

Here are some simple functions that show how these keyboard status operations are used:

```
/*******************************************************
*
* Keyboard status structure
*
*/
struct KbdStatus
  {
  unsigned short size;  /* structure size (10)   */
  unsigned short mode;  /* mode flags */
  unsigned short tchar  /* turnaround character */
  unsigned short iflag; /* interim character flags */
  unsigned short shift; /* shift flags */
  };
/***********************************************************
*
* Set or reset echo mode.  Argument is 0 to reset
* and 1 to set.  Function returns 0 for success
* and -1 for failure.
*
*/
kbecho(s)
int s;
{
struct KbdStatus x;
memset(&x,0,sizeof(struct KbdStatus));   /* clear status */
x.size = sizeof(struct KbdStatus);  /* set length */
x.mode = (s ? 1 : 2);                    /* set flag */
return(KbdSetStatus(&x,0));
}
/***********************************************************
*
* Set or reset raw mode.  Argument is 0 to reset
* and 1 to set.  Function returns 0 for success
* and -1 for failure.
*
*/
kbraw(s)
int s;
{
```

```
struct KbdStatus x;

memset(&x,0,sizeof(struct KbdStatus));     /* clear status */
x.size = sizeof(struct KbdStatus);  /* set length */
x.mode = (s ? 4 : 8);                      /* set flag */
return(KbdSetStatus(&x,0));
}
/***********************************************************
*
* Test if in echo mode.  Function returns 0 if echo is
* not active, 1 if it is active, and -1 for failure.
*
*/
iskbecho()
{
struct KbdStatus x;

x.size = sizeof(struct KbdStatus);  /* set length */
if(KbdGetStatus(&x,0)) return(-1);  /* get status */
return((x.mode & 1) ? 1 : 0);
}
/***********************************************************
*
* Test if in raw mode.  Function returns 0 if ASCII
* mode, 1 if binary (raw) mode, and -1 for failure.
*
*/
iskbraw()
{
struct KbdStatus x;

x.size = sizeof(struct KbdStatus);  /* set length */
if(KbdGetStatus(&x,0)) return(-1);  /* get status */
return((x.mode & 4) ? 1 : 0);
}
```

And now here are some functions that illustrate how to read the keyboard using *KbdCharIn* and *KbdPeek*. These, as well as the preceding status functions, are simplified versions of these same functions from the Lattice C Compiler library, and they are used with permission of Lattice, Inc.

```
struct KbdData
  {
  unsigned char acode;     /* ASCII code */
  unsigned char scode;     /* scan code */
```

```
  unsigned short status;  /* status code */
  unsigned short shift;   /* shift code */
  unsigned long time;     /* time stamp */
  };
/***********************************************************
*
* Static area to save one character
*
*/
char _cpush = 0;
/***********************************************************
*
* Test if keyboard character is present
*
*/
kbhit()
{
struct KbdData x;

if(c = _cpush) return(c);
if(KbdPeek(&x,0)) return(-1);
if(x.status) return(x.acode);
return(0);
}
/***********************************************************
*
* Get a character without echoing it
*
*/
getch()
{
int c,echo;
struct KbdData x;

if(c = _cpush)
   {
   _cpush = 0;
   return(c);
   }
if(echo = iskbecho()) if(kbecho(0)) return(-1);
if(KbdCharIn(&x,0,0)) return(-1);
if(echo) if(kbecho(1)) return(-1);
if((x.acode == 0) || (x.acode == 0xe0))
  {
  _cpush = x.scode;
  return(0);
```

```
    }
return((int)x.acode);
}
/************************************************************
*
* Get a character and echo it
*
*/
getche()
{
int c,echo;
struct KbdData x;

if(c = _cpush)
    {
    _cpush = 0;
    return(c);
    }
if((echo = iskbecho()) == 0) if(kbecho(1)) return(-1);
if(KbdCharIn(&x,0,0)) return(-1);
if(echo == 0) if(kbecho(0)) return(-1);
return((int)x.acode);
}
/************************************************************
*
* Push a character back onto the 1-level keyboard stack
*
*/
ungetch(c)
int c;
{

if(_cpush) return(-1);
_cpush = c;
return(c);
}
```

As promised in Chapter 7, here's an improved version of the *list* and *xfer* programs. This version copies the standard input file to the standard output, but it pauses after each group of 25 lines and then continues when the user presses any key. The *getch* function is called for this keyboard wait, since it does not return until a key is struck, and it does not echo the key to the screen.

```
#include <stdio.h>
main()
{
int i;
char buffer[256];

while(feof(stdin) == 0)   /* loop till EOF */
  {
  for(i = 0; i < 25; i++)   /* loop till screen full */
    {
    if(fgets(buffer,sizeof(buffer),stdin) == NULL) break;
    fputs(buffer,stdout);
    }
  if(i == 25)
    {
    getch();    /* pause after 25 lines */
    i = 0;    /* reset loop counter */
    }
  }
}
```

Notice that I've used *fgets* and *fputs* instead of *DosRead* and *DosWrite*. Also, *feof* is used to detect the end of the input file. These are ANSI-standard C functions that you will find in every commercial C compiler for OS/2, and they call *DosRead* and *DosWrite* internally. When you must process file input one line at a time, you'll find it much more convenient to use the ANSI functions instead of calling the API routines directly.

8.2.2 String Input

The OS/2 keyboard subsystem provides a handy routine named *KbdStringIn* which gets a string of characters. The most similar service in DOS is interrupt 21H, function 10. The following example shows how *KbdStringIn* works:

```
/*******************************************************
*
* Get a character string
*
*/
char *cgets(b)
char *b;
{
int size = 255;
char *p;
```

```
if(KbdStringIn(b,&size,0,0))
for(p = b; size-- > 0; p++)
  if(*p == '\r') break;
*p = '\0';
return(b);
}
```

The *cgets* function, which is also from the Lattice library, obtains a string of up to 255 characters via *KbdStringIn*. Then it searches through the string for a carriage return and replaces it with a null byte. If no carriage return is present, then a null byte is placed after the last byte returned by *KbdStringIn*. The caller's buffer must be at least 256 bytes long. Note that OS/2 changes the value in *size* to indicate how many characters were actually read into the buffer.

KbdStringIn is actually the function that the File Manager uses to access the keyboard, and so the earlier discussion about ASCII and ANSI translation applies here as well.

8.2.3 Translation Control

KbdSetStatus provides the means to activate and deactivate the ASCII translation mode. In addition, the keyboard subsystem includes three other functions involved with the translation of scan codes.

KbdSetCP activates one of the system's preconfigured code pages, while *KbdSetCustXt* activates a customized code page. *KbdGetCP* returns the identity of the current code page. These three functions are part of the National Language Support (NLS) feature described in Chapter 14.

KbdXlate accepts a keyboard data record and translates the scan code and shift state into an ASCII code, if possible. NLS coding is taken into account during the translation.

8.2.4 Keyboard Buffers

OS/2 "virtualizes" the keyboard for each session, just as it does with the video screen. In other words, each session has its own keyboard buffer. However, since keystrokes normally come only from the user, not much keyboard processing can go on in background sessions. When your session goes into the background, it can process any characters that remain in the buffer, but it will be suspended if it tries to read a keyboard data record when the buffer is empty.

Again, as in the video subsystem, keyboard buffers are identified by handles. The default keyboard in each session is referenced via handle 0. You can create additional buffers by calling *KbdOpen*, and these buffers can be released by calls to *KbdClose*. This allows you to create multiple *logical keyboards* within a session. For instance, if several processes or threads in a session need to read the keyboard, you might want each one to have its own buffer. That way, one process could operate in ASCII mode while another could be in binary mode, and so on.

KbdGetFocus and *KbdFreeFocus* are the functions that you use to manage logical-to-physical keyboard connection. These names come from some OS/2 jargon whereby the buffer currently receiving the user's keystrokes is said to have the *keyboard focus*. So when you call *KbdGetFocus*, the physical keyboard is connected to the handle that you specify, which must have been previously assigned by *KbdOpen*. *KbdGetFocus* also allows you to specify that you want your thread to wait until the keyboard becomes free, if it is currently attached to another thread. The alternative is to get an immediate return indicating that someone else has the keyboard focus.

8.2.5 Replacing the Keyboard Subsystem

The API functions of keyboard subsystem can be replaced on a per-session basis with custom versions. As I mentioned in Chapter 7 when we discussed video subsystem replacement, this is the way that the Presentation Manager hooks into OS/2 while still allowing existing OS/2 applications to run at the same time. The two functions that support this feature are *KbdRegister* and *KbdDeregister*, both of which are described in the Appendix.

8.3 Keyboard Monitors

Under DOS, a class of applications known as *pop-up utilities* became very popular (no pun intended). These programs continuously monitor the keyboard character stream and swing into action when they sense their particular "hot key" combinations. For example, Lotus Metro monitors the keyboard data stream and pops up a telephone directory screen when it sees the SHIFT-ALT-P combination.

Now, as I mentioned in Chapter 5, many utilities that function as pop-ups under DOS can be converted to OS/2 sessions which are activated via the Session Manager's hot keys and menus. However, some pop-up utilities cannot use this approach because they need to examine the current contents of the physical screen in order to determine what they are supposed to do. Two examples are spelling checkers and context-sensitive help systems, both of which base their actions on the word that is closest to the screen cursor. Also, some users may not like to constantly pass through the Session Manager in order to activate frequently used utilities. I know that I would be annoyed if it took a lot of keystrokes to get to my phone list or my appointment calendar.

Under DOS, it's pretty easy for pop-up programs to monitor the keyboard data stream. Once the program insinuates itself into the system as a TSR, it simply hooks onto the keyboard interrupt and looks at each keystroke before passing it on to the original interrupt handler. Well-behaved TSRs can cascade this interrupt-hooking in such a way that each keystroke is passed from one TSR to the next. If none of them recognize it as their hot key, then the keystroke finally arrives at the original DOS keyboard handler, which translates it to ASCII and passes it to the application program.

Surprisingly, the OS/2 designers came up with a scheme that works much the same in the protected multitasking environment. That is, several processes can hook themselves into the keyboard subsystem as *monitors* and still remain isolated from each other and from the subsystem. Furthermore, these monitors are able to use all of the normal process services of OS/2, whereas DOS TSRs often have difficulties using API services because DOS does not recognize that these utilities are trying to force it to multitask.

Figure 8-1 shows how keyboard monitors work. Each monitor process must go through the following procedure to hook into the monitor chain and process keystrokes:

1. Call *DosMonOpen* to obtain a *monitor handle* for the KBD device.
2. Call *DosMonReg* to register your input and output buffers with the KBD driver, using the monitor handle returned by *DosMonOpen*. In this call, you can also specify that you want to be first or last in the monitor chain, or that you don't care about your position.
3. Call *DosMonRead* to get a keyboard monitor record. This call does not return until a record is available.
4. Examine the record. If it is something that you should act on, take the action as quickly as possible. Consider activating a different thread or process if the action is a lengthy one and you don't want to lock up the keyboard while it is taking place.

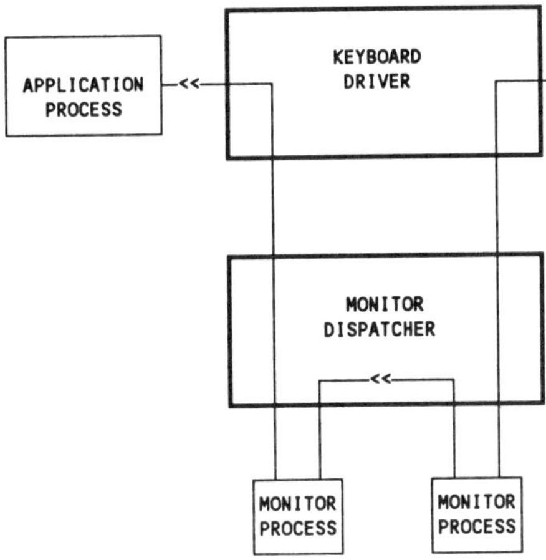

Figure 8-1. Keyboard Monitor Linkages

5. If you do not see anything special about the original record, pass it on to the next monitor by calling *DosMonWrite*. If you did process the keystroke as above, you can also call *DosMonWrite* to pass on the original data, a replacement keystroke, or even a sequence of keystrokes. This is the method that would be used by a keyboard macro package.

6. When you want to get out of the monitor chain, call *DosMonClose*. If you terminate before calling this function, OS/2 automatically removes you from the chain.

This procedure isn't really as difficult as it appears, as the following example illustrates. This example also shows the format of the keyboard monitor data record.

```
struct KbdMonBuff           /* keyboard monitor buffers */
  {
  int size;                 /* buffer size */
  char resv[18];            /* reserved */
  char data[16];            /* key data */
  } ibuff,obuff;

struct KbdMonData           /* keyboard monitor data record */
  {
  int mflags;               /* monitor flags */
  char acode;               /* ASCII code */
  char scode;               /* scan code */
```

```
    int nls;                  /* NLS flags */
    int shift;                /* shift state */
    long time;                /* timestamp */
    int kflags;               /* keyboard flags */
    } key;

main()
{
int mh;                               /* monitor handle */
int keysize;                          /* data record size */

DosMonOpen("KBD$",&mh);               /* get monitor handle */

ibuff.size = obuff.size =             /* initialize buffers */
  sizeof(struct KbdMonBuff);

DosMonReg(mh,&ibuff,&obuff,0,-1); /* register */

while(1)
  {
  keysize = sizeof(struct KbdMonData);
  DosMonRead(&ibuff,0,&key,&keysize);
  if((key.mflags & 4) == 0)
    if(isalpha(key.acode))
      key.acode = toupper(key.acode);
  DosMonWrite(&obuff,&key,keysize);
  }

DosMonClose(mh);
}
```

This monitor looks at each keystroke and converts all lower case letters to upper case. While this is not very useful, I'm sure you can see how a more ambitious version could serve as a keyboard macro package.

Incidentally, the monitor feature is not really restricted to the keyboard, although that is where it will probably be used the most. Any character I/O driver, such as the one for serial communication ports or the one for printers, can be designed to support monitors. In fact, the standard OS/2 printer driver supports them, and the print spooler is actually implemented as a monitor. Naturally, the format of the monitor data record varies from one driver to another, depending on the design of the I/O driver.

8.4 Summary

As with the video subsystem, the OS/2 designers have provided a keyboard subsystem that enables you to provide the same responsive human interface that is possible under DOS. The monitor feature is particularly innovative because it allows pop-up utilities to function in a protected multitasking environment without resorting to potentially disruptive tricks.

Chapter 9

Mouse Interface

Neither DOS nor the PC ROM BIOS provides any built-in support for a mouse, which has become the most popular pointing device. However, when Microsoft began selling a mouse several years ago, they commandeered software interrupt 33H for the mouse driver. In other words, when your system has a Microsoft-compatible mouse installed, interrupt 33H looks just like any other BIOS interrupt, even though the mouse driver is not really in read-only memory.

OS/2 provides a mouse subsystem which replaces and enhances the services handled via interrupt 33H under DOS. As with the video and keyboard subsystems, the biggest challenge that the OS/2 designers faced with the mouse subsystem was how to maintain a high bandwidth to the application programs in a multitasking environment.

9.1 Mouse Subsystem

OS/2 includes drivers for a variety of mice, and if your system has a mouse, the appropriate driver is selected via a DEVICE command in the *config.sys* file. Regardless of which driver you install, the mouse API functions remain the same, as shown in the following table:

INT 33H	NAME	DESCRIPTION
	MouClose	Close mouse device
	MouDeRegister	Deregister a mouse subsystem
01H	MouDrawPtr	Draw a pointer
	MouFlushQue	Flush mouse event queue
	MouGetDevStatus	Get mouse device status flags
	MouGetEventMask	Get mouse event mask
	MouGetNumButtons	Get number of mouse buttons
	MouGetNumMickeys	Get number of mickeys per centimeter
	MouGetNumQueEl	Get number of mouse event queue elements
03H,0BH	MouGetPtrPos	Get mouse pointer position
	MouGetPtrShape	Get mouse pointer shape
	MouGetScaleFact	Get mouse scaling factors
	MouInitReal	Initialize real-mode mouse driver
00H	MouOpen	Open mouse device
05H,06H	MouReadEventQue	Read mouse event queue
	MouRegister	Register a mouse subsystem
10H	MouRemovePtr	Remove mouse pointer from a screen area
0FH	MouSetDevStatus	Set mouse device status flags
0CH	MouSetEventMask	Set mouse event mask
04H	MouSetPtrPos	Set mouse pointer position
09H,0AH	MouSetPtrShape	Set mouse pointer shape
	MouSetScaleFact	Set mouse scaling factors
	MouShellInit	Initialize shell linkage
	MouSynch	Synchronize mouse subsystem

Now let's look at these functions in more detail.

9.2 Basic Mouse Operations

The mouse becomes active in an OS/2 session when a process in that session calls *MouOpen*. After that point, the process can obtain information about mouse movement from the mouse event queue (MEQ), change the position of the mouse pointer on the screen, and change the shape of the pointer. By adjusting the scaling factors, the process can also control the sensitivity of the mouse.

9.2.1 Opening the Mouse

There are two ways to open the mouse, as follows:

```
int error;                                /* error code */
int handle;                               /* mouse handle */
```

```
error = MouOpen(NULL,&handle);              /* method 1 */

error = MouOpen("mydraw.sys",&handle);      /* method 2 */
```

The first method is probably the most common, since it specifies that the normal OS/2 pointer draw driver should be used. Method 2 is used in special applications where a simple block-style pointer is not drawn. For example, many computer-aided drafting (CAD) programs provide a special mouse pointer in the form of intersecting vertical and horizontal lines, which extend the full height and width of the screen, respectively. This type of pointer cannot be drawn by the normal pointer driver, and so you must identify the name of the device driver that will perform this task.

Custom pointer drivers are best covered in a detailed explanation of device drivers, which is not a part of this book. The *IBM OS/2 Technical Reference* gives a fairly thorough description of this complex topic.

It is not necessary to use a custom pointer driver if all you want to do is change the pointer shape. *MouGetPtrShape* and *MouSetPtrShape* can accomplish this. The shape is specified in a bit map whose format depends on the video display mode and on the particular pointer driver being used.

When you are finished with the mouse, you should call *MouClose*. OS/2, of course, takes care of this if the process terminates without closing the mouse.

9.2.2 Mouse Characteristics

The mouse subsystem includes two functions that you can use to determine the characteristics of the mouse device. *MouGetNumButtons* indicates whether the mouse has 1, 2, or 3 buttons. *MouGetNumMickeys* returns the number of mickeys per centimeter. The *mickey* is the basic unit of mouse movement.

The following example displays this information:

```
int handle;                          /* mouse handle */
int buttons;                         /* number of buttons */
int mickeys;                         /* number of mickeys */

MouGetNumButtons(&buttons,handle);   /* get buttons */
MouGetNumMickeys(&mickeys,handle);   /* get mickeys */

printf("The mouse has %d buttonsn",buttons);
printf("The mouse resolution is %d mickeys/cmn",mickeys);
```

9.2.3 Mouse Events

Mouse actions are reported via 10-byte event records placed in the MEQ. An event record has the following format:

OFFSET SIZE	INFORMATION	
00	2	mouse state
02	4	time stamp
06	2	row position
08	2	column position

The time stamp is expressed in milliseconds since system initialization.

The pointer coordinates are normally expressed in either character positions or pixel positions, just as with the *Vio* functions that we discussed in Chapter 7. Character positions are used in the text video modes, while pixels are used in the graphics modes. In either case, the upper left corner of the screen is row 0, column 0. You can also configure the mouse subsystem to return the row and column as the number of vertical and horizontal mickeys since the last event. This selection is made via the *MouSetDevStatus* function, which is described a little later.

The mouse state word contains the following flags:

BIT	MEANING (when set)
00	motion, no buttons down
01	motion, button 1 down
02	no motion, button 1 down
03	motion, button 2 down
04	no motion, button 2 down
05	motion, button 3 down
06	no motion, button 3 down

An event record is placed in the MEQ whenever an unmasked state change occurs. The exact nature of the event can be determined by comparing the state word with the one from the previous event.

MouSetEventMask is used to mask and unmask the various state bits, and *MouGetEventMask* reads the current event mask. For example, the following statements save the current mask and then disable all events caused by button 3.

```
int handle;                        /* mouse handle */
unsigned mask;                     /* saves current mask */

MouGetEventMask(&mask,handle);     /* get current mask */
MouSetEventMask(0x1f,handle);      /* kill button 3 */
```

where *handle* is the mouse handle returned by *MouOpen*. The event mask word is set of 0x1f, thereby unmasking (i.e., enabling) state bits 0 through 4 and masking (i.e., disabling) bits 5 and 6. If you do not change the mask after calling *MouOpen*, all events will be reported.

The following example prints the information associated with each mouse event:

```
struct MouEvent              /* mouse event */
  {
  unsigned state;            /* mouse state */
  unsigned long time;        /* time stamp */
  unsigned row;              /* pointer row */
  unsigned col;              /* pointer column */
  } far *buffer;

unsigned handle;             /* mouse handle */

while(1)
  {
   MouReadEventQue(buffer,0,handle);
   printf("Mouse event at %ldn",buffer.time);
   printf("  State flags: %04xn",buffer.state);
   printf("  Row %d, Column %dn",buffer.row,buffer.col);
   }
```

The *MouReadEventQueue* is self-explanatory except for its second argument. This should be 0 if you want to wait until a mouse event occurs. Otherwise, it should be 1, and if the MEQ is empty, the function returns an error code.

If you want to determine how many elements are in the MEQ, call *MouGetNumQueEl*. Also, it is sometimes necessary to flush all events from the MEQ, which can be accomplished by calling *MouFlushQue*. This is particularly useful just after you force the pointer to a new position with *MouSetPtrPos*, which is described next.

9.2.4 Mouse Pointer Status

The mouse subsystem (specifically, the pointer draw driver) automatically moves the pointer on the screen as the user moves the mouse, and it reports the current pointer position with each mouse event, as we saw earlier. Sometimes you want to know the pointer location even though no mouse event has occurred. At at other times you will want to reposition the pointer independently of the user. These two tasks can be accomplished by *MouGetPtrPos* and *MouSetPtrPos*, respectively.

Here's a simple example that saves the current pointer position and then moves the pointer to row 10, column 25:

```
int handle;                          /* mouse handle */
int oldptr[2];                       /* old pointer position */
int newptr[2] = {10,25};             /* new pointer position */

MouGetPtrPos(oldptr,handle);         /* get old position */
MouSetPtrPos(newptr,handle);         /* set new position */
```

9.2.5 Mouse Scaling Factors

Mouse sensitivity can be an important human interface factor in your applications. If the mouse is too sensitive, then the user may not be able to point accurately, especially if the objects on the screen are small. On the other hand, if the mouse is not sensitive enough, the the user will feel that the program is sluggish.

This aspect of the mouse subsystem can bc controlled via *MouSetScaleFact*, and *MouSetScaleFact*, which set and get the mouse scale factors, respectively. Scale factors can be specified for both horizontal and vertical movement in terms of the number of mickeys required to move 8 pixels, where a *mickey* is the basic unit of movement reported by the mouse and a pixel is a single dot on the screen. The default factors are 8 mickeys per 8 pixels in the vertical direction and 16 mickeys per 8 pixels in the horizontal direction. This combination makes the mouse less sensitive when moving horizontally, which has proven to give a more natural feel to the device.

Here's a strip of C code that saves the current scale factors and then increases the sensitivity of the mouse:

```
int handle;                          /* mouse handle */
int old[2];                          /* old scale factors */
```

```
int new[2] = {4,8};                 /* new scale factors */

MouGetScaleFact(old,handle);       /* get old scale factors */
MouSetScaleFact(new,handle);       /* set new scale factors */
```

Here we set the vertical factor to 4 mickeys per 8 pixels and the horizontal factor to 8 mickeys per 8 pixels, making the pointer move twice as fast as the default factors specify.

9.2.6 Mouse Device Status

MouGetDevStatus and *MouSetDevStatus* get and set the device status, consisting of the following flags in the status word:

BIT	MEANING (when set)
00	Event queue is busy
01	Block read in progress
02	Flush in progress
03	Unsupported video mode
08	No interrupt pointer draw
09	Return position in mickeys

Bits 0 to 3 are primarily of interest to those who write their own pointer draw drivers or are otherwise intimately connected to the mouse driver. Only bits 8 and 9 can be changed via *MouSetDevStatus*. For example, here's the code to save the current status and then cause the position to be returned in relative mickeys instead of absolute screen coordinates:

```
int handle;                        /* mouse handle */
unsigned old;                      /* current status */

MouGetDevStatus(&old,handle);      /* get current status */
MouSetDevStatus(0x0200,handle);    /* set mickey position */
```

After bit 9 is set, *MouReadEventQue* will supply the row and column information as the number of mickeys that have been moved since the previous event.

9.2.7 Restricting Pointer Movement

In some applications it is necessary to define an area of the screen that should never contain a mouse pointer. This can be done with *MouRemovePtr* and *MouDrawPtr* as follows:

```
int handle;                        /* mouse handle */
int area[4] =                      /* restricted area */
  {10,15,20,30};

MouRemovePtr(area,handle);         /* restrict the pointer */

/*** Restriction is now active ***/

MouDrawPtr(handle);                /* remove restriction */
```

The *area* array defines the rectangular area in which the pointer will not be displayed. The first two words are the upper left row and column, respectively, and the next two words are the lower right row and column. These should be expressed in characters or pixels, depending on the current video display mode. In this example, the restricted area is the rectangle whose corners are at row 10, column 15 and row 20, column 30.

When the user attempts to move the pointer into the restricted area, it disappears from the screen. The mouse driver, however, continues to track the pointer and redraws it as soon as it leaves the restricted area.

As previously shown, you simply call *MouDrawPtr* to remove the restricted area and redraw the pointer.

9.3 Replacing the Mouse Subsystem

OS/2 allows you to replace some or all of the mouse subsystem, using the same technique as we previously examined for the video and keyboard subsystems. The two functions that support this are *MouRegister* and *MouDeregister*, both of which are described in the Appendix.

9.4 Summary

It took a long time for the mouse to become popular in the DOS environment, primarily because the operating system did not provide any standardized support for this pointing device. Mouse-based applications are much easier to design under OS/2 because of the *Mou* functions, which make all mice and similar pointing devices look alike. As a result, many OS/2 interactive programs will be designed to be "mouse aware" even if they do not utilize the Presentation Manager.

Chapter 10

Multitasking

As I pointed out in Chapter 3, OS/2 offers a rich multitasking environment suitable for a broad range of applications. At the highest level, the multi-session capability makes OS/2 a powerful base for business, scientific, and engineering workstations where the user frequently switches from one application context to another. At the lowest level, the multi-threading capability enables OS/2 to provide efficient service in real-time applications such as file servers, network managers, factory automation and point-of-sale systems.

In its initial versions, OS/2 did not include a multiuser capability amongst its multitasking features. However, as OS designers like to say, "The hooks are all there." This implies that OS/2 can and undoubtedly will evolve to include multiuser support, at least as an option.

Since DOS has no "official" multitasking capability, we are now entering virgin territory; most of the API services described from this point on have no counterparts in DOS. So, if you incorporate these services into your program, it will only run under OS/2, unless you use some of the tricks described in Chapter 15.

10.1 Session Management

A session, as we've already seen, is a "virtual PC" having its own "logical devices". OS/2 offers two standard session managers, which obviate the need for most applications to perform any session management on their own.

The Base Session Manager, also called the Program Selector, is included with both OS/2 Standard Edition 1.0 and OS/2 Extended Edition 1.0 from IBM, as was described in Chapter 3. The Program Selector provides the user with the ability to start multiple character-oriented sessions. The application programs running in these sessions can place the display into graphical modes, but the Program Selector does not automatically save and restore graphical displays when the user switches sessions.

The Presentation Manager is an advanced session manager included with Version 1.1 of IBM's Standard and Extended Editions of OS/2. It provides full support for graphical displays and also includes many services that can simplify and standardize the design of graphical applications. Because the Presentation Manager also provides a full complement of character-oriented display services, most applications that run under the Base Session Manager will work correctly in the Presentation Manager environment.

Programs communicate with either of these session managers via the four API functions named *DosStartSession*, *DosStopSession*, *DosSetSession*, and *DosSelectSession*. However, since most applications require only a single session, these functions are rarely used. Therefore, I'll just briefly review them here. See the Appendix for more details.

DosStartSession creates a new session which can be a child of the current one or can be independent. If you specify that the new session is to be independent, then you lose control over it. However, if you create a child session, then you can control its state and can eliminate it when it is no longer needed. The standard session managers already mentioned usually create child sessions.

As part of the *DosStartSession* parameter list, you specify the name of a program that is to become the base process in the session. You also indicate whether you want the session to begin in the foreground or in the background. If this API call is successful, it returns a session identifier and a process identifier. Note that the base process in the new session is not considered to be a descendant of the process calling *DosStartSession*.

When the base process terminates, its session is automatically eliminated, and the completion code is returned via a queue that was previously specified in the *DosStartSession* parameter list. If you start the session as a child, you can also call *DosStopSession* to eliminate it.

DosSetSession changes the status of a child session. With this function, you can make the child selectable or nonselectable. In the former case, the child session name will appear in the "select list" that the Session Manager displays to the user, while the latter case requires that the parent session bring the child to the foreground at the appropriate time. This function also allows you to bond the child session to the parent so that when the parent is selected, the child actually moves to the foreground.

DosSelectSession simply places the specified child session in the foreground so that it is visible to the user.

10.2 Process Management

In OS/2, a process is an entity having the following characteristics:

- It belongs to one and only one session.
- It is a child of another process, which may be in another session.
- It is associated with a specific executable file.
- It can be associated with one or more dynamic link libraries.
- It can own system resources such as memory segments and file handles.
- It contains at least one execution thread, to which OS/2 allocates slices of processor time.
- It can communicate with other processes via a variety of interprocess communication, or IPC, techniques.
- It has a unique 16-bit process identifier, or PID.

Many applications can be greatly simplified if they are split up into multiple processes. For example, consider an electronic bulletin board system (EBBS) handling several phone lines. Under DOS, the EBBS program would probably use a polling loop to periodically examine each phone line. Upon receipt of a complete command message, this loop would call a routine to parse the command and perform the appropriate action. However, the action routine would have to be careful not to take too much time, or else the polling rate would decrease to the point where the system would appear sluggish. Furthermore, some data could actually be lost if the polling loop did not regain control in time to empty the modem buffers.

Under OS/2 you could design an EBBS as a parent process having a set of relatively simple child processes. The parent creates one child for each phone line. These children all run the same program; that is, the children share the same code segments but have different data segments. The function of each child is to read a command from its phone line, analyze it, perform the necessary action, and loop back to read another command. While this is going on, OS/2 dynamically adjusts the priorities of the children so that no user input is lost and they all get equitable amounts of processor time.

The parent process just sits there patiently waiting for a child to request some action that it cannot handle on its own. For example, when a user types a password, the child could send an IPC message to the parent asking it to consult the password file for validation. Similarly, when a user disconnects, the child process handling that phone line terminates, which causes OS/2 to alert the parent. The parent then creates a new child when another user connects to that line.

Now even though multiple processes can simplify certain applications and make them perform more consistently, this is not a "no-brainer." Without the proper planning, you can easily create an application architecture that crumbles under heavy workloads as more and more processor time is consumed in process management.

For instance, I once did some performance analysis of a UNIX-based message switching system in which a new process was created for each message. After routing the message to the appropriate output channel, the process died. Everything worked fine in the laboratory under light loads, and the program design was elegantly simple. However, the first time the system encountered heavy loading after it was placed into service, it choked. We found that under these heavy loads, over ninety percent of the CPU time was being spent by the operating system setting up and tearing down processes. The moral of the story is: *Don't create processes with short life spans or for frivolous reasons.*

10.2.1 Process Creation

DosExecPgm is the OS/2 API call that creates a child process. Its parameters are described in the Appendix. You can specify that the child is to run synchronously or asynchronously. In the former case, the function does not return until the child is finished, while in the latter case, the function returns immediately, and the parent and child then contend for processor time.

The parent can specify the environment variables for the child, or it can pass its own environment on. Also, the parent can give the child several ASCII strings resembling command line arguments.

The child also inherits all of the parent's open file handles except those that were opened with the "private" flag set, as was described in Chapter 6. In many situations, the parent manipulates file handles 0 and 1 via *DosDupHandle* so that it can control the child's standard input and output files.

10.2.2 Process Termination

When the child process terminates, its completion code is usually returned to the parent. For a synchronous child, this code is available when *DosExecPgm* returns. For an asynchronous child, the parent must call *DosCWait* to wait for the child and get its completion code. When creating an asynchronous child, the parent can indicate that it does not want to receive the completion code. In that case, the child process is said to be *detached.*

The parent can also use *DosKillProcess* to forcibly terminate any or all of its child processes.

10.2.3 Some Examples

Here's a simple example of process creation. This is a form of the *system* function usually provided with C compilers. It invokes the command processor (a program named *cmd.exe*) to execute the command string supplied by the caller.

```
system(cmd)
char *cmd;
{
int error;                    /* error code */
unsigned ret[2];              /* return codes */
char buffer[128];             /* command buffer */
char *p;                      /* miscellaneous */
/*
*
```

```
* Form argument array for command processor by terminating
* the verb.
*
*/
for(p = buffer; *cmd != '\0'; *p++ = *cmd++)
  if(*cmd == ' ') break;
*p++ = '\0';
while(*cmd != '\0') *p++ = *cmd++;
*p = '
/*
*
* Call the command processor as a synchronous child
*
*/
error =
  DosExecPgm(obj,sizeof(obj),0,buffer,0L,ret,"cmd.exe");
if(error) return(-1);
return(0);
}
```

Here's a more complicated example that uses the file transfer program originally presented in Chapter 6. If you recall, you can execute this program by typing the following command:

```
xfer <input >output
```

where *input* and *output* are the input and output file names, respectively. In the following example, we create a child process which runs the *xfer* program asynchronously to copy file *abc* to file *def*.

```
main()
{
int error;                  /* error code */
unsigned pid[2];            /* process identifier */
unsigned cpid;              /* completed process ID */
unsigned ret[2];            /* return information */
unsigned input=0;           /* standard input handle */
unsigned output=1;          /* standard output handle */
unsigned fh;                /* file handle */

error =                     /* open the input file */
  DosOpen("abc",&fh,&action,0L,0,1,0,0L);
if(error) exit(error);
```

```
error =                    /* force input to handle 0 */
  DosDupHandle(fh,&input);
if(error) exit(error);

error =                    /* open the output file */
  DosOpen("def",&fh,&action,0L,0,0x11,1,0L);
if(error) exit(error);

error =                    /* force output to handle 1 */
  DosDupHandle(fh,&output);

error =                    /* create the child process */
  DosExecPgm(obj,objlen,2,0L,0L,pid,"xfer.exe");
if(error) exit(error);

/*** Other processing can be done here ***/

error =                    /* wait for child process */
  DosCWait(0,0,ret,&cpid,pid[0]);
if(error) exit(error);

if(ret[0]) exit(-1);       /* exit -1 if abnormal terminate */
exit(ret[1]);              /* exit with xfer code */
}
```

Notice how we use *DosDupHandle* to coerce the handles returned from *DosOpen*. This is necessary because *xfer* wants its input file to be handle 0 and its output to be handle 1. *DosDupHandle* is described more thoroughly in Chapter 13.

Also, as the program comments indicate, you can proceed with other work while *xfer* goes about its job of copying the file. In the next section we'll see how to accomplish this overlapped copy operation using threads, and in Chapter 13 we'll do it again using the asynchronous read and write functions provided in the OS/2 API.

10.3 Thread Management

Thread management is an unusual feature of OS/2 that can greatly facilitate the construction of high-performance applications. Each process has at least one execution thread, but OS/2 allows you to create additional threads quickly. All threads within a process share the same memory. The only items that are kept on a per-thread basis are the stack and the register contents, including the current instruction address.

The API functions directly related to thread management are: *DosCreateThread*, *DosSuspendThread*, and *DosResumeThread*. In addition, there are several API functions concerned with thread priorities, critical sections, and timing.

10.3.1 File Transfer Example

Let's jump right in and see how threads work by reprogramming the file transfer example that we just examined:

```
/************************************************************
*
* This static data area is used for communication between
* the parent and child threads.
*
*/
static int ifh;          /* input file handle */
static int ofh;          /* output file handle */
int terror;              /* thread error code */
int tid = 0;             /* thread identifier */
/************************************************************
*
* This is the file transfer routine, which runs as a child
* thread.
*
*/
static void xfer()
{
char buffer[1024];       /* file transfer buffer */
int rsize;               /* DosRead actual size */
int wsize;               /* DosWrite actual size */

while(1)                 /* copy input to output */
  {
  terror = DosRead(ifh,buffer,sizeof(buffer),&rsize);
  if(terror) break;
  terror = DosWrite(ofh,buffer,rsize,&wsize);
  if(terror) break;
  if(rsize == wsize) continue;
  terror = -1;
  break;
  }
DosClose(ifh);           /* close input file */
```

```
DosClose(ofh);           /* close output file */
tid = 0;
}
/***********************************************************
*
* This is the asynchronous file copy routine, which opens
* the input and output file and then creates a thread
* that runs the file transfer function.  The tid item
* in the static area above is nonzero when the thread
* is active.
*/
acopy(iname,oname)
char *iname;             /* input file name */
char *oname;             /* output file name */
{
int error;
unsigned action;         /* action code */
char stack[3000];        /* stack for thread */

if(tid) return(-1);      /* return -1 if xfer is busy */

error =                  /* open the input file */
  DosOpen(iname,&ifh,&action,0L,0,1,0,0L);
if(error) return(error);

error =                  /* open the output file */
  DosOpen(oname,&ofh,&action,0L,0,0x11,1,0L);
if(error)
  {
  DosClose(ifh);
  return(error);
  }

error =                  /* create the thread */
  DosCreateThread(xfer,&tid,stack+sizeof(stack));
if(error)
  {
  DosClose(ifh);
  DosClose(ofh);
  return(error);
  }

return(0);               /* success return */
}
```

In this example, the function *acopy* is called with an input and output file name as its two arguments. It opens the files and saves their handles in *ifh* and *ofh*, respectively. These two integers are defined in the static data area so that they can be accessed by both *acopy* and the child thread, which is the function named *xfer*.

If *acopy* successfully opens the two files, it starts *xfer* as a child thread and saves the thread identification in another static integer named *tid*. Then *acopy* returns with a value of 0 to indicate success. Form that point on, OS/2 arranges for the original thread and the *xfer* thread to share the processor.

DosCreateThread is quite simple when compared to the *DosExecPgm* function that is used to create processes. It accepts three arguments. The first is the address of the routine that OS/2 is to call as the child thread. The next two arguments specify the stack that the child should use. In the *acopy* routine, we just grab a portion of the current stack and give it to the child. We could have also have used a static data area for this purpose, or we could have allocated a new segment using the methods described in Chapter 11. The general rule is that each child needs its own stack space of at least 2 kilobytes. Of course, the stack may have to be larger, depending on how the child uses it.

If *acopy* is unsuccessful in opening either file or in starting the child thread, it returns the OS/2 error code. Also, if *tid* is nonzero when *acopy* is called, a value of -1 is returned to indicate that the file transfer thread is already active.

The *xfer* function simply copies the input to the output, using thc file handles supplied in *ifh* and *ofh*. When the thread finishes or aborts, it closes both files, resets *tid*, and dies by returning to OS/2. In the case of an abort, the global integer named *terror* contains the OS/2 error code causing the abort.

The program calling *acopy* should occasionally check *tid* to see if the transfer operation is finished. This is a fairly crude form of interthread communication, and we'll see better ways to do it in Chapter 12.

The most important thing to note in this example is the use of static data to communicate between threads within a process. All threads share the same data area, and even though each thread has its own stack, the stacks can be addressed by all threads. The primary hazard of multithreading is that the threads can easily interfere with each other's data. We'll discuss thread interference more thoroughly a little later in this chapter.

The test of *tid* at the beginning of *acopy* is a simple example of a safeguard against thread interference. Without this test, *acopy* could initiate a second instance of *xfer* before the first one was finished. By changing *ifh* and *ofh* for the second instance, *acopy* would pull the rug out from under the first *xfer* thread. The first transfer would be incomplete and its files would be left open. The second transfer would produce a garbled output file, because two threads would be copying to the output file at the same time.

10.3.2 Video Buffer Example

In Chapter 7 I mentioned that threads are required when you are directly controlling the physical video buffer in a graphical mode. Here's an abbreviated version of the *box* function which shows this:

```
unsigned *dsave;         /* saves box dimension pointer */

/*********************************************************/

box(d)                   /* Primary box-drawing function */
unsigned short *d;
{
char stat;               /* screen lock status */
int error;               /* OS/2 error code */
unsigned tid1;           /* mode control thread id */
unsigned tid2;           /* redraw thread id */
char stack1[2048];       /* stack for mode control thread */
char stack2[2048];       /* stack for redraw thread */

if(checkbox(d)) return(-1);  /* fail if bad box */

error =                  /* create mode control thread */
  DosCreateThread(modectrl,&tid1,stack1+sizeof(stack1));
if(error) return(error);

error =                  /* create redraw thread */
  DosCreateThread(redraw,&tid2,stack2+sizeof(stack2));
if(error)
  {
  VioModeUndo(1,1,0);
  return(error);
  }

setmode();               /* establish graphics mode */
VioScrLock(1,&stat,0);   /* lock the screen */
draw();                  /* draw the box */
```

```
VioScrUnlock(0);          /* unlock the screen */
pause();                  /* pause */
VioModeUndo(1,1,0);       /* kill mode control thread */
VioSavRedrawUndo(1,1,0);/* kill redraw thread */
return(error);            /* exit */
}

/**********************************************************/

void modectrl()           /* Mode control thread */
{
while(1)
  {
  VioModeWait(0,0,0);
  setmode();
  }
}

/**********************************************************/

void redraw();            /* Redraw thread */
{
unsigned action;
while(1)
  {
  VioSavRedrawWait(1,&action,0);
  draw();
  }
}
```

The code to check the box dimensions, set the graphics mode, and draw the box is not shown here, but is assumed to reside in the functions named *checkbox*, *setmode*, and *draw*. Notice that since *draw* is called from the *box* thread and from the *redraw* thread, we save the box pointer in a static data area named *dsave* which can be easily accessed by both threads.

The flow here is actually quite easy to understand. When *box* is called, it first checks for a valid box. Next it creates two threads, which are the functions named *modectrl* and *redraw*. Each of these threads calls the appropriate *Vio* wait routine, which does not return until the specified event has occurred. In *modectrl*, *VioModeWait* returns when the thread must restore the graphics mode, which it does by calling *setmode*. Similarly, *VioSavRedrawWait* does not return to *redraw* until the screen must be repainted, which is accomplished by a call to *draw*.

After creating the threads, *box* sets the graphics mode, locks the screen, draws the box, unlocks the screen, and pauses until the user presses a key. The screen locking and unlocking should not be done in the *draw* function, because these operations are not allowed within the *redraw* thread.

10.3.3 Thread Priorities

Whenever a thread reaches a point where it can relinquish control of the processor, OS/2 must decide which thread gets to use the processor next. This decision is based upon a priority algorithm in which each thread has a *priority class* and a *priority level*. The three classes are:

> **Class 3 – Time-Critical**
> Used for threads that must run as soon as possible after they become ready.
>
> **Class 2 – Regular**
> Used for threads that can tolerate some delay in their access to the processor.
>
> **Class 1 – Idle-Time**
> Used for threads that should run when the system is idle, that is, when no regular or time-critical threads are ready.

Within each class there are 32 priority levels, with level 31 having the highest priority. Time-critical and idle-time threads have static priority levels that are not varied by OS/2. The level of each regular thread, however, is dynamically varied by OS/2 in order to keep the system as busy as possible. Regular threads that are in the foreground session or are using a lot of I/O services will be moved to higher levels, while threads that are just using a lot of processor time will go to lower levels. This strategy ensures that requests from the system user and the I/O devices get serviced quickly.

When a new thread is created, it inherits the priority class and level of its parent. You can call *DosGetPrty* to obtain this information for any thread, and *DosSetPrty* can be used to change the class or level of a single thread or of all threads within a process family. These API functions are described in the Appendix.

10.3.4 Timing Services

Many applications require actions to be performed on a timed basis. The easiest way to do this in OS/2 is to start a thread and then have the thread start a timer and go to sleep. When the timer expires, the thread wakes up and performs the necessary action.

OS/2 provides four timer functions. *DosSleep* simply delays for the specified number of milliseconds. For instance, here's a thread that performs some operation every 30 seconds:

```
wait30()
{
while(DosSleep(30000L) == 0)
  {

/*** DO THE 30-SECOND WORK HERE ***/

  }
}
```

The other three functions are a little more sophisticated, but they are also more difficult to use. *DosTimerAsync* starts a "one-shot" timer that resets a semaphore when after the specified number of milliseconds. *DosTimerStart* starts a timer that resets a semaphore periodically. *DosTimerStop* stops either type of timer.

Semaphores are an interprocess communication technique discussed in Chapter 12. By using this technique, the *DosTimer* functions enable the thread to continue executing while the timer runs, unlike *DosSleep*. Then when the thread can do no more until the next timeout, it waits for the semaphore. *DosSleep*, in fact, is nothing but a call to *DosTimerAsync* followed by a call to *DosSemWait*.

Here's an example of a thread that displays a help message on the screen if the user doesn't type something within 10 seconds:

```
unsigned long sh;              /* semaphore handle */
int helpcode;                  /* help message code */
int keycode;                   /* input key code */

void userhelp()
{
int th;                        /* timer handle */
```

```
int error;                      /* OS/2 error code */

DosSemSet(sh);                  /* set the semaphore */

error =                         /* start the timer */
  DosTimerAsync(10000L,sh,&th);
if(error) return(error);

while(DosSemWait(sh,500L))      /* check for timeout */
  if(kbhit())                   /* check KBD if no timeout */
    {
    DosTimerStop(th);           /* stop timer if key hit */
    keycode = getch();          /* get input character */
    return;                     /* return to kill thread */
    }

keycode = -1;                   /* indicate help needed */
showhelp(helpcode);             /* show help message */
```

The *userhelp* thread is started by another thread which could be performing some computation while waiting for the user to press a key. Before starting *userhelp*, the parent places a semaphore handle into *sh*, a help message code into *helpcode*, and clears *keycode*.

Upon entry, *userhelp* sets the semaphore via *DosSemSet* and starts a 10-second one-shot timer via *DosTimerAsync*. Next, a loop is entered to check the keyboard every half-second until either a key is pressed or the timer expires. In the former case, the timer is stopped, the input character is placed into *keycode*, and the thread terminates. In the latter case, a value of -1 is placed into *keycode* to inform the parent that no user input occurred. Then the *showhelp* function is called with the help message code supplied by the parent thread. This function displays one or more help screens, and when it returns, the thread terminates.

Notice that the *while-loop* is broken when *DosSemWait* returns a value of 0, indicating that the semaphore has been reset because the timer has expired. This function returns a nonzero value, specifically 121, when it waits the specified amount of time and still finds the semaphore set. In this case, we specify 500 milliseconds as the second argument to *DosSemWait*, just so the thread doesn't consume a lot of processor time repeatedly testing the semaphore.

10.3.5 Thread Interference

Because all threads within a process share the same data area, it is quite possible for them to interfere with one another in ways that are very difficult to detect. As I mentioned earlier, you must be extremely careful to design threads in such a way that they cannot clobber each other accidentally. For instance, if one thread is putting stuff on a linked list and the other is removing it, they must carefully coordinate their activities so that the linkages remain correct.

One way to achieve this coordination is for each thread to call *DosEnterCritSec*, thereby entering a "critical section", before it manipulates a shared data area. This function prevents any other thread in the process from running until *DosExitCritSec* is called.

Semaphores, which are discussed in Chapter 12, can also be used to prevent thread interference. With this technique, each thread requests ownership of the semaphore before accessing the shared data controlled by that semaphore. If another thread currently owns the semaphore, the others that are requesting it will wait until the current owner releases it.

Canny programmers realize that critical sections, semaphores, or other thread synchronization techniques are not needed if shared data items are always read and written via "atomic operations." An atomic operation is one that cannot be interrupted, which, of course, means that the shared data cannot become inconsistent. In effect, *DosEnterCritSec* makes a sequence of instructions appear to be an atomic operation to other threads in the process.

There is a subtle trap here, however: *Operations that appear atomic to the C programmer often do not appear that way to OS/2.* For example, consider this assignment statement:

```
float x,y;

x = y;
```

Now if *x* is being accessed by two threads, you might assume that it can never contain invalid data because the assignment statement is so simple. However, look at the code that a typical C compiler generates for this "simple" statement:

```
MOV     AX,y
MOV     x,AX
MOV     AX,y+2
MOV     x+2,AX
```

What happens if OS/2 switches to the other thread after the second instruction of this sequence? The floating point variable *x* will contain the first 16 bits of *y*, but its second word will contain old data. In other words, *x* will contain an invalid number when the second thread uses it.

You can probably conjure up examples even more horrible than this one, but they all are rooted in the same misconception. Operations which appear atomic to one who programs in a high-level language are rarely atomic from the operating system's viewpoint. Therefore, explicit thread synchronization techniques are needed.

Incidentally, the preceding discussion also applies to processes that use shared data segments, which we'll discuss in the next chapter.

10.4 Summary

When IBM and Microsoft designed OS/2, they provided a very stylish replacement for all the *ad hoc* multitasking techniques that had arisen in the DOS world. Furthermore, by spanning a broad range from sessions to threads, the OS/2 multitasking feature gives you more flexibility than similar systems such as UNIX. As the underlying hardware evolves, OS/2 could even become an important player in real-time applications.

Chapter 11

Memory Management

As you can probably imagine, memory management is one of the most complex parts of OS/2. This is partly due to the Intel processors, which have some truly bizarre schemes for taking what is basically a 16-bit machine and making it behave like one with 24-bit or even 32-bit addresses. The low-level aspects of the Intel processors were discussed in Chapter 2. In this chapter we'll see how the OS/2 designers, working within the constraints of the 8086 real-mode and 80286-protected mode, came up with a memory management approach that is reasonably efficient and includes a pretty good set of API services.

11.1 Physical Memory Organization

If you recall from Chapter 2, the 80286 processor can access 16 megabytes of physical memory. The lowest megabyte is often called *real memory* because it is the only portion that can be reached when the processor is in real mode and generating 20-bit addresses using the 8086 *segment:offset* format. Likewise, the remaining 15 megabytes are called *protected memory* because they can only be reached when the processor is running in protected mode using the *selector:offset* format to generate 24-bit addresses. Of course, the first megabyte can also be addressed in protected mode.

Since OS/2 is required to run existing DOS programs, it must support both real and protected modes. This leads to the fairly complicated physical memory organization shown in Figure 11-1.

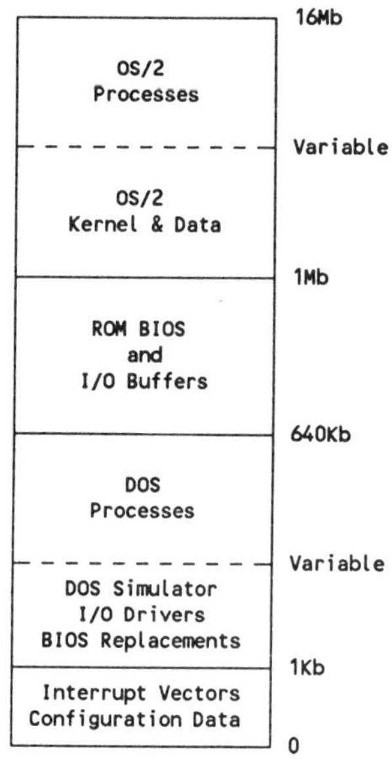

Figure 11-1. OS/2 Physical Memory Organization

The first megabyte closely resembles the memory map used by DOS, except that DOS isn't really present. In its place, OS/2 provides a DOS simulator which converts the various DOS API services into their OS/2 equivalents.

Also, OS/2 replaces many of the ROM BIOS routines with more robust versions that are re-entrant and interrupt driven. This does not mean that the actual ROM routines are removed, since that would require surgery on the system hardware. Rather, the BIOS interrupt vectors in the first kilobyte of memory are rerouted so that they point to the replacement BIOS routines.

The first megabyte also contains much of the OS/2 driver code. This enables I/O interrupts to be handled efficiently regardless of whether the processor is currently running in real mode or in protected mode. In other words, the I/O drivers are *bimodal*. While this greatly complicates their design, it is responsible for OS/2's excellent I/O performance.

Most of OS/2 actually resides just above the first megabyte. This is often called the *kernel*. Above that are various dynamically-allocated data areas used by the kernel and some of the I/O drivers. Whatever memory remains is then available for protected-mode processes. These processes can also use memory in the first megabyte if the system is configured without the DOS simulator, or if DOS is given less space than the maximum 640 kilobytes.

Now what is the significance of all this? Very little if you only work in protected mode, since your program will never see the physical memory layout. That is, when you are running as an OS/2 process, the operating system uses the 80286 memory management facilities to give your program a 30-bit, or one-gigabyte, addressing spectrum all to itself.

However, if you run any DOS programs under OS/2, the layout shown in Figure 11-1 has great significance because it shows that some essential parts of the operating system are not protected. If a DOS program scribbles below its alloted space, it will mutilate the DOS simulator, an I/O driver, a BIOS routine, or some other important system area. If it tampers with memory above the DOS boundary (assuming that the boundary is below the 640-kilobyte mark), then a protected-mode process may be injured.

So, you must remain aware that even though OS/2 can offer a lot of security and protection to its application processes, a rogue DOS program can bring the entire system down. This is a necessary result of the requirement to support the DOS environment on the 80286. A much more secure real-mode partition can be constructed on the 80386, and OS/2 or its successor will surely take advantage of that improvement in the future.

11.2 Logical Memory Organization

As I previously mentioned, a protected-mode process "sees" a 30-bit addressing spectrum, which means that each process has a "logical memory" of one gigabyte (i.e., 1024 megabytes). This is due to the *selector:offset* addressing method which we discussed in Chapter 2. If you recall, the selector contains a 13-bit index and a 1-bit table selector, as shown in Figure 11-2. The 30-bit logical address if formed by the combination of the table selector, index, and the 16-bit offset.

The table bit is reset to indicate that the index refers to one of the 8192 possible entries in the Global Descriptor Table (GDT). If the bit is set, the index refers to the Local Descriptor Table (LDT). OS/2 places all application segment descriptors into the LDT and reserves the GDT for system segments that are generally accessed only by the API routines. Therefore, the theoretical 1-gigabyte application address space is cut in half to 512 megabytes.

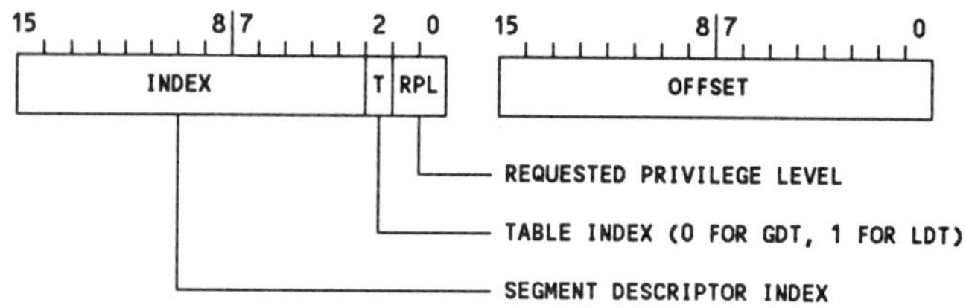

Figure 11-2. Protected-Mode Segment Selector

When a process is initiated, OS/2 does not allocate adjacent LDT slots to its segments. Typically, the odd-numbered slots are used for private segments of that process, while the even-numbered ones are treated as a system resource for the management of such features as shared memory and dynamic libraries. This means that an application's theoretical address space is further reduced to 256 megabytes, which is still a generous size.

To be more specific, private segments for a process are typically assigned selectors in the sequence 0x0F, 0x1F, 0x2F, and so on. The rightmost two bits are set because applications usually operate at privilege level 3, as we discussed in Chapter 2. Bit 2 is set to select the LDT, and bit 3 specifies an odd-numbered index. When a process is created, OS/2 builds its environment in segment 0x0F. The program is then loaded starting at segment 0x1F, and the program segments are followed by the data and stack segments.

Public segments that are shared by all processes have selector values in the sequence 0x07, 0x17, 0x27, and so on. So, if a load module (i.e. an EXE file) is sharable, it will occupy a unique range of selectors within this sequence. Then when a new process is created to run that load module, the descriptors for that range are simply copied into the new LDT. The same thing is true of shared data segments, as we'll see next.

Note that this slot-assignment scheme may change in future versions of OS/2, and so you should not build any assumptions about specific selector numbers for code or data segments into your application programs.

11.3 Allocating Data Segments

Once the process has started running, it can request OS/2 to allocate additional data segments. These can be private, or nonshared, in which case they are assigned selectors with odd-numbered indices. The process can also request the allocation of shared segments, which causes OS/2 to assign even-numbered selectors that are unique throughout the system. Then when a shared segment is accessed by another process, OS/2 uses exactly the same selector, which makes the 32-bit addresses of shared data identical throughout the system.

The following table lists the API functions used to allocate and release data segments:

NAME	DESCRIPTION
DosAllocHuge	Allocate a multisegment block
DosAllocSeg	Allocate an unnamed segment
DosAllocShrSeg	Allocate a named segment
DosFreeSeg	Free a segment or block
DosGetHugeShift	Get intersegment spacing
DosGetSeg	Get access to an unnamed segment
DosGetShrSeg	Get access to a named segment
DosGiveSeg	Give access to an unnamed segment
DosLockSeg	Lock a discardable segment
DosMemAvail	Get size of largest available block
DosReallocHuge	Reallocate a multisegment block
DosReallocSeg	Reallocate a segment
DosUnlockSeg	Unlock a discardable segment

With these functions, you can allocate private (i.e., nonshared), public (i.e., shared), and discardable data segments.

11.3.1 Private Data Segments

DosAllocSeg obtains a single segment (i.e., up to 64 kilobytes) and maps it into the LDT using the next available selector. For example, here's the code to obtain a private segment containing 10,000 bytes:

```
int error;                  /* OS/2 error code */
unsigned seg;               /* selector is placed here */

error = DosAllocSeg(10000,&seg,0);
```

The first argument specifies the size, with a value of 0 indicating a full segment. The second argument points to a word into which OS/2 places the selector for the new segment. The third argument is 0 because we are requesting a private segment. Later, we'll see that it can have several valid non-zero values as well when requesting shared or discardable segments.

DosAllocHuge obtains a block of memory larger than one segment and assigns the next available selector range to it. For example, let's allocate a 100,000-byte block:

```
int error;               /* OS/2 error code */
unsigned huge;           /* base selector is placed here */
unsigned shift;          /* shift factor for huge blocks */
unsigned step;           /* selector step factor */

error = DosAllocHuge(100000L,&huge,4,0);
DosGetHugeShift(&shift);
step = 1 << shift;
```

The first argument is a 32-bit size instead of the 16-bit size used for *DosAllocSeg*. The second argument points to a word that will receive the selector for the first segment in the block. The third argument specifies the maximum number of segments to which this block can grow as a result of subsequent *DosReallocHuge* requests. Finally, the fourth argument is 0 for a private block.

Since *DosAllocHuge* obtains more than one segment, OS/2 must assign several LDT entries (i.e., several selectors). It returns the first of these as previously described. You can then find the rest of them by using the information supplied by *DosGetHugeShift*. This function returns a "shift factor," which is simply the bit number that must be added to a huge block's base selector in order to obtain the next one. To actually get the selector step, shift the value 1 left by the shift factor, as shown in the preceding example.

The initial versions of OS/2 use a shift factor of 4, resulting in a step of 16. This is consistent with the selector sequences discussed earlier. However, you should not assume that this value applies to all versions, or to all processes in the same system. In fact, if you write a family application and run it under DOS or in the OS/2 DOS partition, *DosGetHugeShift* returns a value of 12. This is because you must add 1000H to a real-mode segment address in order to advance to the next segment.

After a segment or a huge block has been allocated, you can change the size via *DosReallocSeg* or *DosReallocHuge*. The following example shows how you would use these functions to expand the blocks that were allocated in the preceding two examples:

```
unsigned seg,huge;          /* selectors */

error = DosReallocSeg(20000,seg);

error = DosReallocHuge(120000,huge);
```

Of course, you can also decrease the size of a private block; this is not allowed for shared blocks.

When changing the size of a huge block, you must supply the base selector that was originally returned by *DosAllocHuge*. Also, you cannot expand a huge block beyond the maximum number of segments that was specified by the third argument to *DosAllocHuge*.

11.3.2 Shared Segments

Shared segments come in two flavors: named and unnamed. The latter are obtained by *DosAllocSeg* and *DosAllocHuge*, while you must use *DosAllocShrSeg* to obtain named segments. It is not possible to allocate a named huge block. *DosReallocSeg* and *DosReallocHuge* can be used on shared segments, but the size cannot be decreased.

Unnamed Shared Segments

If you set either bit 0 or bit 1 in the last argument to *DosAllocSeg* or *DosAllocHuge*, then OS/2 makes the segment(s) sharable. These two bits specify two different ways that other processes can gain access to the shared area.

If bit 0 is set, then the only processes that can access the area are those that you explicitly identify in calls to *DosGiveSeg*. For example, let's allocate a 10,000 as above and give access permission to another process:

```
int error;                  /* OS/2 error code */
unsigned seg;               /* selector is placed here */
int upid;                   /* user process id */
unsigned useg;              /* user segment */

error = DosAllocSeg(10000,&seg,0);
```

```
error = DosGiveSeg(seg,upid,&useg);
```

On the call to *DosGiveSeg*, we specify the segment that we want to share and the process with whom we want to share it. OS/2 then returns the selector that that process should use. This might seem strange in the light of our earlier discussion of even-odd selector indices. Aren't all shared segments assigned a unique even-numbered selector index from the system pool? The answer is yes, at least for the initial versions of OS/2. However, *DosGiveSeg* is defined in a general way to allow for the possibility of two processes sharing segments whose selector indices do not come from the system pool. If that were allowed, then OS/2 could not guarantee that the selectors would be identical amongst all the sharers, which is why the *useg* argument is necessary above.

The second method for allocating unnamed shared segments is by setting bit 1 in the last *DosAllocSeg* or *DosAllocHuge* argument. This bit informs OS/2 that the sharers will use *DosGetSeg* to gain access to the shared area. When you use this method, OS/2 always assigns selectors that are unique throughout the system, as discussed earlier. Then when a sharing process calls *DosGetSeg*, it need only mention the selector. That is, the process that allocates the shared area does not need to explicitly give the shared area to each of the sharers.

Both of these methods are very easy to use and are quite appropriate for groups of closely cooperating processes which have already established some other form of communication among themselves. They will need this other form of communication so that a process creating a shared segment can transmit the appropriate selector to the other processes. When you use the first method, you must give each sharer the user selector returned from the corresponding call to *DosGiveSeg*. For the second method, you must put the shared memory selector someplace where the other processes can obtain it for inclusion in their calls to *DosGetSeg*.

Chapter 12 discusses the various forms of interprocess communication that OS/2 provides. Message queues are particularly well-suited for transmitting shared-memory selectors, but often the best approach is to use a named shared memory area and place in it the selectors for the other shared segments.

Named Shared Segments

DosAllocShrSeg enables you to obtain a sharable segment and assign it a name by which other processes will know it. Here's how you would obtain a 10,000-byte shared segment named *\sharemem\stuff*:

```
int error;                    /* OS/2 error code */
unsigned seg;                 /* selector is placed here */

error = DosAllocShrSeg(10000,"\\sharemem\\stuff",&seg);
```

A process desiring to share this segment would do so via *DosGetShrSeg* as follows:

```
int error;                    /* OS/2 error code */
unsigned seg;                 /* selector is placed here */

error = DosGetShrSeg("\\sharemem\\stuff",&seg);
```

Notice that the names of shared memory segments look like file names in the *\sharemem* directory. All segment names must be placed in this pseudo-directory, and subdirectories are also allowed. For instance, if your application were named *payables*, you could place its shared segment names in *\sharemem\payables* to ensure that they did not conflict with the names from other applications. Of course, if you attempt to assign a name that is already in use, *DosAllocShrSeg* returns an error code.

11.3.3 Freeing Segments

Segments allocated by any of these techniques can be released by calling *DosFreeSeg* with the appropriate selector. When a private segment is freed, it immediately becomes available to fulfill other memory requests. A shared segment, however, is not truly freed until all sharers call *DosFreeSeg*. All segments being used by a process are automatically freed when the process terminates.

11.3.4 Discardable Segments

Discardable segments are used by nice programmers who want to help the operating system work as efficiently as possible. When OS/2 runs out of memory for such activities as starting new processes or allocating new data segments, it first looks for segments that can be discarded. If that fails, then it then begins swapping segments to disk, which can cause the entire system to slow down.

Discardable segments are created by setting bit 2 in the last argument to *DosAllocSeg* or *DosAllocHuge*. Then you must call *DosLockSeg* before using that area and *DosUnlockSeg* when you no longer need it. If *DosLockSeg* fails, then OS/2 has discarded the segment, and you must call *DosReallocSeg* or *DosReallocHuge* to get the memory area back. Since the contents of the area have been discarded, you must also regenerate them after the space has been reallocated.

This probably sounds like a useless feature. After all, what good is a memory area that occasionally loses its contents? And if I only need an area for short periods, why not use *DosAllocSeg* and *DosFreeSeg*?

Answering the second question first, it is much less work for OS/2 to lock and unlock segments than to allocate and free them. As for the usefulness of this feature, it all depends on how you design your application. For example, if a spreadsheet program needs a large block of memory when plotting data, this block could be discardable. It would be locked only when the spreadsheet user requested that the graph be drawn.

11.4 Suballocation

Many programs need to frequently allocate and release small blocks of memory. For example, a spreadsheet program typically allocates less than 100 bytes for each active cell, and a busy spreadsheet can contain thousands of these. Since it would be extremely inefficient to use segment allocation for each of these small blocks, OS/2 provides a *suballocation* mechanism.

Suballocation occurs within a segment that was obtained via *DosAllocSeg* or *DosAllocShrSeg*. First you call *DosSubSet* to initialize the segment. Then *DosSubAlloc* and *DosSubFree* are used to allocate and release small blocks within this segment. A process can have many segments set up for suballocation, and these segments can be shared with other processes, since the suballocation routines use semaphores (see Chapter 12) to avoid interference with one another.

Here is a simple program that allocates a segment and then suballocates 100 blocks from it, printing the address of each block:

```
int error;                  /* OS/2 error code */
unsigned seg;               /* selector is placed here */
int i;                      /* loop counter */
unsigned offset;            /* offset of suballocated block */

error = DosAllocSeg(10000,&seg,0);
DosSubSet(seg,1,10000);
for(i = 0; i < 100; i++)
  {
  error = DosSubAlloc(seg,&offset,50);
  if(error) printf("DosSubAlloc error %d\n",error);
  else printf("Block offset: %04x\n",offset);
  }
```

The second argument on the *DosSubSet* call is 1 to indicate that we are initializing a new segment. If this argument is 0, it indicates that the size of a previously initialized segment has been increased via *DosReallocSeg*.

A common use of suballocation is in conjunction with message queues, a form of interprocess communication discussed in the next chapter. As we'll see, the queue elements must reside in shared segments so that they can be accessed by the sending process, called the requester, and the receiving process, called the server. Typically, the queue server creates a shared segment and sets it up for suballocation. Then the requester uses *DosSubAlloc* to obtain a message block, which it places on the queue. The server processes the message in turn and then uses *DosSubFree* to release the block.

11.5 Allocating Code Segments

You may be wondering if it is at all possible for an application process to allocate code segments. This might be necessary, for example, in a compile-and-go system, where the compiler constructs a program in a data segment and then wants to execute it.

The OS/2 designers thoughtfully provided *DosCreateCSAlias* for this purpose. The following sequence shows how this function works:

```
unsigned dataseg;        /* data selector */
unsigned codeseg;        /* code selector */

error = DosCreateCSAlias(dataseg,&codeseg);
```

If *dataseg* contains a valid selector for a private data segment, this function call will create a new code selector describing the same segment. The code selector is returned in *codeseg*, and from that point on, you can execute programs in that segment. Use *DosFreeSeg* to get rid of the selector in *codeseg* when you no longer need it.

11.6 Summary

The OS/2 memory manager is well designed for the peculiar 80286 environment, and the associated API functions are general enough that evolution to the 80386 and beyond should not be difficult. In addition to basic segment allocation, the API supports allocation of multisegment blocks and suballocation within a segment. This broad range of allocation techniques, together with OS/2's efficient implementation of shared memory, enables you to design memory-intensive applications that perform well in the multitasking environment.

Chapter 12

Interprocess Communication

Many people judge a multitasking operating system by the quality of its interprocess communication features. This is because the true utility of multitasking cannot be realized unless the operating system enables cooperating tasks to communicate efficiently.

For instance, let's recall an example I've cited before, namely a multitasking spreadsheet program. One task executes in the foreground, accepting the user's keyboard input and placing it into the appropriate spreadsheet cells. The other scurries around in the background, recalculating the formulas in the dependent cells that are effected by this input. Clearly, these two tasks must communicate frequently and in a variety of ways. The foreground task must inform the background the user has changed a cell. The background task must then inform the foreground about the resulting changes in the dependent cells so that the screen display can be updated. If these information exchanges are too time consuming, then the spreadsheet seems sluggish, and the usefulness of multitasking is diminished.

OS/2 has been blessed with a broad variety of interprocess communication techniques, ranging from low-bandwidth signals to high-bandwidth shared memory. All of these are covered in this chapter, although most of the details about shared memory were presented in Chapters 10 and 11.

12.1 Shared Memory

Shared memory is the interprocess communication technique that offers the highest bandwidth and the lowest operating system overhead. That is, after several tasks arrange with OS/2 to share the same data area, they can exchange information very rapidly with no further involvement of the operating system.

As we discussed in Chapter 10, this is the natural way for the threads within a process to communicate with each other, since they all use exactly the same memory map. Different processes, however, must explicitly request access to shared segments using the API functions described in Chapter 11.

When several threads or processes are accessing a shared data area, they must carefully coordinate their actions so that they do not wind up working with inconsistent data. For instance, if one process or thread is adding a element to a linked list in shared memory, then it must lock out the other users until the linkage pointers are back in a consistent state.

Since threads are so tightly coupled, they often use *ad hoc* techniques for synchronizing their activities. Chapter 10 showed an example of this in the *xfer* thread. Cooperating processes usually employ one of the other interprocess communication techniques as a more general, but slower, coordination method. Semaphores are particularly well suited for this purpose, as we'll see next.

12.2 Signals

The *signal* is a simple interprocess communication mechanism normally used to alert processes that some unusual event has occurred. OS/2 generates three standard signals to application processes, and three others are available for application definition. These signals have the following names and numbers:

NUMBER	NAME	DESCRIPTION
1	SIGINTR	User interrupted via CTRL-C
3	SIGTERM	Program was terminated
4	SIGBREAK	User interrupted via CTRL-BREAK
5		Event flag A
6		Event flag B
7		Event flag C

A process must call *DosSetSigHandler* before it can receive any signals. Otherwise, any standard signal sent to the process causes it to terminate, while the three application-defined signals are ignored. For instance, if the user presses CTRL-C while your process is in the foreground session, OS/2 sends the SIGINTR signal. If you have not previously called *DosSetSigHandler* to intercept this signal, the process is terminated.

The process sending a signal uses either *DosSendSignal* or *DosFlagProcess*. The latter sets one of the event flags, while the former sends the SIGINTR or SIGBREAK signal just as if the user had pressed those keys. The SIGTERM signal is sent when a process calls *DosKillProcess* to terminate a process.

12.3 Semaphores

A semaphore is most often used to provide serial access to a resource, although it can also be employed as a signaling mechanism. This is best understood by considering where the name *semaphore* originated. The term as used here really comes from the railroads, where a semaphore was a wooden arm that could be raised and lowered to indicate whether a particular stretch of track was in use. Often a single track had to carry traffic in both directions, and the state of the semaphore would alert the engineer to pull onto a siding because an oncoming train was using the track.

This is exactly how semaphores are typically used in OS/2. Before accessing a shared resource, you request control of its semaphore, and OS/2 grants the request if the semaphore is free. Otherwise, OS/2 either blocks your task until the semaphore is released, or else it returns, indicating that the semaphore is busy.

Of course, it is extremely important that the task controlling a semaphore eventually release it so that other tasks can proceed. During normal operation this is usually not a concern, since the tasks sharing a resource should be well designed to cooperate graciously with each another. However, if a task terminates prematurely, perhaps because of an error or a user abort, then someone should release all semaphores controlled by that task. OS/2 allows you to choose between two semaphore types, depending on how important this clean-up operation is to your application. *System semaphores* are cleaned up automatically by OS/2, while *RAM semaphores* must be cleaned up by the application.

12.3.1 System Semaphores

A *system semaphore* is administered by OS/2 and has a name by which other processes can gain access to it. Because it has a public name, this type is also called a *public semaphore*.

To create one of these, call *DosCreateSem*, specifying a name for the semaphore and whether it is to be exclusive or nonexclusive. In the former case, only the threads within your process will be able to access it, while the latter allows any other process to access the semaphore via *DosOpenSem*. *DosCreateSem* returns a 32-bit *semaphore handle* that you use when referring to the semaphore in API calls.

System semaphore names are administered like file names. They must begin with *\sem* and can be constructed just like file names. For example, *\sem\test* and *\sem\mystuff\test* are valid names that refer to two different system semaphores.

When you are finished with a system semaphore, you can call *DosCloseSem* to notify OS/2. This is done automatically if your process terminates for any reason. That is why the system semaphore is considered a safe way to control resources, because OS/2 guarantees that no process will die and leave a system semaphore locked up. Note however, that this guarantee does not extend to the resource that is actually being controlled. For example, if a process dies while adding an element to a linked list in shared memory, OS/2 releases the system semaphore that controls the list, but it cannot guarantee that the list is valid. To help you detect this situation, *DosSemRequest* returns an error code indicating that the previous owner died.

12.3.2 RAM Semaphores

A *RAM semaphore* is simply a 32-bit integer within the address space of a process. Your program can initialize this integer to zero, indicating that the semaphore is not busy. A better way to initialize a RAM semaphore is to call *DosSemClear* to make it idle or *DosSemSet* to make it busy. This will prevent problems if IBM or Microsoft changes OS/2 in such a way that an idle semaphore does not contain zero.

A RAM semaphore has no name; it is known only by its 32-bit *selector:offset* address, and only processes having access to that address can use the semaphore. That is why this type is often called a *private semaphore*.

Since OS/2 is not aware of your RAM semaphores, it cannot clean things up if a process terminates and leaves one of them locked up. If this is a problem, then you can use *DosExitList* to define your own clean-up function to be called during the termination sequence.

12.3.3 Using Semaphores for Resource Control

To control a resource with a semaphore, simply call *DosSemRequest* before using the resource, and call *DosSemClear* when your are finished. For example, here are two routines that push and pop elements on a first-in first-out (FIFO) list:

```
struct ELT
  {
  struct ELT *next;         /* points to next element */
  ..                        /* element data */
  ..
  ..
  };

struct ELT *head = 0;       /* head of list */
unsigned long sem = 0;      /* semaphore for list */

push(elt)                   /* function to push an element */
struct ELT *elt;
{
DosSemRequest(&sem,-1L);    /* lock the list */
elt->next = head;           /* push an element */
head = elt;
DosSemClear(&sem);          /* unlock the list */
}

struct ELT *pop();          /* function to pop an element */
{
struct ELT *elt;
DosSemRequest(&sem,-1L);    /* lock the list */
if((elt = head) != 0)       /* pop an element */
  head = head->next;
DosSemClear(&sem);
return(elt);
}
```

This example uses a RAM semaphore. To use a system semaphore, add a list initialization routine that sets things up by calling *DosCreateSem*.

This example might also seem a bit sloppy because it does not check for API error codes and it uses a timeout value of -1 when calling *DosSemRequest*, indicating that the thread should block as long as the semaphore is busy. Actually, however, this type of programming is often quite appropriate in a well crafted application program. None of the API calls should fail, since they do not require OS/2 to allocate any memory or perform any I/O. Furthermore, each *DosSemRequest* call should eventually return, since the semaphore is only used by *push* and *pop*, which are simple, straight line functions.

12.3.4 Using Semaphores for Signaling

An alternative way to use semaphores is for intertask signaling, as an extension of the signal and event mechanism described earlier. In this case, one thread calls *DosSemSet* and *DosSemWait*, or just *DosSetSemWait*, to set a semaphore and wait for someone to reset it. The signaling thread then calls *DosSemClear* to wake up the one that is waiting.

You can use system or RAM semaphores in this way, but you should not intermix the resource control technique and the signalling technique on the same semaphore without careful forethought.

12.4 Pipes

The *pipe* mechanism is useful when a process must pass a sequential data stream to another process. This could be done by buffering the data in a shared disk file, with one process writing to the file while the other reads from it. A pipe has exactly this appearance, although the data is buffered in memory.

When you call *DosMakePipe*, OS/2 returns two file handles. One of these is for output to the pipe, and the other is for input from it. Usually you pass one of these handles to a child process. For example, suppose you're designing a program source code editor and a compiler in such a way that the editor can feed the source program from its memory directly to the compiler. The editor could create a pipe and spawn the compiler as a child process, passing it the pipe read handle. Then the editor would proceed to write the source code into the pipe, and the compiler would read it just as if it were coming from a disk file.

By creating a second pipe and passing the write handle to the compiler, the editor could read the compiler error messages and display them to the user on the editing screen.

The major drawback of pipes is that you must figure out a way to let the child process know which file handles are being used. A simple way to do this is to use *DosDupHandle* to force the pipe handles into agreed upon values. For example,

```
int input = 0;  /* standard input handle */
int output = 1;  /* standard output handle */
int inpipe,outpipe; /* pipe handles */

DosMakePipe(&inpipe,&outpipe,1024);
DosDupHandle(inpipe,&input);
DosDupHandle(outpipe,&output);
```

creates a pipe and duplicates its read and write handles to the standard input and output handles, respectively. These are handles 0 and 1, as we discussed in Chapter 6.

12.5 Queues

Queues are a flexible form of interprocess communication particularly suitable for transaction processing. For instance, a database manager could have a request queue that would hold messages from the processes that are using the database. These messages would request transactions such as "fetch a record," "fetch a record and lock it for updating," or "update a record." The database manager can process the requests in chronological order (i.e., FIFO, which stands for "first in, first out") or reverse chronological order (i.e., LIFO, which stands for "last in, first out"). OS/2 also allows the requests to be retrieved in priority order using a 16-level priority scheme.

You might think that a FIFO queue is simply a pipe containing structured data. Actually, pipes and queues have some major differences:

- Pipes can only connect parent and child processes, but queues can connect any processes, even if they are unrelated.
- The information passing through a pipe is buffered in the operating system, but queue elements are passed via shared memory. That is, piped data must be copied from the sender to OS/2 and then from OS/2 to the receiver. Queued information is not copied, since it resides in memory that is shared by the sender and receiver.

12.5.1 Creating a Queue

A queue is usually created by a *server*, which is a process whose primary function is to handle the transactions it receives through the queue. The server initializes the queue by calling *DosCreateQueue*. This function accepts the queue name and the queue type. The queue type is one of the following codes:

TYPE	SEQUENCE
0	FIFO (first in, first out)
1	LIFO (last in, first out)
2	Priority

As with semaphores and pipes, OS/2 treats queue names as files in a special directory. Each queue name must begin with *\queues*, such as *\queues\test* and *\queues\mystuff\test*.

If *DosCreateQueue* is successful, it returns a 16-bit queue handle which must be used in all other API functions that refer to the queue.

Usually a queue server also creates one or more shared memory segments that the requesters use to construct messages. The techniques for doing this were discussed in Chapter 11.

12.5.2 Adding Elements to a Queue

In order to add an element to a queue, you need to know the name of the queue, the name of the shared segment, and the message formats that are acceptable to the queue server. OS/2 imposes no constraints here; a queue server process is free to define any message formats that it needs for its particular job. If more than one format is needed, the server typically assigns a type code to each format.

Assuming that you know the queue name, segment name, and message types, you can interact with the queue server by first calling *DosOpenQueue*, specifying the queue name. If it is successful, this function returns a queue handle. Usually you must also call *DosGetShrSeg* in order to gain access to the shared segment created by the queue server.

After this bit of initialization, you construct each message by calling *DosSubAlloc* to get a block of the appropriate size in the shared segment. Then after loading the message into this block, you send it via the *DosWriteQueue* function, specifying the queue handle, the message type, the priority (if a type 2 queue), the message address, and its length. Typically, the server frees the shared memory block after it processes the message.

Notice that OS/2 provides no feedback mechanism to inform you about the state of the message. In a sense, you're just "throwing it over the wall" and hoping that the server handles it correctly. Furthermore, there is no predefined way for the server to send data back to the requester. This would surely be necessary in the database manager example cited earlier.

However, the need for message status and other information from the server can be easily accommodated. The server simply defines the messages in such a way that the requester must always pass the identity of a semaphore and the address of a return buffer in the shared segment. The requester then sets the semaphore prior to the *DosWriteQueue* call, and the server clears it after loading the status and other return data.

Incidentally, as we'll see in a minute, some queue servers define a semaphore that must be cleared whenever a message is placed in the queue. In that case, the requester needs to know the semaphore name so that *DosOpenSem* can be called to gain access to the semaphore. Then *DosWriteQueue* will automatically clear the semaphore each time a message is sent.

12.5.3 Removing Elements From a Queue

Only the server can remove elements from a queue. Typically, the server calls *DosReadQueue* with the queue handle and specifies that the function should not return until a message is present. Alternatively, the server can occasionally check the queue via *DosQueryQueue* or *DosPeekQueue* to see if any elements have been added. A third method is to set a semaphore and wait until a requester clears it after writing a message.

If the queue is not empty, *DosReadQueue* returns the next message according to the queue type: FIFO, LIFO, or priority. In special cases, the server can request the next message of a certain type. Also, *DosPeekQueue* can be used to scan through the queue to find messages that have special significance, although this is not as efficient as using the built-in priority mechanism.

12.6 Summary

In this chapter we've briefly covered interprocess communication, which is one of OS/2's most important features. The available techniques cover a broad performance range and are easy to use. The OS/2 implementation of shared memory and queues is particularly powerful, making the operating system quite acceptable in transaction processing applications with tight timing constraints.

Chapter 13

Advanced I/O

Chapter 6 presented the most common I/O services, which are associated with the File Manager. In this chapter, we'll examine some of OS/2's advanced I/O facilities which give application programmers much more control over the peripheral devices.

Most of these advanced features are completely innocuous insofar as system integrity is concerned. For instance, there is no way your program can crash the system by requesting the current status of an I/O device. However, in order to accommodate DOS programmers, OS/2 goes so far as to provide a means for you to directly access peripheral devices without having to undertake the difficult task of writing I/O drivers. Of course, when application programs perform low-level I/O operations, system malfunctions and crashes can occur because of programming bugs. OS/2 makes a valiant attempt to maintain a modicum of protection even in those trying times, but you take on the ultimate responsibility for system sanity when you use some of these advanced I/O features.

13.1 Asynchronous I/O

DosRead and *DosWrite* are *synchronous* operations, which means that they do not return to the caller until the data transfer is complete. In a multitasking operating system like OS/2, it is also possible to have *asynchronous* I/O operations which allow the caller to continue working while the data are being transferred. This mode of operation is provided by the API functions named *DosReadAsync* and *DosWriteAsync*. To see how these work, let's examine a double-buffered file copy routine:

```
copy(from,to)
int from;                   /* source file handle */
int to;                     /* destination file handle */
{
int i = 0;                  /* buffer toggle */
char b[2][4096]             /* I/O buffers */
unsigned long s[2];         /* semaphores */
int ret = 0;                /* return codes */
unsigned rsize[2];          /* actual read sizes */
unsigned wsize[2];          /* actual write size */

rsize[0] = wsize[0] = 0;            /* reset buffer 0 sizes */
rsize[1] = wsize[1] = 0;            /* reset buffer 1 sizes */
DosSemClear(&s[0]);                 /* clear semaphores */
DosSemClear(&s[1]);
while(1)
  {
  DosSemWait(&s[i],-1L);            /* wait for write */
  if(error = ret) break;            /* break on error */
  if(rsize[i] != wsize[i])          /* break on size error */
    {
    error = -1;
    break;
    }
  error =                           /* do synchronous read */
    DosRead(from,&b[i],sizeof(b)/2,&rsize[i]);
  if(error) break;                  /* break on read error */
  if(rsize[i] == 0) break;          /* break on end of file */
  DosSemSet(&s[i]);                 /* set the semaphore */
  error =                           /* do asynchronous write */
    DosWriteAsync(to,&s[i],&retcodes[i],&b[i],rsize[i],
      &wsize[i]);
  if(error)                         /* break on write error */
    {
    DosSemClear(&s[i]);
    break;
    }
  i ^= 1;                           /* toggle the buffer */
  }
DosSemWait(&s[0]);                  /* wait for buffer 0 */
DosSemWait(&s[1]);                  /* wait for buffer 1 */
```

```
  return(error);
  }
```

The *copy* function is called with two file handles. The *from* file is copied to the *to* file using a simple loop containing a synchronous read and an asynchronous write. This loop uses two buffers, each of which is controlled by a semaphore. The loop variable *i* is toggled between 0 and 1 to select the buffer for the read operation. After this buffer is loaded, its semaphore is set and an asynchronous write operation is initiated. The loop then cycles back to wait for the other buffer's semaphore to clear. That buffer then becomes the target for the next read operation.

The loop terminates when no bytes are read, indicating that the input file is exhausted. After waiting for both semaphores to clear, the function returns a value of 0. Note that only one of the semaphores can possibly be set, because only one asynchronous write operation can be active. However, it's easiest just to wait for them both.

Loop termination also occurs if the read or write operation fails, in which case the function returns the OS/2 error code. If the amount of data actually written does not match the amount requested, the loop terminates with an error code of -1.

DosWriteAsync uses two more arguments than *DosWrite*, which was covered in Chapter 6. One of these is a semaphore handle. You must set this semaphore via *DosSemSet* before calling *DosWriteAsync*. The other new argument points to a word that will receive the return code when the write operation finishes or aborts. OS/2 also resets the semaphore at that time.

Although this example does not show how to use *DosReadAsync*, it could be easily modified to do so. That function, like *DosWriteAsync*, requires a semaphore and a return code address. However, if you introduced an asynchronous read into this loop, performance would not improve. Think about it, and you'll see why.

13.2 Status Operations

Next let's look at some API functions that enable you to obtain and change the status of individual files and file handles, as well as the overall file system. Most of the status-read functions begin with *DosQ*, where the Q means *query*, and the status-change operations usually begin with *DosSet*, as shown below:

NAME	OPERATION
DosQFHandState	Query file handle state
DosQFileInfo	Query file information
DosQFileMode	Query file mode
DosQFSInfo	Query file system information
DosQHandType	Query file handle type
DosQVerify	Query disk verify mode
DosSetFHandState	Set file handle state
DosSetFileMode	Set file mode
DosSetFileInfo	Set file information
DosSetFSInfo	Set file system information
DosSetVerify	Set disk verify mode

13.2.1 Disk Verify Status

Normally OS/2 trusts the disk hardware to reliably record and check each data block as it is written. In certain critical applications, such as database managers, additional checking may be desirable. Both DOS and OS/2 provide an automatic verification mode in which each block is read back immediately after being written. Of course, this slows down the entire file system, and so it should be used only when absolutely necessary.

Here's a piece of code which saves the current state of disk verification and then activates it:

```
int verify;                /* saves old verify mode */

DosQVerify(&verify);       /* save verify mode */
DosSetVerify(1);           /* activate verification */
```

The *verify* word will contain 0 if verification is not active or 1 if it is. *DosSetVerify* uses the same values.

13.2.2 File System Information

DosQFSInfo is used to obtain information about a logical drive, as shown in the following example. This function is named *prfsinfo* because it prints the information about the file system whose drive number is supplied by the caller. The drive number is 0 for the current drive, 1 for drive A, 2 for drive B, and so on.

```
prfsinfo(drive)
int drive;                  /* drive code */
{
int error;                  /* error code */

struct FSINFO1              /* Level 1 information */
  {
  long fsid;                /* file system identification */
  long spau;                /* sectors per allocation unit */
  long nau;                 /* number of allocation units */
  long fau;                 /* free allocation units */
  unsigned bps;             /* bytes per sector */
  } info1;

struct FSINFO2              /* Level 2 information */
  {
  long resv;                /* reserved */
  unsigned char vsize;      /* size of volume name */
  char vname[64];           /* volume name */
  } info2;

error = DosQFSInfo(drive,1,&info1,sizeof(struct FSINFO1));
if(error) printf("DosQFSInfo error: %dn",error);
else
  {
  error = DosQFSInfo(drive,2,&info2,size(info2));
  if(error) printf("DosQFSInfo error: %dn",error);
  else
    {
    printf("nnInformation for drive %dn",drive);
    if(info2.vsize)
      printf("  Volume name: %sn",info2.vname);
    else printf("No volume labeln");
    printf("  File system ID: %ldn",info1.fsid);
    printf("  Sectors per cluster: %ldn",info1.spau);
    printf("  Number of clusters: %ldn",info1.nau);
    printf("  Number of free clusters: %ldn",info1.fau);
    printf("  Bytes per sector: %dn",info1.bps);
    }
  }
}
```

Notice that two types, or levels, of file system information are available. Level 1 includes the file system identification code and the basic size parameters. The identification code is not used in early versions of OS/2. Presumably it is intended to be assigned when the volume is initially formatted and never changed after that unless the volume is reformatted. In fact, none of the level 1 information can be changed.

The volume label is returned in the level 2 information block. The label can be assigned when the volume is formatted, and *DosSetFSInfo* provides a means to change it after that. For example, suppose you want the label of the diskette in drive A to be "MYDISK". Here's how you can accomplish this with *DosSetFSInfo*:

```
struct FSINFO2              /* Level 2 information */
  {
  long resv;                /* reserved */
  unsigned char vsize;      /* size of volume name */
  char vname[64];           /* volume name */
  } info2;

strcpy(info2.vname,"MYDISK");
info2.vsize = strlen(info2.vname);
error = DosSetFSInfo(drive,2,&info2,6+info2.vsize);
```

Pay particular attention to the two length items here. The size of the volume name string, not including the terminating null, must be placed into *vsize*. Then when you call *DosSetFSInfo*, the last argument must specify the total size of the information structure, including the null terminator on the volume name.

13.2.3 File Information

Each file has a directory record that contains the file name and other information such as the file attributes and the date and time that the file was created, most recently written, and most recently read. Chapter 6 showed how you can obtain this information by searching directories with file name patterns. You can also obtain the directory record for an open file via *DosQFileInfo*, and the date fields in the record can be changed by calling *DosSetFileInfo*.

DosQFileMode and *DosSetFileMode* enable you to read and change just the attribute word in a file's directory record. It's not clear why the OS/2 designers used the term *Mode* instead of *Attr* in these functions.

Here's an example showing how to set a file's archive bit, which normally causes the file to be saved the next time you run a backup program:

```
int error;                  /* error code */
char *name;                 /* points to file name */
unsigned attr;              /* file attribute */

error = DosQFileMode(name,&attr,0L);
if(error == 0)
  DosSetFileMode(name,attr | 0x20,0L);
```

If *DosQFileMode* is successful in finding the directory entry for *name*, it returns the attribute in *attr*. *DosSetFileMode* is then called with the same attribute word, except that 0x20 is OR'ed in to set the archive bit.

13.2.4 Handle Type

DosQHandType returns a code indicating whether the handle is associated with a disk file, a character device, or a pipe. This code also contains a bit specifying whether the file, device, or pipe is local or remote. Remote files, devices, and pipes are accessed via a local area network or its equivalent. The type codes are listed in the following table:

CODE	MEANING
0x0000	Local disk file
0x0001	Local character device
0x0002	Local pipe
0x8000	Remote disk file
0x8001	Remote character device
0x8002	Remote pipe

For a local character device, *DosQHandType* also returns the 16-bit driver attribute word, which provides the following information about the device's characteristics:

Bit 15 – Device Type
Set for a character device.

Bit 13 – Output-Until-Busy Support
Set for output-until-busy support, which means that the device can accept multiple bytes until it indicates that it is busy.

Bit 12 – Sharability
Set if device is sharable via the File Manager. Reset if device is not sharable or if sharing is managed within the driver.

Bit 11 – Open/Close Required
Set if driver must receive open and close requests, otherwise reset.

Bits 9 to 7 – Function Level
Contains 001 to indicate an OS/2 device driver.

Bit 6 – IOCTL Supported
Set if driver supports I/O control (IOCTL) operations.

Bit 3 – Clock
Set if this is the system clock device, otherwise reset.

Bit 2 – NULL
Set if this is the NULL device, otherwise reset.

Bit 1 – Standard Output
Set if this is the standard output device, otherwise reset.

Bit 0 – Standard Input
Set if this is the standard input device, otherwise reset.

13.2.5 Handle State

The file handle state is 16 bits of information that you normally supply as the seventh argument to *DosOpen*. This is also known as the *file processing mode* or *file access mode*, as we discussed in Chapter 6. The following snippet of code shows how you could change a file's state such that the handle will not be inherited by child processes:

```
int handle;                   /* file handle */
unsigned state;               /* file state */

DosQFHandState(handle,&state);  /* get file state */
state &= 0x7f88;                /* reset access, share */
state |= 0x0080;                /* set private flag */
DosSetFHState(handle,state);
```

Note that only bit 3 and bits 7 to 14 can be changed. When you call *DosSetFHState*, the other bits should be zero. In this case we preserve the values returned by *DosQFHandState* except for bit 7, which we set in order to make this a private (i.e. non-inherited) file handle. See Chapter 6 and the Appendix for more details on the various items packed into the state word.

13.3 Device Control

Sometimes you need to deal directly with an I/O driver, bypassing the File Manager. DOS provided an I/O control (IOCTL) function for this purpose, and OS/2 has greatly improved upon that approach in the *DosDevIOCtl* function. This is an extremely rich and complicated API service, and we'll just touch the surface here.

DosDevIOCtl is called in the following way with a file handle, a category code, a function code, a parameter area, and a data area.

```
DosDevIOCtl(data,parm,function,category,handle);
```

The file handle, also called the device handle, must apply to a device that was opened via *DosOpen*. The category code generally specifies the type of I/O driver being accessed, and OS/2 defines this item in such a way that it can be extended to support user-supplied drivers. The function code specifies the operation that the driver is to perform, and the parameter area contains further information needed to carry out the operation. The data area can supply information to the driver or receive information from it.

13.3.1 IOCTL Category Codes

The category code is a byte whose high bit is 0 for a standard category and 1 for a user-defined category. The standard categories defined in OS/2 SE 1.0 are:

CATEGORY	DESCRIPTION	DEVICE NAME
01	Serial device control	COM1, COM2, etc.
03	Pointer draw control	MOUSE$
04	Keyboard control	KBD$
05	Printer control	LPT1, LPT2, etc.
06	Light pen control	
07	Mouse control	MOUSE$
08	Logical disk control	
09	Physical disk control	
10	Monitor control	
11	General device control	

Note that categories 10 and 11, unlike the others, apply to all drivers. Category 11 is particularly important because it provides some frequently used capabilities in a way quite different than DOS. Specifically, the functions in category 11 enable you to flush the input and output buffers associated with the device.

13.3.2 IOCTL Function Codes

Each category contains one or more functions, which are identified with an 8-bit code. The function code is strucutured in the following way:

BIT	STATE	MEANING
7	0	Return error if unsupported
	1	Ignore if unsupported
6	0	Intercepted by OS/2
	1	Passed to driver
5	0	Send data/commands to device
	1	Query data/status from device
4:0		Operation

If you define new categories for your own I/O drivers, the associated function codes should conform to this structure.

Now let's examine the functions provided by the standard OS/2 IOCTL categories. As I said earlier, this is a very complex part of the OS/2 API, and space constraints do not permit an exhaustive treatment here. The full details can be found in the *OS/2 Technical Reference*.

13.3.3 Serial Device Control

Unlike DOS, OS/2 includes a sophisticated I/O driver for serial devices, that is, for devices that are attached via RS-232 adaptors. DOS provides only the simplest support for these devices, and so DOS communication programs usually supply their own I/O drivers. While this is still possible under OS/2, it is probably not necessary because the OS/2 driver has the features needed for high-speed computer-to-computer and computer-to-terminal communication.

The function codes for IOCTL category 1 follow:

FUNCTION	DESCRIPTION
0x41	Set baud rate
0x42	Set line characteristics
0x44	Transmit byte immediately
0x45	Break off
0x46	Set modem controls
0x47	XOFF (stop transmission)
0x48	XON (start transmission)
0x4B	Break on
0x53	Set device control block parameters
0x61	Return current baud rate
0x62	Return line characteristics
0x64	Return COM status
0x65	Return transmit data status
0x66	Return modem controls
0x67	Return modem inputs
0x68	Return bytes in receive queue
0x69	Return bytes in transmit queue
0x6D	Return COM error information
0x72	Return COM event information
0x73	Return device control block parameters

To give you an idea of how *DosDevIOCtl* works, here's an example that saves the current baud rate and changes the rate to 9600:

```
int com;                  /* COM device handle */
int error;                /* error code */
unsigned oldrate;         /* old baud rate */
unsigned newrate=9600;    /* new baud rate */
error =                   /* get old baud rate */
  DosDevIOCtl(&oldrate,NULL,0x61,1,com);

if(error == 0)            /* change to 9600 */
  DosDevIOCtl(NULL,&newrate,0x41,1,com);
```

The *com* item is assumed to be a valid file handle resulting from a previous call to *DosOpen* with one of the serial devices (e.g., COM1) as the file name. If *com* is not a serial device handle, then the first call to *DosDevIOCtl* will return an error code.

Notice how the first call obtains the old baud rate in a word whose address is supplied as the data pointer. Since no parameters are required for this function, the parameter pointer must be NULL. On the second call, the reverse is true. That is, the data pointer is NULL because function 0x41 returns no information. The parameter pointer refers to a word containing the baud rate.

13.3.4 Pointer Draw Control

Category 3 supports one function whose code is 0x72. This function is typically used only by the mouse subsystem (see Chapter 9) to obtain the address of the pointer draw routine and of the pointer image.

Keyboard Control

Category 4 contains the following function codes for controlling the keyboard device:

FUNCTION	DESCRIPTION
0x50	Set code page
0x51	Set input mode
0x52	Set interim character flags
0x53	Set shift state
0x54	Set typematic rate and delay
0x55	Notify of foreground change
0x56	Set session manager hot key
0x57	Set keyboard control block parameters
0x58	Set code page identifier
0x5C	Set NLS and custom code page
0x71	Get input mode
0x72	Get interim character flags
0x73	Get shift state
0x74	Read character data records
0x75	Peek at character data record
0x76	Get session manager hot key
0x77	Get keyboard type
0x78	Get code page identifier
0x79	Translate scan code to ASCII

You will seldom need to use any of these because application programs are expected to access the keyboard via the *Kbd* functions described in Chapter 8. However, the *DosDevIOCtl* function lets you do several things that cannot be done with the *Kbd* functions. In particular, you can obtain the keyboard type (function code 0x77), set the typematic rate and delay (function code 0x54), and query or change the session manager hot key (function codes 0x76 and 0x56).

13.3.5 Printer Control

Category 5 contains the following codes for controlling printers:

FUNCTION	DESCRIPTION
0x42	Set page and line sizes
0x44	Set retry mode
0x46	Initialize printer
0x48	Activate font
0x62	Get page and line sizes
0x64	Get retry mode
0x66	Get printer status
0x69	Query active font
0x6A	Verify font

These operations are typically used only by the OS/2 print spooler, which is usually activated to buffer all printer output. However, if you run the system without the spooler, then your application program can control the printer directly via *DosDevIOCtl*.

13.3.6 Mouse Control

Category 7 contains the following functions for controlling the mouse pointing device:

FUNCTION	DESCRIPTION
0x50	Notify of screen switch
0x51	Notify of display mode change
0x52	Notify of pending screen switch
0x53	Re-assign scaling factors
0x54	Assign new event mask
0x56	Set pointer shape

0x57	Remove collision area
0x58	Define collision area
0x59	Specify pointer position
0x5A	Specify OS/2 pointer draw address
0x5B	Specify DOS pointer draw address
0x5C	Set driver status flags
0x60	Get number of buttons
0x61	Get mickeys/centimeter
0x62	Get driver status flags
0x63	Read event queue
0x64	Get event queue status
0x65	Get event mask
0x66	Get scaling factors
0x67	Get pointer position
0x68	Get pointer shape

As with the keyboard control functions, these mouse controls are usually employed only by the mouse subsystem which was described in Chapter 9. Application programs normally use the *Mou* functions from the mouse subsystem. However, *DosDevIOCtl* does give you a lower-level method to control the mouse, which can occasionally be useful.

13.3.7 Logical Disk Control

Category 8 includes a number of functions related to *logical disk drives*. The file handle used in these functions must be the one returned by a call to *DosOpen* specifying that you want the entire volume opened. See the *DosOpen* description in the Appendix for information on how to do this.

The following functions are associated with category 8:

FUNCTION	DESCRIPTION
0x00	Lock logical drive
0x01	Unlock logical drive
0x02	Re-determine media type
0x03	Set logical map
0x20	Query removability
0x43	Set device parameters
0x44	Write logical track

0x45	Format and write logical track
0x63	Get device parameters
0x64	Read logical track
0x65	Verify logical track

Some of these functions, such as lock and unlock, can be used only if no other files are open on the logical drive. Generally, you should lock the drive before performing any functions that change the logical drive contents or parameters.

Notice that these category 8 functions allow you to access the logical drive by tracks. A track is simply the collection of sectors that can be read or written from one disk surface in a single revolution. Use function 0x63 to obtain the sector size and the number of sectors per track. Tracks are numbered from 0 to some maximum value which depends on the size of the logical drive. This information is also returned by function 0x63.

When you access a logical drive via *DosDevIOCtl*, you are completely bypassing the File Manager. One hazard is that you can easily step on critical data such as directories and the File Allocation Table (FAT) that the File Manager uses to allocate file space on the drive.

13.3.8 Physical Disk Control

Category 9 is similar to category 8, except that it gives you access to physical, rather than logical, disks. A physical disk always contains at least one logical disk, but it may contain more if it is defined as a partitionable drive. For instance, a 64-megabyte physical disk is typically organized as two 32-megabyte logical disks, or partitions.

In order to use a category 9 function, you must first call *DosPhysicalDisk* to obtain a handle for the physical disk. This function has a calling format similar to *DosDevIOCtl* and is described in the Appendix.

The category 9 functions are:

FUNCTION	DESCRIPTION
0x00	Lock physical drive
0x01	Unlock physical drive
0x44	Write physical track
0x63	Get physical drive parameters
0x64	Read physical track

0x65	Verify physical track

Notice that the track access functions in this category use track numbers that are relative to the beginning of the physical disk, starting at physical track 0. The category 8 functions also begin at track number 0, but a logical track number is always relative to the beginning of the partition.

13.3.9 Monitor and General Device Control

Category 10 contains a single function, number 0x40, which does exactly the same thing as *DosMonReg*, which was described in Chapter 8.

Category 11 provides the following three useful functions intended for use with character devices:

FUNCTION	DESCRIPTION
0x01	Flush input buffer
0x02	Flush output buffer
0x60	Query monitor support

The flush functions delete any data that the driver has stored up in its internal buffers, including data that are currently passing through the input or output monitor chain.

13.4 IOPL Segments

Normal application processes are not allowed to execute I/O instructions directly, nor are they allowed to block I/O interrupts. OS/2 imposes this restriction so that processes cannot accidentally interfere with one another or with the operating system and its I/O drivers.

But what if a process has a legitimate reason for performing direct I/O? For example, the Enhanced Graphics Adaptor (EGA) has some special display modes that are not supported by the standard OS/2 video subsystem but are useful in some graphics applications. Such an application could, of course, supply its own video driver, but this would not be an easy programming task. Fortunately, OS/2 provides a better method in the form of the *IOPL segment*.

An IOPL segment is a code segment that has been given I/O privileges. In other words, that code segment runs at privilege level 2, while normal process segments run at level 3. As we discussed in Chapter 2, OS/2 grants I/O privileges only to levels 0, 1, and 2. Normal processes run at level 3, and the operating system (including I/O drivers) uses levels 0 and 1. Level 2, then, is reserved for those portions of a normal process which need I/O privileges.

In order to employ the IOPL segment feature, you must include the command

```
IOPL=YES
```

in *config.sys*. Also, you must use some special directives when linking the program. These directives identify the segment(s) that should run at level 2 and cause the linker to set up the necessary level transitions as described in Chapter 2.

An IOPL segment has some of the characteristics of a thread, which we discussed in Chapter 10. Threads and IOPL segments are both treated as functions entered via far calls and operating with their own stacks. Arguments are typically passed via a common data area, since threads and IOPL routines both share in the caller's address space. However, an IOPL segment does not actually execute asynchronously relative to its caller. Furthermore, the IOPL stack is assigned by OS/2 instead of by the caller, and the IOPL stack is always just 512 bytes. Because of this small stack and other factors, an IOPL routine cannot call or jump to any other segments, nor can it use any OS/2 API services.

Although an IOPL routine can freely access any I/O port, the application process should inform OS/2 about the particular ports being used. This is done via *DosPortAccess*. Here is an example in which we notify OS/2 that the IOPL routine named *senddata* will block interrupts and will use I/O ports 0x3C0 through 0x3CF:

```
error =                     /* request port access */
  DosPortAccess(0,0,0x3c0,0x3cf);

senddata();                 /* call IOPL routine */

error =                     /* release port access */
  DosPortAccess(0,1,0x3c0,0x3cf);
```

If the IOPL routine blocks interrupts but does not perform any I/O, you should call *DosCLIAccess* to inform OS/2.

The use of *DosPortAccess* is voluntary, since the 80286 processor provides no means for OS/2 to restrict an IOPL process to only those ports. However, you should get into the habit of using this API function as well as *DosCLIAccess*, because the 80286's successors will enable OS/2 to provide finer-grained protection.

13.5 Summary

OS/2 provides an impressive set of I/O services, including the fundamental file operations described in Chapter 6 and the advanced operations presented in this chapter. These services go well beyond the needs of most applications, and they even allow you to directly control the I/O ports via IOPL segments.

However, if you do find yourself cramped, OS/2 also allows its I/O drivers to be replaced and new drivers to be added. The rules for writing I/O drivers are not simple, but they are covered reasonably well in the IBM documentation. Because of space and time constraints, I won't get into that topic in this book.

Chapter 14

International Features

DOS-based PCs have become ubiquitous not just in the USA, but throughout the world. This international success has created great opportunities for software product developers, but it has also turned the spotlight on an area previously ignored in most operating systems. In the past, the typical operating system was quite chauvinistic, reflecting the language, practices, and biases of the country in which it originated. Even UNIX, which is arguably the most portable operating system yet devised, has often been criticized for being tied to the USA computing community and ignoring the needs of European and Asian users.

In recognition of the growing international market, IBM and Microsoft began to introduce some international features into DOS Version 2. Specifically, they provided API services whereby a program can access a set of country-dependent information in order to adapt itself to the data representations of the country in which it is being used. In addition, they introduced operating system support for code pages, thereby insulating programs from keyboard, video display, and printer differences among various countries.

For instance, by using the country-dependent information services, an accounting program can show money amounts with dollar signs in the USA and pound signs in the United Kingdom. Similarly, the program could automatically adjust date formats to month-day-year in the USA and day-month-year in Europe.

International application support has steadily improved in the DOS releases since Version 2, and OS/2 continues that evolution. With a small amount of effort, you can now make many applications truly country-independent, even to the point of supporting countries which use dual-byte character sets, such as Japan.

14.1 Country Codes and Code Pages

DOS and OS/2 identify different countries or language regions by means of a *country code*. Within a country, several different I/O translations are usually available, and each of these is represented by a *code page identifier*. The following table lists thc country codes and code pages that are defined for IBM OS/2 SE 1.0:

COUNTRY	COUNTRY CODE	CODE PAGE	KEYBOARD CODE
Arabic	785		
Asia	099		
Australia	061	437,850	
Belgium	032	437,850	BE
Canada (English)	001	437,850	
Canada (French)	002	863,850	CF
China	086		
Denmark	045	865,850	DK
Finland	358	437,850	SU
France	033	437,850	FR
Germany	049	437,850	GR
Hebrew	972		
Italy	039	437,850	IT
Japan	081		
Korea	082		
Latin America	003	437,850	LA
Netherlands	031	437,850	NL
Norway	047	865,850	NO
Portugal	351	860,850	PO
Spain	034	437,850	SP
Sweden	046	437,850	SV
Switzerland	041	437,850	SF,SG

Taiwan	088		
United Kingdom	044	437,850	UK
United States	001	437,850	US

This table also shows the keyboard codes associated with the different countries or regions. The user must enter a KEYB command to inform OS/2 that a special keyboard is attached. Without this command, OS/2 assumes that the United States keyboard is being used. I won't discuss special keyboards any further, because they make no difference from a programming viewpoint. That is, if the user correctly identifies the keyboard, then OS/2 will translate the scan codes into the correct ASCII codes.

You probably recognize that many country codes are the same as the country prefixes used for international telephone dialing. However, non-telephone codes are used when it is necessary to differentiate among various language regions within a single international dialing area.

Now let's look at country codes and code pages in more detail.

14.1.1 Country Codes

OS/2 includes a file named *country.sys* which contains a *country-dependent information*, or CDI, record for each country code. This record contains the following items:

- Time and date formats
- Currency symbol
- Decimal separator
- Lower-to-upper case mapping table
- Collating sequence table
- Dual-byte character set (DBCS) vector table

OS/2 selects the appropriate entry from this file during system initialization when it reads the COUNTRY command in *config.sys*. For example, to use the Norwegian CDI, insert the following command into *config.sys*:

```
COUNTRY=047
```

This country selection applies to all sessions and cannot be changed by application programs. This is slightly different than DOS, which does allow its application programs to change the current country.

If no country is explicitly selected during system initialization, IBM OS/2 defaults to the USA. Other computer manufacturers may choose different default settings in their versions of the operating system.

14.1.2 Code Pages

Code pages are tables used by the keyboard, video, and printer subsystems to translate from internal codes to the appropriate human-readable characters. IBM OS/2 SE 1.0 defines five code pages:

PAGE	USAGE
437	USA (IBM PC)
850	Multi-lingual
860	Portuguese
863	Canadian (French)
865	Nordic

Figures 14-1 through 14-5 at the end of this chapter show how these code pages cause certain internal 8-bit codes to be treated as different displayable characters. Notice that the letters, numbers, and common punctuation characters are the same in all code pages. These characters have values between 32 and 128 and use the ASCII encoding scheme. Characters with values below 32, which are IBM PC extensions to ASCII, are also common to all code pages.

Many of the characters with values from 128 to 255 are also the same in these five code pages. However, if you look closely, you'll see a few differences. For instance, the character Á has the value 0xB5 in code page 850 and 0x86 in code page 860. It does not appear in the other code pages. Similarly, character û is 0x9E in code page 863 and 0xEA in code page 850, but is absent from the other pages.

In general, these code pages differ in the number of accented characters that they provide and in the values they assign to those characters. And except for code page 850, all of them provide the complete set of PC line drawing characters, as well as most of the other ASCII extensions that were introduced with the IBM PC. So, it appears that pages 860, 863, and 865 were produced by "tweaking" the original IBM PC encoding scheme, which is code page 437.

Code page 850, however, is not the result of a few simple changes to page 437. It sacrifices many of the PC line drawing characters and other special PC characters in order to pick up the accented characters needed to cover the major languages in Europe, North America, and South America. In other words, code page 850 is an amalgam of pages 437, 860, 863, and 865. Its purpose is to enable application programs to easily move data files from one country to another.

For example, suppose a French-Canadian user types the character û, which is captured by your program and written to a disk file. If this occurred with code page 863 active, which would be the normal situation when the user employs a French-Canadian keyboard, then the character would be stored in the file as a byte containing 0x9E. The USA computer, using code page 437, would display this byte as · (a dot). However, if both users activated code page 850 then the file would contain 0xEA for this character, and both users would see it displayed correctly.

14.1.3 Activating Code Pages

OS/2 normally provides only one code page (often called the "national" or "local" code page), depending on the country that is selected during system initialization. For instance, if you select Norway via country code 47 as shown earlier, then code page 865 is automatically activated.

OS/2 also allows you to activate a second code page in order to produce internationally portable files. As shown in the country code table presented earlier, IBM OS/2 SE 1.0 only allows code page 850 to be selected as an alternative to the local page. This is done via the CODEPAGE command as shown below:

```
CODEPAGE=865,850
```

This command requires that you specify both the national and the international code pages, which in this case are 865 and 850, respectively. When OS/2 sees this command, it prepares both code pages so that the user or any application process can switch between them. The user does this via the CHCP command, while the process can call *DosSetCP* or *DosSetProcCP*, which will be described later.

OS/2 needs several other pieces of information before it can correctly manage code pages. Specifically, *config.sys* must contain one or more DEVINFO statements describing the characteristics of the keyboard, video display, and printer. For instance, the DEVINFO statements related to the previous COUNTRY and CODEPAGE commands might be:

```
DEVINFO=KBD,NO,C:\KEYBOARD.DCP
DEVINFO=SCR,VGA,C:\VIOTBL.DCP
DEVINFO=LPT1,4201,C:\4201.DCP,ROM=(865,0)
```

The first line specifies a Norwegian keyboard, and the second specifies a normal VGA display. The third line specifies an IBM Proprinter (which IBM calls the 4201 printer) using a ROM cartridge that contains the Norwegian character font.

DEVINFO statements can get very complicated, and can also be quite different from one computer manufacturer to another. For that reason, I won't get into any more details here. Consult the *OS/2 User's Reference* for the particular computer you will be using.

14.1.4 Code Pages and File Names

The active code page governs the translation of all characters typed by the user. OS/2 will allow the user to create files whose names contain characters that are only available in the local code page. This can cause problems if such a file is shipped to another country, since a user in that country might not be able to correctly display or type the file name.

To avoid this problem, file names should generally be restricted to the letters from A to Z and the digits from 0 to 9.

14.2 Accessing Country-Dependent Information

There are four API functions that enable you to access the current CDI record and code page or other combinations of CDI records and code pages: *DosGetCtryInfo*, *DosCaseMap*, *DosGetCollate*, and *DosGetDBCSEv*. Unlike DOS, OS/2 has no API function to change the current country selection, although there are functions to change the current code page, as we'll see later.

14.2.1 Basic Country-Dependent Information

DosGetCtryInfo obtains the basic CDI items for the current country or a the specified country. This record can be declared in the following way for use in C programs:

```
struct CDI
  {
  unsigned cc;        /* country code */
  unsigned cp;        /* code page */
  unsigned fdate;     /* date format, as follows
                         0 = mm/dd/yy
                         1 = dd/mm/yy
                         2 = yy/mm/dd
                      */
  char curr[5];       /* currency symbol */
  char sthou[2];      /* thousands separator */
  char sdec[2];       /* decimal separator */
  char sdate[2];      /* date separator */
  char stime[2];      /* time separator */
  char fcurr;         /* currency format, as follows
                         Bit 0 = 0 if symbol precedes value
                               = 1 if symbol follows value
                         Bit 1 = number of spaces
                         Bit 2 = replace decimal symbol
                      */
  char dcurr;         /* number of decimals in currency */
  char ftime;         /* time format, as follows
                         Bit 0 = 0 if 12-hour clock
                               = 1 if 24-hour clock
                      */
  long r1;            /* reserved */
  char sdata[2];      /* data list separator */
  unsigned r2[5];     /* reserved */
  };
```

Here's an example showing how you can use this information to properly display a date:

```
int error;                  /* error code */
int cc[2] = {0,0};          /* country code and code page */
struct CDI cdi;             /* country-dependent info */
int asize;                  /* actual size of data */
int day,month,year;         /* date components */
int f1,f2,f3;               /* date fields for printf */

error =                     /* get country info */
  DosGetCtryInfo(sizeof(struct CDI),cc,&cdi,&asize);
if(error == 0) switch(cdi.fdate)
  {
  case 0:                   /* 0 for mm/dd/yy */
```

```
    f1 = month;
    f2 = day;
    f3 = year;
    break;

    case 1:                     /* 1 for dd/mm/yy */
    f1 = day;
    f2 = month;
    f3 = year;
    break;

    case 2:                     /* 2 for yy/mm/dd */
    default:                    /* trap unknown date code */
    f1 = year;
    f2 = month;
    f3 = day;
    }

  printf("%d%s%d%s%d\n",f1,cdi.sdate,f2,cdi.sdate,f3);
  }
```

After obtaining the CDI record for the current country, we use a *switch* statement on the date format to select the proper date components into *f1*, *f2*, and *f3*. These components are then formatted and displayed via *printf*. Notice that we include the proper date field separator by using the *%s* formatting directive with *cdi.sdate*. This illustrates that the various CDI symbols and separators are all stored as null-terminated strings.

The *cc* array contains two integers specifying the country code and the code page. If these are both zero, then the CDI record for the current country and currently selected code page is returned.

14.2.2 Case Mapping

DosCaseMap converts all lower case characters in an ASCII string into upper case characters, using the mapping rules for the specified country and code page. Here's how you use this function:

```
int error;                  /* error code */
int cc[2] = {0,0};          /* country code and code page */
char buffer[80];            /* string buffer */

while(1)
  {
  gets(buffer);
```

```
DosCaseMap(strlen(buffer),cc,buffer);
puts(buffer);
}
```

This little program reads a string of characters from the keyboard, converts it to upper case via *DosCaseMap*, and then displays the converted string. So, if the user types the string abc, that will be displayed on the screen with ABC just below it. While this doesn't seem particularly useful, consider the case where the user types some accented characters, such as äëöü, when code page 865 is active. In that case, *DosCaseMap* would return ÄEÖÜ. Notice that accented lower case characters for which there is no accented upper case equivalent get converted into unaccented upper case characters.

14.2.3 Collation Table

DosGetCollate gets a 256-byte collation table which indicates how characters are to be sorted. This function is used as follows:

```
int error;                /* error code */
int cc[2] = {0,0};        /* country code and code page */
char table[256];          /* collation table */
int length;               /* actual table length */
int a,b;                  /* test characters */
int c;                    /* test result */
char *p;                  /* phrase pointer */

error = DosGetCollate(256,cc,table,&length);
while(1)
  {
  printf("\nEnter 1st character: ");
  a = getchar();
  printf("\nEnter 2nd character: ");
  b = getchar();
  c = table[a] - table[b];
  if(c < 0) p = "less than";
  if(c > 0) p = "greater than";
  if(c == 0) p = "equal to";
  printf("\n'%c' is %s '%c'\n",a,p,b);
  }
}
```

In this example, we first get the collation table. Then we obtain two characters from the user, determine their collating sequence via the collation table, and display the result. Determining the collating sequence is a simple matter of comparing the collation table values that correspond to the two character values.

14.2.4 Dual-Byte Character Set Vector

Some countries, such as Japan and Korea, require more than 256 characters to represent their native written language. In such a situation, a dual-byte character set, or DBCS, is used. A DBCS contains both one-byte and two-byte characters, with the latter being recognized by certain lead-in values.

For instance, Japanese dual-byte characters begin with the values from 0x81 to 0x9F and from 0xE0 to 0xFC. In effect, when one of these values is encountered in a character string, the following byte gets translated through a different 256-byte code page. This means that the Japanese character set requires 29 code pages, since there is one main code page and 28 alternate pages selected by the DBCS lead-in values.

The *DosGetDBCSEv* function returns a "DBCS environment vector" for the current country and code page. This vector is simply a list of ranges for the lead-in characters. Here's a simple routine that prints the DBCS vector:

```
int error;              /* error code */
int cc[2] = {0,0};      /* country code and code page */
unsigned char dbcs[32]; /* DBCS environment vector */
int i;                  /* loop index */

error = DosGetDBCSEv(sizeof(dbcs),cc,dbcs);
for(i = 0; (dbcs[i]+dbcs[i+1]) != 0; i += 2)
  {
  if(i == 0) printf("DBCS environment vector...\n");
  printf("Start = 0x%02x  Stop = 0x%02x\n",
    dbcs[i],dbcs[i+1]);
  }
if(i) printf("End of vector\n\n");
else printf("No DBCS environment vector\n\n");
}
```

The vector consists of a number of two-byte entries. The first byte of each entry specifies the starting value for a range of lead-in characters, and the second byte is the ending value for the range. The last entry in the vector is followed by two bytes containing zero.

By now you've probably concluded that writing an application program to work in DBCS and non-DBCS countries is a pretty tough chore. When you have to accommodate dual-byte characters, many simple chores become quite difficult.

Consider, for example, how to measure the length of a character string. The ANSI-standard method for C programmers is to call *strlen*, which counts the number of bytes in a string up to but not including the null terminator. However, if the string contains dual-byte characters, it's possible that a second byte of a dual-byte pair could be null (i.e. could have a value of 0). In that case, *strlen* would stop counting and would return an incorrect value.

Okay, then, suppose we change *strlen* so that it senses the DBCS lead-in characters and counts correctly. We would then be measuring the *memory length* of a string, not its *display length*. In other words, even though a dual-byte character occupies two bytes in memory, it only occupies one character position when it is displayed or printed. If your program uses *strlen* to compute display lengths, it will reserve one extra display position for each dual-byte character.

Clearly, we need a second function similar to *strlen* for measuring the display length. The same is true of several other ANSI-defined string manipulation functions. Japanese vendors of C compilers often include such functions in their libraries, but few American and European programmers are familiar with this problem.

14.3 Manipulating Code Pages

Even though OS/2 does not allow the country selection to be changed after system initialization, it does allow the user or any process to change the code page. The user does this via the CHCP command, while a process has several API functions to manipulate code pages. Both of these techniques can only switch between the two code pages that were specified during system initialization via the CODEPAGE command that we discussed earlier.

DosGetCP, *DosSetCP*, and *DosSetProcCP* are the API functions that you normally use to get the code page status and to switch to a different code page. For example, the following routine prints the current code page, the available code pages, and then allows the user to select a different page:

```
int pages[20];                  /* code page table */
int length;                     /* actual length */
int i;                          /* loop counter */
```

```
DosGetCP(sizeof(pages),pages,&length);
if(length)
  {
  printf("Current code page: %d\n",pages[0]);
  length = length/2;
  for(i = 1; i < length; i++)
    {
    if(i == 1) printf("Prepared code pages:");
    printf(" %d",pages[i]);
    }
  if(length > 1)
    {
    printf("\nSelect code page: ");
    scanf("%d\n",&i);
    error = DosSetCP(i,0);
    if(error) printf("DosSetCP error %d\n",error);
    }
  }
else printf("No code pages available\n");
}
```

DosGetCP returns a list containing the current code page in the first word and all available code pages in the remaining words. In the initial version of OS/2, this list only needs to be three words long, since a maximum of two code pages can be specified during system initialization. This example uses a table containing twenty entries, just in case the two-page limit is increased in a future version. Notice that *DosGetCP* returns the actual number of bytes in the *length* word. We divide this by two in order to convert it to a word count.

After printing the code pages, the example program obtains a code page number from the user via *scanf*, a standard C input function. We could check if this number is valid by examining the list produced by *DosGetCP*. However, here we just take the easy way and feed the new code page number to *DosSetCP*, which will fail if the number is not valid.

If *DosSetCP* is successful, it switches the code page for the current session. After that point, the print spooler uses that code page to translate any new print files opened by that process. Furthermore, any child processes created after that point inherit the new code page instead of the one that is currently defined for the session. Finally, *DosSetCP* changes the code page used by the default logical keyboard and display within that session.

DosSetProcCP is almost the same as *DosSetCP*, except that it does not change the keyboard and display code pages. In addition, the keyboard and display subsystems provide API functions named *KbdGetCP*, *KbdSetCP*, *VioGetCP*, and *VioSetCP*. These are not normally used by application programs because it would be very unusual to want the keyboard using one code page while the display was using another.

14.4 Message Files

While country-dependent information and code pages are of great help in translating variable input and output, they don't offer much assistance with the many canned messages that an application program must produce. For instance, it would be very nice if your error messages would appear in the local language: English, French, German, or whatever. However, such messages are often embedded within the program as constants. OS/2 provides a neat method to separate such messages from the program so that the user can select the language without needing a different version of the program. In fact, most of the OS/2 messages and prompters use this facility so that OS/2 can be easily customized and adapted to local languages.

The following steps are necessary to use the OS/2 message facility in your application:

1. Prepare an ASCII text file containing the messages in the format that is described in the next section.
2. Convert the text file to an indexed format via the MKMSGF utility, which is provided in the IBM OS/2 Programmer's Toolkit.
3. If you want the messages to reside in memory, bind them to your executable file via the MSGBIND utility, which is also part of the Programmer's Toolkit. However, do not perform this step if you want to allow your users to easily switch message files.
4. Within your program, use *DosGetMessage*, *DosInsMessage*, and *DosPutMessage* to retrieve, format, and display messages.

Now let's look at these steps in more detail.

14.4.1 Message Text Files

A message file is identified by a three-character code, such as XYZ, and each message in the file begins with that code, followed by four digits and a message type code. Here's a simple example:

```
XYZ
XYZ0100E: This is an error message
XYZ0101I: This is an information message
XYZ0102P: This is a prompt for input on the next line
XYZ0103P: This is a prompt for input on the same line%0
XYZ0104W: This is a warning message
XYZ0105I: Variable A is %1, Variable B is %2
```

Notice that the letters E, I, P, and W are the message type codes. As shown in the last message, you can use %1 through %9 to indicate where variable data should be placed by *DosInsMessage*. Also, XYZ0103P shows how %0 is used at the end of the line to suppress the carriage return and line feed.

If these messages are in the file named *xyz.txt*, the following command will convert them into the indexed format:

```
mkmsgf xyz.txt xyz.msg
```

The first argument is the input file name, and the second is the output file name. While the input file can have any name, the output file name must be the same as the message group, represented by the letters XYZ in the preceding example. Furthermore, the output file must have the MSG extension.

14.4.2 Message API Functions

DosGetMessage retrieves a message and, optionally, inserts variables into it. For instance, the following statements fetch and display message XYZ0105I, supplying "Hello" and "Goodbye" as the variables:

```
int error;                          /* error code */
char *vars[2] =                     /* variables */
  {"Hello","Goodbye"};
char buffer[256];                   /* message buffer */
int length;                         /* message length */
int fh;                             /* file handle */

error =
  DosGetMessage(vars,2,buffer,sizeof(buffer),105,
```

```
                  "xyz.msg",&length);
error = DosPutMessage(fh,buffer,length);
```

DosGetMessage retrieves the message into *buffer*, substituting the two strings in *vars* for %1 and %2, respectively. The actual message length is returned in *length*. Then *DosPutMessage* sends the formatted message out to the file represented by handle *fh*. You could simple write the message via *DosWrite*, but *DosPutMessage* makes sure that words are not broken if the message requires multiple lines on the display screen or printer.

This example does not show the use of *DosInsMessage*. That function is similar to *DosGetMessage*, except that it inserts variables into a message that was previously fetched without variable insertion. See the Appendix for details.

14.4.3 Binding Messages to the EXE File

As I mentioned earlier, you can bind a message file to your executable file if you do not want to retrieve messages from the disk. This is especially appropriate for messages that you might want to display when encountering some problem with the disk device.

For example, suppose your executable is named *myprog.exe*. Then the following command will bind messages XYZ0100 and XYZ0104 to it, together with a third message from file *pdq.msg*:

```
msgbind xyz.pro
```

where the file *xyz.pro* contains these statements:

```
>xyz.exe
<xyz.msg
XYZ0100
XYZ0104
<pdq.msg
PDQ0999
```

MSGBIND attaches a new data segment to the executable file and stores the specified messages there. If *DosGetMessage* sees that this special segment is present, it looks for messages there before searching the message file. This means that your program can be coded the same way no matter where the messages are stored.

14.5 Summary

I know of no other operating system that includes as many international programming features as OS/2. For that matter, the later versions of DOS outshine many larger operating systems in this area. If you take the time to use these features, you'll eliminate many of the barriers that previously made it difficult or impossible to adapt your programs so that they can be easily used in other countries. Not only will this increase the market for your software products, but it will greatly ease your maintenance burden.

Code page 437 (US English)

Hex Digits 1st → 2nd ↓	0-	1-	2-	3-	4-	5-	6-	7-		8-	9-	A-	B-	C-	D-	E-	F-
-0		►		0	@	P	`	p		Ç	É	á	░	└	╨	α	≡
-1	☺	◄	!	1	A	Q	a	q		ü	æ	í	▒	┴	╤	β	±
-2	☻	↕	"	2	B	R	b	r		é	Æ	ó	▓	┬	╥	Γ	≥
-3	♥	‼	#	3	C	S	c	s		â	ô	ú	│	├	╙	π	≤
-4	♦	¶	$	4	D	T	d	t		ä	ö	ñ	┤	─	╘	Σ	⌠
-5	♣	§	%	5	E	U	e	u		à	ò	Ñ	╡	┼	╒	σ	⌡
-6	♠	▬	&	6	F	V	f	v		å	û	ª	╢	╞	╓	µ	÷
-7	•	↨	'	7	G	W	g	w		ç	ù	º	╖	╟	╫	τ	≈
-8	◘	↑	(	8	H	X	h	x		ê	ÿ	¿	╕	╚	╪	Φ	°
-9	○	↓	)	9	I	Y	i	y		ë	Ö	⌐	╣	╔	┘	Θ	•
-A	◙	→	*	:	J	Z	j	z		è	Ü	¬	║	╩	┌	Ω	•
-B	♂	←	+	;	K	[	k	{		ï	¢	½	╗	╦	█	δ	√
-C	♀	∟	,	<	L	\	l	|		î	£	¼	╝	╠	▄	∞	^{n}
-D	♪	↔	-	=	M	]	m	}		ì	¥	¡	╜	═	▌	φ	^{2}
-E	♫	▲	.	>	N	^	n	~		Ä	Pt	«	╛	╬	▐	ε	■
-F	☼	▼	/	?	O	_	o	⌂		Å	ƒ	»	┐	╧	▀	∩	

Figure 14-1. Code Page 437 (USA IBM PC)

Code page 850 (Multilingual)

Hex Digits 1st → 2nd ↓	0-	1-	2-	3-	4-	5-	6-	7-	8-	9-	A-	B-	C-	D-	E-	F-
-0		►		0	@	P	`	p	Ç	É	á	░	└	ð	Ó	-
-1	☺	◄	!	1	A	Q	a	q	ü	æ	í	▒	┴	Ð	ß	±
-2	☻	↕	"	2	B	R	b	r	é	Æ	ó	▓	┬	Ê	Ô	=
-3	♥	‼	#	3	C	S	c	s	â	ô	ú	│	├	Ë	Ò	¾
-4	♦	¶	$	4	D	T	d	t	ä	ö	ñ	┤	─	È	õ	¶
-5	♣	§	%	5	E	U	e	u	à	ò	Ñ	Á	┼	ı	Õ	§
-6	♠	▬	&	6	F	V	f	v	å	û	ª	Â	ã	Í	µ	÷
-7	•	↨	'	7	G	W	g	w	ç	ù	º	À	Ã	Î	þ	¸
-8	◘	↑	(	8	H	X	h	x	ê	ÿ	¿	©	╚	Ï	Þ	°
-9	○	↓	)	9	I	Y	i	y	ë	Ö	®	╣	╔	┘	Ú	¨
-A	◙	→	*	:	J	Z	j	z	è	Ü	¬	║	╩	┌	Û	·
-B	♂	←	+	;	K	[	k	{	ï	ø	½	╗	╦	█	Ù	¹
-C	♀	∟	,	<	L	\	l	|	î	£	¼	╝	╠	▄	ý	³
-D	♪	↔	-	=	M	]	m	}	ì	Ø	¡	¢	═	¦	Ý	²
-E	♫	▲	.	>	N	^	n	~	Ä	×	«	¥	╬	Ì	¯	■
-F	☼	▼	/	?	O	_	o	⌂	Å	ƒ	»	┐	¤	▀	´	

Figure 14-2. Code Page 850 (Multilingual)

Code page 860 (Portuguese)

Hex Digits 1st → 2nd ↓	0-	1-	2-	3-	4-	5-	6-	7-	8-	9-	A-	B-	C-	D-	E-	F-
-0		►		0	@	P	`	p	Ç	É	á	░	└	╨	α	≡
-1	☺	◄	!	1	A	Q	a	q	ü	À	í	▒	┴	╤	β	±
-2	☻	↕	"	2	B	R	b	r	é	È	ó	▓	┬	╥	Γ	≥
-3	♥	‼	#	3	C	S	c	s	â	ô	ú	│	├	╙	π	≤
-4	♦	¶	$	4	D	T	d	t	ã	õ	ñ	┤	─	╘	Σ	⌠
-5	♣	§	%	5	E	U	e	u	à	ò	Ñ	╡	┼	╒	σ	⌡
-6	♠	▬	&	6	F	V	f	v	Á	Ú	ª	╢	╞	╓	µ	÷
-7	•	↨	'	7	G	W	g	w	ç	ù	º	╖	╟	╫	τ	≈
-8	◘	↑	(	8	H	X	h	x	ê	Ì	¿	╕	╚	╪	Φ	°
-9	○	↓	)	9	I	Y	i	y	Ê	Õ	Ò	╣	╔	┘	Θ	∙
-A	◙	→	*	:	J	Z	j	z	è	Ü	¬	║	╩	┌	Ω	·
-B	♂	←	+	;	K	[	k	{	Ì	¢	½	╗	╦	█	δ	√
-C	♀	∟	,	<	L	\	l	|	Ô	£	¼	╝	╠	▄	∞	^{n}
-D	♪	↔	-	=	M	]	m	}	ì	Ù	¡	╜	═	▌	φ	^{2}
-E	♫	▲	.	>	N	^	n	~	Ã	Pt	«	╛	╬	▐	ε	■
-F	☼	▼	/	?	O	_	o	⌂	Â	Ó	»	┐	╧	▀	∩	

Figure 14-3. Code Page 860 (Portuguese)

Code page 863 (Canadian-French)

Hex Digits 1st → 2nd ↓	0-	1-	2-	3-	4-	5-	6-	7-	8-	9-	A-	B-	C-	D-	E-	F-
-0		►		0	@	P	`	p	Ç	É	¦	░	└	╨	α	≡
-1	☺	◄	!	1	A	Q	a	q	ü	È	´	▒	┴	╤	β	±
-2	☻	↕	"	2	B	R	b	r	é	Ê	ó	▓	┬	╥	Γ	≥
-3	♥	‼	#	3	C	S	c	s	â	ô	ú	│	├	╙	π	≤
-4	♦	¶	$	4	D	T	d	t	Â	Ë	¨	┤	─	╘	Σ	⌠
-5	♣	§	%	5	E	U	e	u	à	Ï	¸	╡	┼	╒	σ	⌡
-6	♠	▬	&	6	F	V	f	v	¶	û	³	╢	╞	╓	µ	÷
-7	•	↨	'	7	G	W	g	w	ç	ú	¯	╖	╟	╫	τ	≈
-8	◘	↑	(	8	H	X	h	x	ê	¤	Î	╕	╚	╪	Φ	°
-9	○	↓	)	9	I	Y	i	y	ë	Ô	⌐	╣	╔	┘	Θ	∙
-A	◙	→	*	:	J	Z	j	z	è	Ü	¬	║	╩	┌	Ω	·
-B	♂	←	+	;	K	[	k	{	ï	¢	½	╗	╦	█	δ	√
-C	♀	∟	,	<	L	\	l	|	î	£	¼	╝	╠	▄	∞	ⁿ
-D	♪	↔	-	=	M	]	m	}	‗	Ù	¾	╜	═	▌	φ	²
-E	♫	▲	.	>	N	^	n	~	À	Û	«	╛	╬	▐	ε	■
-F	☼	▼	/	?	O	_	o	⌂	§	ƒ	»	┐	╧	▀	∩	

Figure 14-4. Code Page 863 (French Canadian)

Code page 865 (Norwegian)

Hex Digits 1st → 2nd ↓	0-	1-	2-	3-	4-	5-	6-	7-		8-	9-	A-	B-	C-	D-	E-	F-
-0		►		0	@	P	`	p		Ç	É	á	░	└	╨	α	≡
-1	☺	◄	!	1	A	Q	a	q		ü	æ	í	▒	┴	╤	β	±
-2	☻	↕	"	2	B	R	b	r		é	Æ	ó	▓	┬	╥	Γ	≥
-3	♥	‼	#	3	C	S	c	s		â	ô	ú	│	├	╙	π	≤
-4	♦	¶	$	4	D	T	d	t		ä	ö	ñ	┤	─	╘	Σ	⌠
-5	♣	§	%	5	E	U	e	u		à	ò	Ñ	╡	┼	╒	σ	⌡
-6	♠	▬	&	6	F	V	f	v		å	û	ª	╢	╞	╓	µ	÷
-7	•	↨	'	7	G	W	g	w		ç	ú	º	╖	╟	╫	τ	≈
-8	◘	↑	(	8	H	X	h	x		ê	ÿ	¿	╕	╚	╪	Φ	°
-9	○	↓	)	9	I	Y	i	y		ë	Ö	⌐	╣	╔	┘	Θ	•
-A	◙	→	*	:	J	Z	j	z		è	Ü	¬	║	╩	┌	Ω	·
-B	♂	←	+	;	K	[	k	{		ï	ø	½	╗	╦	█	δ	√
-C	♀	∟	,	<	L	\	l	|		î	£	¼	╝	╠	▄	∞	^{n}
-D	♪	↔	-	=	M	]	m	}		ì	Ø	¡	╜	═	▌	φ	^{2}
-E	♫	▲	.	>	N	^	n	~		Ä	Pt	«	╛	╬	▐	ε	■
-F	☼	▼	/	?	O	_	o	⌂		Å	ƒ	¤	┐	╧	▀	∩	

Figure 14-5. Code Page 865 (Nordic)

Chapter 15

Family Mode

IBM and Microsoft have taken extraordinary steps to build bridges between the old world of DOS and the new world of OS/2. They could have made a "great leap forward" and designed OS/2 to run only on the 80386; this would have brought us all of the advantages of 32-bit linear addressing and multiple DOS partitions. But, in deference to the millions of people who use the IBM AT and its clones, they targeted OS/2 for the 80286, despite all of that chip's shortcomings. Furthermore, they didn't take the easy path and just design an 80286 protected-mode operating system. Instead, they tackled the thorny problem of providing DOS compatibility and, after much frustration, figured out how to provide a single DOS partition.

DOS compatibility is both a great strength and a notable weakness of OS/2. The fact that many DOS programs can run under OS/2 with no changes will certainly help the new operating system gain acceptance. However, since it can only handle one DOS program at a time, OS/2's popularity depends even more on the availability of significant protected-mode applications. After all, why move to OS/2 if you can still only run one DOS program at a time? DOS extensions such as Desqview and alternative operating systems such as PC-MOS can satisfy your desire to multitask existing DOS programs. And eventually there will be an OS/3 for the 80386 offering multiple DOS partitions.

This situation causes a dilemma for software product developers. Should you be a pioneer and start designing for OS/2 protected mode? Or should you continue writing DOS applications with the hope that the emerging 80386 operating systems will eventually overcome many of the DOS limitations?

One solution to this dilemma is to do both, that is, to design applications that can run in OS/2 protected mode as well as in DOS real mode. Such an application is said to operate in *family mode*, a term that IBM and Microsoft coined to promote the idea that DOS and OS/2 are members of a compatible operating system family. Family mode is an extremely valuable OS/2 feature, and the IBM/Microsoft team should be congratulated for having the foresight and ingenuity to include it.

In this chapter, I'll explain how family mode works and how you can use it effectively in your applications. Some of the topics covered here re-echo the detailed discussions of the DOS and OS/2 APIs and conversion rules which were presented in Chapters 4 and 5.

15.1 What Is Family Mode?

A family-mode application is one which uses only those OS/2 API features which are supported under DOS. But, you say, there are no such features, because the OS/2 API is accessed via function calls, while the DOS API uses software interrupts. This is where the OS/2 Programmer's Toolkit and the dynamic linking feature come into play.

The toolkit contains a library named *api.lib* in which you will find DOS versions of the following OS/2 API functions:

DosAllocHuge	DosAllocSeg	DosBeep	DosCaseMap
DosChDir	DosChgFilePtr	DosCLIAcess	DosClose
DosCreateCSAlias	DosCWait	DosDelete	DosDevConfig
DosDevIOCtl	DosDupHandle	DosErrClass	DosError
DosExecPgm	DosExit	DosFileLocks	DosFindClose
DosFindFirst	DosFindNext	DosFreeSeg	DosGetCollate
DosGetCtryInfo	DosGetDateTime	DosGetEnv	DosGetHugeShift
DosGetMachineMode	DosGetMessage	DosGetVersion	DosHoldSignal
DosInsMessage	DosMkDir	DosMove	DosNewSize
DosOpen	DosPortAccess	DosPutMessage	DosQCurDir
DosQCurDisk	DosQFHandState	DosQFileInfo	DosQFileMode
DosQFSInfo	DosQVerify	DosRead	DosReallocHuge
DosReallocSeg	DosRmDir	DosScanEnv	DosSearchPath
DosSelectDisk	DosSetDateTime	DosSetFHAndState	DosSetFileInfo
DosSetFileMode	DosSetFsInfo	DosSetSigHandler	DosSetVec
DosSetVerify	DosSubAlloc	DosSubFree	DosSubSet
DosWrite	KbdCharIn	KbdFlushBuffer	KbdGetStatus

KbdPeek	KbdSetStatus	KbdStringIn	VioGetBuf
VioGetCurPos	VioGetCurType	VioGetMode	VioGetPhysBuf
VioReadCellStr	VioReadCharStr	VioScrollDn	VioScrollLf
VioScrollRt	VioScrollUp	VioSetCurPos	VioSetCurType
VioSetMode	VioShowBuf	VioWrtCellStr	VioWrtCharStr
VioWrtCharStrAttr	VioWrtNAttr	VioWrtNCell	VioWrtNChar
VioWrtTTY			

That is, *api.lib* contains functions that look like the OS/2 API but actually generate the corresponding DOS software interrupts. When constructing a family application, you use a toolkit utility called *bind* to incorporate the necessary parts of *api.lib* into the executable, or EXE, file in a special way. The *bind* utility also attaches a *stub loader* to the EXE file which makes the necessary connections between the application program and the *api.lib* functions when the EXE file is loaded under DOS.

The OS/2 protected-mode program loader is smart enough to ignore the extra stuff that *bind* tacks onto the EXE file. As it loads the program, it resolves all calls to OS/2 API functions via the dynamic linking facility discussed in Chapter 3.

The DOS loader, however, brings the *api.lib* functions and the stub loader into memory first; this is also true of the loader used in OS/2's DOS compatibility mode. Then the stub loader gets control, loads the application program, links that program's OS/2 API function calls to the *api.lib* routines, and then passes control to the application using the OS/2 initiation protocol that was described in Chapter 4. From that point on, the application's calls to the OS/2 API are translated into the equivalent DOS services by the *api.lib* functions.

And so, a family application can run in OS/2 protected mode, OS/2 real mode, and on DOS computers. Furthermore, when a family application is running in protected mode, it enjoys the primary benefits of OS/2, namely, multitasking and access to more than 640 kilobytes of memory. Of course, family applications cannot freely use these and other advanced OS/2 features, such as the Presentation Manager, because they are not available under DOS.

15.2 Converting From DOS to Family Mode

Most of the interest in family mode probably comes from those who want to adapt their DOS programs to OS/2 without losing DOS compatibility. In other words, if you can produce a single executable file that will run in any mode, your production and maintenance costs will be lower and your users will be less confused.

It's fairly easy to adapt a DOS program to family mode if the program is *well behaved*, which is a term whose definition varies from one programming language to another. Since C and assembly language are arguably the most popular PC programming languages, we'll concentrate on them.

Chapter 5 pointed out that a well-behaved C program originally designed for DOS has the following characteristics:

1. All DOS interfaces are handled through the compiler's standard library.
2. The program does not use low-level DOS interface functions from the library, such as *int86*, *intdos*, *bdos*, or *bios*.
3. The program does not hook into any DOS hardware or software interrupts.
4. Keyboard and screen interactions use the simple "glass TTY" approach, or else the ANSI.SYS driver is used for any complex screen operations.
5. The program always treats 32-bit pointers as atomic objects; that is, it does not manipulate the segment and offset portions separately.

If your DOS program conforms to this description, then you'll probably just need to re-compile it with the appropriate OS/2 compiler, link it, and bind it to *api.lib*. And even if you deviate slightly from these rules, the conversion to family mode can still be relatively easy.

For example, many screen-oriented programs write directly to the video display buffer or, at least, call the BIOS services instead of going through DOS. Referring to the API function list in the preceding section, notice that many of the OS/2 keyboard and video functions (i.e., those beginning with *Kbd* and *Vio*) are available in family mode. Furthermore, many interactive programs were designed with their keyboard and screen interfaces isolated into a few modules. If your program has that structure, you just need to rewrite those modules so that they use the family-mode API functions. Chapter 5 presented the general techniques for such rewrites.

15.3 Designing New Family-Mode Programs

While there are some technical challenges in converting existing DOS programs to family mode, it's more of an emotional challenge to design new OS/2 applications that will remain compatible with DOS. Even if you avoid the Presentation Manager, you'll quickly develop a taste for new OS/2 features such as multitasking and advanced interprocess communication. But if you succumb to temptation and let these features creep into your design, you can kiss family mode goodbye. Instead, you should remember the following simple rules:

1. Use a high-level language, such as C, as much as possible.
2. Use whatever compiler options are necessary to cause only family-mode (i.e., 8086) instruction sequences to be generated.
3. Use only those library functions which restrict their OS/2 API calls to the family subset listed earlier.
4. Do not rely upon multitasking or upon access to more than 640 kilobytes of memory. On the other hand, do not prevent the program from using more than 640 kilobytes.

The OS/2 C compilers with which I am familiar (i.e., those from IBM, Lattice, and Microsoft) tend to favor family-mode programming. That is, the compilers typically generate 8086 code unless you tell them otherwise, and the majority of the library functions typically use only family-mode API services. For instance, the initial release of the Lattice C Compiler for OS/2 contained 335 functions, of which 306 could be used in family mode. What is even more important is that the family-mode group includes all of the Lattice functions that are in the ANSI C standard.

The other compilers have roughly the same ratio, although their function repertoires are somewhat different. In other words, in most OS/2 C compilers the popular C functions, including the portable functions defined by ANSI, are compatible with family mode. The relatively small set of DOS-only functions have very special purposes, such as generating software interrupts or supporting Terminate-and-Stay-Resident (TSR) applications.

Returning to the preceding list of rules, it might seem that Rules 3 and 4 are redundant. After all, if you stick to the family-mode API functions, you can't possibly multitask or allocate memory beyond the 640K limit, right? *Wrong.*

It is possible to violate Rule 4 while conforming to Rule 3. For example, if you declare a one-megabyte buffer area in the following way,

```
static huge char buffer[1000000];
```

the program will compile, link, and run fine under OS/2, but it will not be a family application because it exceeds the DOS memory limit. Similarly, you could construct an OS/2 application consisting of two EXE files that are expected to be running simultaneously and exchanging data via shared files. Even though each EXE conforms to Rule 3, the application is not DOS-compatible because it relies upon OS/2 multitasking for the concurrent execution of the two component programs.

And so, the safest way to design a new family-mode application is to do all the work under DOS, using the family-mode API functions and the *bind* utility. Then, when the software is running correctly in the DOS environment, you'll be certain that it has no hidden dependencies on new OS/2 features, and the conversion to OS/2 should be trivial.

15.4 Assembly Language Considerations

Assembly-language routines that are to be used in family applications must obey the same rules as DOS C programs. However, as we discussed in Chapter 5, it's usually more difficult to tell if assembly-language functions are well behaved by just eyeballing them. Furthermore, without a compiler to generate the low-level code sequences, it's easy for an assembly-language programmer to accidentally employ instructions that are not allowed in family mode. Specifically, you must avoid the following common DOS coding practices, which will cause problems when you try to run in protected mode:

1. Use of INT instructions, which generate software interrupts;
2. Use of IN and OUT instructions, which directly access the I/O ports;
3. Use of CLI and STI instructions, which change the state of the interrupt enable flag;
4. Instruction sequences that change segment register contents, such as

```
MOV     AX,DS     ; advance to next paragraph
INC     AX
MOV     DS,AX
```

which is guaranteed to fail because segment register arithmetic is different in protected mode;

5. Timing loops, such as

```
          MOV     CX,1000   ; wait awhile
DELAY:    LOOP    DELAY
```

which are risky even under DOS because they often become invalid when you upgrade to a faster computer.

The first three of these practices will cause protection violations because OS/2 does not allow normal processes to execute INT, IN, OUT, CLI, and STI instructions. The fourth will usually cause addressing exceptions because the process will attempt to load an invalid selector into a segment register. The fifth just causes the program to behave erratically because the time delay may be quite different between real mode and protected mode, even on the same computer.

15.5 How to Cheat

Now that I've given you a lot of rules for programming in family mode, I'll explain how to cheat; that is, I'll show how to include DOS-specific and/or OS/2-specific features into a family application. You see, so far we've assumed that the goal is to let the application remain blissfully unaware of whether it is running under DOS or OS/2, and so we came up with rules that forced us to use API services and programming techniques that are common to both environments. But sophisticated programmers (*Aren't we all?*) will sometimes want to design family applications that behave differently in real mode and protected mode.

For example, a spreadsheet program could use a simple calculation algorithm under DOS, where the size of the spreadsheet is constrained by the 640K limit. In the OS/2 environment, where spreadsheets can get much larger than 640K, it might be more appropriate to create a separate thread that performs the calculations in the background while the user continues to enter data via the main thread running in the foreground. This would reduce the keyboard delay that the user sees when a recalculation is needed.

Now this type of behavior makes a lot of sense, and it's actually quite easy to implement because none of the rules mentioned earlier are *coercive*. That is, there is nothing in either DOS or OS/2 that prevents the loading of an EXE file containing "illegal" API calls and instruction sequences, although the *bind* utility will warn you if it detects any nonfamily API calls.. If you hit a real-mode instruction sequence under OS/2, such as some segment register arithmetic, the operating system will abort your program. It's not as clean under DOS, where a protected-mode instruction sequence can cause a system crash or garbled results.

The point is, you can design a family application containing some instruction sequences that will execute only under DOS and others that will execute only under OS/2. However, you must make sure that each of these sequences is entered only after the appropriate mode tests are made. Here's a simple C function which you call to ask, "Is this OS/2 protected mode?" It returns 0 if called in DOS mode and 1 if called in OS/2 mode:

```
extern far pascal DosGetMachineMode(char far *);

int isos2p();
{
char mode;
DosGetMachineMode((char far *)(&mode));
return((int)mode);
}
```

Note that the *isos2p* function calls *DosGetMachineMode*, which is in the family API. The only argument to this API function is a pointer to a single byte, which is set to 0 for DOS and 1 for OS/2.

So, if you reach a point in your program where you must use different logic depending on the mode, you could use the following approach:

```
if(isos2p())        /* OS/2 logic */
        {
        *
        *
        *
        }

else                /* DOS logic */
        {
        *
        *
        *
```

```
        }
```

It's really only necessary to call *DosGetMachineMode* once, since an application cannot change modes after it is started. So, there are more efficient ways to write this conditional code than calling *isos2p* each time. Lattice C, for instance, gets the machine mode as part of its startup procedure and places the indicator into a global variable named *_PMODE*, meaning *processor mode*. So you can use the following test instead of the *if* statement in the previous example:

```
extern char _PMODE;

if(_PMODE) ...      /* OS/2 logic */
```

With other compilers, you can call *isos2p* once in your *main* program and place its results into your own version of *_PMODE*.

As programmers become more comfortable with OS/2, I expect we'll see a lot of applications that automatically adapt their behavior using techniques such as this. The gold medal, however, will be awarded to the first person who designs a family application that adapts itself to Microsoft Windows in the DOS environment and to the Presentation Manager in OS/2.

15.6 Building a Family-Mode Program

As I mentioned earlier, you build a family-mode executable by linking your object modules in the normal way and then *binding* them to *api.lib* via the *bind* utility. Consider the following simple program:

```
        EXTRN   DosExit:FAR
        EXTRN   VioWrtTTY:FAR

STACK   SEGMENT STACK PARA 'STACK'
        DB      2048 DUP(?)
STACK   ENDS

DGROUP  GROUP   DATA
DATA    SEGMENT WORD PUBLIC 'DATA'
MSG     DB      'GOODBYE!'
DATA    ENDS

TEXT    SEGMENT BYTE PUBLIC 'CODE'
        ASSUME  CS: TEXT
```

```
START:  MOV     AX,SEG MSG          ; send a message
        PUSH    AX
        MOV     AX,OFFSET MSG
        PUSH    AX
        MOV     AX,8
        PUSH    AX
        XOR     AX,AX
        PUSH    AX
        CALL    VioWrtTTY
        XOR     AX,AX               ; terminate
        PUSH    AX
        PUSH    AX
        CALL    DosExit
CODE    ENDS
        END     START
```

in the file named *quit.asm*. All the program does is print **GOODBYE!** and then exit to the operating system. Two OS/2 API calls are used, *VioWrtTTY* and *DosExit*, and both are in the family API repertoire. The following commands will build assemble, link, and bind this program:

```
masm quit;
link quit,,,doscalls;
bind quit doscalls.lib api.lib
```

The *masm* command ends with a semicolon in order to tell the assembler to use the defaults for all other arguments, thereby producing an object file named *quit.obj*.

On the *link* command, the second and third arguments are defaulted, causing the executable to be named *quit.exe* and suppressing the production of a map file. The fourth argument, *doscalls*, causes the linker to search *doscalls.lib* for the API function definitions. The functions themselves are not actually in this library file, since the OS/2 API library is dynamically loaded. So all the linker does is extract information from *doscalls.lib* that will be used to complete the API linkages while the program is being loaded. The terminating semicolon after *doscalls* indicates that there is no *module definition file* – a new OS/2 linker feature that gives you a great deal of control over the characteristics of the EXE file.

The *bind* command requires that you first identify the EXE file, which is *quit.exe* in this case. Then you must name the dynamic link libraries used by that program. As mentioned earlier, our example only calls OS/2 API functions, which are defined in *doscalls.lib*. Finally, you must specify *api.lib*, the DOS binding library. Note that the *.lib* extension must be explicitly stated for the library files, although you can write the program name without the *.exe* extension. This is because *bind* can also accept object files, with *.obj* extensions, that are to be bound into the new executable. An example is shown later for the user-replacable *BadDynLink* function.

You might wonder why *doscalls* must be mentioned in both the *link* and *bind* commands. This is because *link* consults *doscalls.lib* in order to convert API names such as *DosExit* into numeric values, called *ordinal references*. In most cases, the names themselves are not carried along in the EXE file, and the OS/2 loader completes the API linkages using the ordinal references. The *bind* utility, however, needs to know the actual API function names in order to extract the DOS versions from *api.lib*. Therefore, it consults *doscalls.lib* to convert the ordinals back into the original names.

The previous example uses the simplest form of the *bind* command, and it replaces the original executable file with a new one that includes the DOS bindings. There are also some useful options for *bind*, as follows:

/O newexe
The **/O** option names the new executable file *newexe*.EXE instead of replacing the original EXE file. The EXE extension is not tacked on if *newexe* includes an extension.

/M mapfile
This option produces a map file named *mapfile*.BM, with the BM extension only added if you don't specify some other extension.

/N func
This option causes the dynamic link symbol *func* to be bound to a function called *BadDynLink* when the program runs under DOS. You can also replace *func* with *@file* to specify a file containing a list of such symbols.

This feature allows you to bind a program that selectively calls non-family API functions only when running under OS/2, as described earlier. Normally, the *bind* utility would complain about such symbols because they are not in *api.lib*. But if you identify them via the **/N** option, *bind* connects those API references to *BadDynLink*, which displays an error message and then aborts.

You can supply your own version of *BadDynLink* in an object module that you mention on the *bind* command just before *api.lib*. For example,

```
bind prog doscalls.lib badlink.obj
     api.lib /n DosCreateThread
```

includes the object file *badlink.obj*, which would presumably contain your own definition of *BadDynLink*. Then if the program *prog* makes any calls to *DosCreateThread* when running under DOS, your version of *BadDynLink* would be called instead. This example is shown on two lines for clarity only; normally, you would type it on one line.

The *bind* utility has one annoying shortcoming. Unlike the linker, *bind* does not use the LIB environment variable to locate libraries that are not in the current directory. I like to keep *doscalls.lib* and *api.lib* in *c:\syslib* and then set the LIB variable to point to this directory. Unfortunately, *bind* requires that you give the complete path for all files.

But, except for that minor glitch, *bind* works well and, as you can see from the preceding example, makes it quite easy to construct family applications.

15.7 How Family Mode Works

The key to understanding how family mode works is to understand the transformation that the *bind* utility makes to the OS/2 EXE file produced by the linker. This was briefly described earlier in this chapter, but let's take a more detailed look.

In order to support new OS/2 features such as segment protection and dynamic linking, the simple DOS EXE file format needed significant changes. Specifically, the DOS format does not include information about individual segments, nor does it include the information needed to interface with dynamic libraries. OS/2 must know about the individual segments in an application, because each one can have different privileges, depending on its use. For instance, code segments are write-protected, while most data segments are not.

The OS/2 designers were clever enough to add this new information in an upward-compatible manner. That is, they made sure that DOS could look at an OS/2 EXE file and recognize it. Figure 15-1 shows the major sections of an OS/2 executable file. Note that the file begins with three DOS-compatible sections: the header, relocation table, and DOS stub program. Then come the new OS/2 sections, beginning with a header and ending with a section for each OS/2 code or data segment. In between are several sections containing descriptive information about the segments, dynamic linkages, and other resources that the program requires.

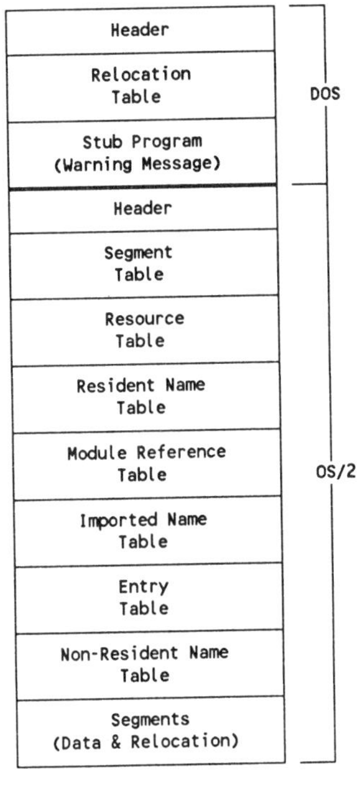

Figure 15-1 OS/2 EXE File Structure

Now as far as DOS is concerned, an OS/2 EXE file consists of everything before the OS/2 header. So, if you try to execute an OS/2 program in real mode, DOS is fooled into loading the stub program, which displays a message indicating that this program can only be run in protected mode.

Figure 15-2 shows what happens to an OS/2 EXE file after it has been processed by the *bind* utility. It looks pretty much the same as Figure 15-1, except that the small DOS stub which displays the warning message is replaced with a much larger DOS program, called the *stub loader*. This loader is followed by the functions extracted from *api.lib* plus any object modules that you explicitly mentioned in the *bind* command. All of the OS/2 sections are simply shoved upward in the EXE file in order to accommodate the expanded DOS section.

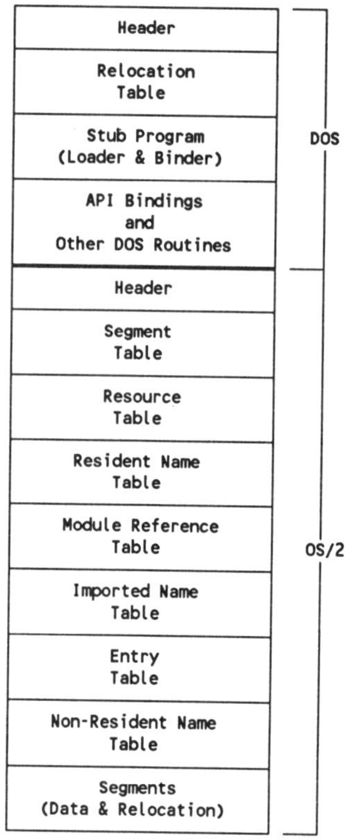

Figure 15-2 Family EXE File Structure

As before, when you attempt to execute this program under DOS, the stub actually gets entered. But instead of displaying an error message as the default stub did, the one supplied by *bind* reopens the EXE file, loads the OS/2 code and data segments, completes all dynamic linkages, and then jumps to the main entry point of the OS/2 program with everything set up just as it would be under OS/2.

That's all there is to it, except for a few dozen nitty-gritty details having to do with the new EXE information, DOS memory allocation, and so on. These details make the stub loader a little bulky. For instance, the EXE file for the previous example program grows from 1077 bytes to 9269 bytes when *bind* processes it. Fortunately, this increase is not proportional to the original EXE size; a spreadsheet program with an OS/2 EXE size of 127,156 bytes grew to 154,804 bytes after being bound, which is only about a 22 percent increase.

Performance of family-mode programs is usually not much of an issue. You don't pay any penalty in loading or execution when the program runs in protected mode. In real mode, loading is slightly slower because of the two-step process discussed earlier, but the application itself generally runs at about the same speed as an equivalent DOS version. In other words, the routines in *api.lib* seem to be pretty efficient.

So, as is usually the case, OS/2 family mode is a trade-off. You'll have to decide if the increase in EXE size and slightly slower loading time under DOS is an acceptable price to pay for having a single EXE file for both modes.

Appendix

OS/2 Application Program Interface

This appendix contains brief descriptions of the functions that comprise the OS/2 Standard Application Program Interface, or SAPI. The descriptions use C calling conventions, as shown in the following example:

```
error = DosRead(fh,buffer,size,asize);

int error;              error code
int fh;                 file handle
char far *buffer;       buffer pointer
unsigned size;          size of buffer in bytes
unsigned far *asize;    returns actual data size
```

The arguments are presented in the way that the API functions expect to see them. For instance, *DosRead* expects four arguments. The first is a 16-bit word containing the file handle. The second is a 32-bit pointer to a buffer area, and the third is a 16-bit word specifying the size of the buffer. The fourth argument is a 32-bit pointer to a 16-bit word that will receive the actual size of the data block read from the file.

All API functions return a 16-bit error code, with a nonzero value indicating success. For the sake of brevity, the descriptions do not mention this error return. Also, to save space and avoid clutter, I've omitted the /* and */ delimiters around the comments.

OS/2 C compilers generally default to 16-bit integers, and so we use the *int* and *unsigned* keywords to declare 16-bit signed and unsigned values, respectively. Some compilers have an option which changes the default integer size to 32 bits in order to simplify the conversion of programs to OS/2 from 32-bit systems like the Motorola 68000 and DEC VAX. If you use this option, then you must declare the API's 16-bit arguments via the *short* and *unsigned short* keywords.

Finally, some of the functions accept pointers to structures, and in those cases I usually define the structure right in line with the argument declaration. If you decide to obtain these structure definitions from the header files provided in the OS/2 Programmer's Toolkit or in your C compiler package, be aware that those definitions may use different structure and field names. I have not adhered to the naming conventions of the toolkit or of any particular compiler, for two reasons. First, the names used in the toolkit are particularly ugly and difficult to remember. Second, because the initial toolkit names are so ugly, the various compiler manufacturers, including Microsoft, are improving the definitions as OS/2 programming catches on.

The functions are described in alphabetical order. Before that, however, is a set of quick reference tables organized into logical groups, such as *multitasking* and *memory management*. These tables also indicate the corresponding services from the DOS API and/or the ROM BIOS. The FAM column contains an F if the function is fully implemented in the Family API, or FAPI. An R in this column indicates that a restricted version of the function is available in the FAPI.

MULTITASKING FUNCTIONS

FAM	INT 21H	NAME	DESCRIPTION
		DosCreateThread	Create a thread
R	4DH	DosCWait	Wait for child process termination
		DosEnterCritSec	Enter a critical section
R	4BH	DosExecPgm	Execute a program
R	00H,4CH	DosExit	Exit a program
		DosExitCritSec	Exit a critical section
		DosExitList	Specify exit function list
		DosGetPid	Get process identification
		DosGetPrty	Get process priority
		DosKillProcess	Kill a process
		DosMonClose	Disconnect device monitor
		DosMonOpen	Connect device monitor
		DosMonRead	Read from monitor structure
		DosMonReg	Register monitor buffers
		DosMonWrite	Write to monitor structure
		DosPtrace	Process debugging interface
		DosResumeThread	Restart a thread
		DosSelectSession	Select foreground session
		DosSetPrty	Set process priority
		DosSetSession	Set session status
		DosSleep	Delay process execution
		DosStartSession	Start a session
		DosStopSession	Stop a session
		DosSuspendThread	Suspend thread execution
		DosSystemService	Request special process services
		DosTimerAsync	Start asynchronous timer
		DosTimerStart	Start interval timer
		DosTimerStop	Stop interval timer

MEMORY MANAGEMENT FUNCTIONS

FAM	INT 21H	NAME	DESCRIPTION
R		DosAllocHuge	Allocate a huge memory block
R	48H	DosAllocSeg	Allocate a segment
		DosAllocShrSeg	Allocate a shared segment
F		DosCreateCSAlias	Create code segment alias for data segment
F	49H	DosFreeSeg	Free a segment
F		DosGetHugeShift	Get shift parameter for huge blocks
		DosGetInfoSeg	Get address of system variable segment
		DosGetSeg	Get access to a segment
		DosGetShrSeg	Get access to a shared segment
		DosGiveSeg	Give access to a segment
		DosLockSeg	Lock a segment in memory
		DosMemAvail	Get size of largest free memory block
R		DosReallocHuge	Change size of huge memory block
R	4AH	DosReallocSeg	Change size of a segment
F		DosSubAlloc	Allocate memory within a segment
F		DosSubFree	Free memory within a segment
F		DosSubSet	Set memory sub-allocation size
		DosUnlockSeg	Unlock a segment

FILE I/O FUNCTIONS

FAM	INT 21H	NAME	DESCRIPTION
F	3BH	DosChDir	Change current directory
F	42H	DosChgFilePtr	Change a file's read/write pointer
F	3EH	DosClose	Close a file
F	41H	DosDelete	Delete a file
F	45H,46H	DosDupHandle	Duplicate a file handle
R		DosFindClose	Close a directory handle
R	4EH	DosFindFirst	Find first matching file
R	4FH	DosFindNext	Find next matching file
F	39H	DosMkDir	Create a directory
F	56H	DosMove	Move a file
F		DosNewSize	Change file size
R	3CH,3DH,5BH	DosOpen	Open a file
F	3FH	DosRead	Read a file
F	3AH	DosRmDir	Remove a directory
F	40H	DosWrite	Write a file

ADVANCED I/O FUNCTIONS

FAM	INT 21H	NAME	DESCRIPTION
	0DH	DosBufReset	Commit a file's cache buffers
F		DosCLIAcess	Request CLI/STI privilege
F		DosDevConfig	Get device configuration
F	44H	DosDevIOCtl	Perform I/O control function
F	45H,46H	DosDupHandle	Duplicate a file handle
R	5CH	DosFileLocks	Lock a file section
F		DosGetMessage	Get system message with variable text
F		DosInsMessage	Insert variable information into message
		DosPhysicalDisk	Request disk partition information
F		DosPortAccess	Request I/O port access
F		DosPutMessage	Put message to specified file handle
F	47H	DosQCurDir	Query the current directory
F	19H	DosQCurDisk	Query the current disk
R		DosQFHandState	Query a file handle state
F	57H	DosQFileInfo	Query file information
F	43H	DosQFileMode	Query file mode
F	36H	DosQFSInfo	Query file system information
		DosQHandType	Query file handle type
F	54H	DosQVerify	Query disk verify setting
		DosReadAsync	Read a file asynchronously
F		DosSearchPath	Search a path for a file name
F	0EH	DosSelectDisk	Select default disk
R		DosSetFHAndState	Set a file handle state
F	57H	DosSetFileInfo	Set file information
F	43H	DosSetFileMode	Set file mode
F		DosSetFsInfo	Set file system information
		DosSetMaxFH	Set maximum file handles
F	2EH	DosSetVerify	Set or reset verify switch
		DosWriteAsync	Write a file asynchronously

INTERPROCESS COMMUNICATION FUNCTIONS

FAM	INT 21H	NAME	DESCRIPTION
		DosCloseQueue	Close a queue
		DosCloseSem	Close a system semaphore
		DosCreateQueue	Create a queue
		DosCreateSem	Create a system semaphore
		DosFlagProcess	Set process external event flag
R	33H	DosHoldSignal	Disable or enable signals
		DosMakePipe	Create a pipe
		DosMuxSemWait	Wait for one of several semaphores
		DosOpenQueue	Open a queue
		DosOpenSem	Open a system semaphore
		DosPeekQueue	Peek at a queue
		DosPurgeQueue	Purge a queue
		DosQueryQueue	Query the size of a queue
		DosReadQueue	Read from a queue
		DosSemClear	Clear a semaphore
		DosSemRequest	Request a semaphore
		DosSemSet	Set a semaphore
		DosSemSetWait	Set a semaphore and wait for clear
		DosSemWait	Wait for a semaphore to clear
		DosSendSignal	Send a signal
R		DosSetSigHandler	Set signal handler
		DosWriteQueue	Write to a queue

MISCELLANEOUS FUNCTIONS

FAM	INT 21H	NAME	DESCRIPTION
F		BadDynLink	Called on bad dynamic link
F		DosBeep	Honk the horn
F		DosCaseMap	Case-map a character string
R	59H	DosErrClass	Classify error code
R		DosError	Enable hard error processing
		DosFreeModule	Free dynamic link module
F		DosGetCollate	Get collating sequence table
		DosGetCp	Get process code page
R	38H	DosGetCtryInfo	Get country-dependent information
F	2AH,2CH	DosGetDateTime	Get system date and time
		DosGetDBCSEv	Get dual-byte character set environment
F		DosGetEnv	Get environment string address
F		DosGetMachineMode	Get processor mode
		DosGetModHandle	Get dynamic link module handle
		DosGetModName	Get dynamic link module name
		DosGetProcAddr	Get dynamic link procedure address
F	30H	DosGetVersion	Get operating system version number
		DosLoadModule	Load dynamic link module
F		DosScanEnv	Scan environment strings
		DosSetCp	Set process code page
F	2BH,2DH	DosSetDateTime	Set system date and time
F	25H	DosSetVec	Specify exception handling function

KEYBOARD FUNCTIONS

FAM	DOS INT 21H	BIOS INT 16H	NAME	DESCRIPTION
F	01H,07H	00H	KbdCharIn	Read character and scan code
			KbdClose	Close logical keyboard
			KbdDeRegister	Deregister keyboard subsystem
			KbdFreeFocus	Free keyboard focus
F			KbdFlushBuffer	Flush keystroke buffer
			KbdGetFocus	Get keyboard focus
F		01H	KbdGetStatus	Get keyboard status
			KbdGetCP	Get keyboard code page ID
			KbdOpen	Open logical keyboard
R	0BH	02H	KbdPeek	Peek at character and scan code
			KbdRegister	Register keyboard subsystem
			KbdSetCP	Set keyboard code page ID
			KbdSetCustXt	Set custom translate table
			KbdSetFgnd	Set foreground keyboard priority
F			KbdSetStatus	Set keyboard status
			KbdShellInit	Initialize shell
F	0AH		KbdStringIn	Read character string
			KbdSynch	Synchronize keyboard access
			KbdXlate	Translate scan code

MOUSE FUNCTIONS

FAM	INT 33H	NAME	DESCRIPTION
		MouClose	Close mouse device
		MouDeRegister	Deregister a mouse subsystem
	01H	MouDrawPtr	Draw a pointer
		MouFlushQue	Flush mouse event queue
		MouGetDevStatus	Get mouse device status flags
		MouGetEventMask	Get mouse event mask
		MouGetHotKey	Get mouse hot key definition
		MouGetNumButtons	Get number of mouse buttons
		MouGetNumMickeys	Get number of mickeys per centimeter
		MouGetNumQueEl	Get number of mouse event queue elements
	03H	MouGetPtrPos	Get mouse pointer position
		MouGetPtrShape	Get mouse pointer shape
		MouGetScaleFact	Get mouse scaling factors
		MouInitReal	Initialize real-mode mouse driver
	00H	MouOpen	Open mouse device
	05H,06H	MouReadEventQue	Read mouse event queue
		MouRegister	Register a mouse subsystem
	02H	MouRemovePtr	Remove mouse pointer from a screen area
		MouSetDevStatus	Set mouse device status flags
	0CH	MouSetEventMask	Set mouse event mask
		MouSetHotKey	Set mouse hot key definition
	04H	MouSetPtrPos	Set mouse pointer position
	09H,0AH	MouSetPtrShape	Set mouse pointer shape
		MouSetScaleFact	Set mouse scaling factors
		MouShellInit	Initialize shell linkage
		MouSynch	Synchronize mouse subsystem

OS/2 VIDEO FUNCTIONS

FAM	DOS INT 21H	BIOS INT 10H	NAME	DESCRIPTION
			VioDeRegister	Deregister video subsystem
			VioEndPopUp	Deallocate pop-up display screen
			VioGetANSI	Get ANSI status
F			VioGetBuf	Get logical video buffer
			VioGetConfig	Get video configuration
			VioGetCp	Get video code page ID
F		03H	VioGetCurPos	Get cursor position
F			VioGetCurType	Get cursor type
			VioGetFont	Get font
F		0FH	VioGetMode	Get display mode
F			VioGetPhysBuf	Get physical display buffer
			VioGetState	Get video state
			VioModeUndo	Cancel mode wait
			VioModeWait	Wait for mode change
			VioPopUp	Allocate pop-up display screen
			VioPrtSc	Print screen
			VioPrtScToggle	Print screen key operation trap
F		08H	VioReadCellStr	Read cell string
F			VioReadCharStr	Read character string
			VioRegister	Register video subsystem
			VioSavRedrawUndo	Cancel save-redraw wait
			VioSavRedrawWait	Wait for save-redraw
			VioScrLock	Lock the screen
F		07H	VioScrollDn	Scroll down
F			VioScrollLf	Scroll left
F			VioScrollRt	Scroll right
F		06H	VioScrollUp	Scroll up
			VioScrUnLock	Unlock the screen

OS/2 VIDEO FUNCTIONS

(continued)

FAM	DOS INT 21H	BIOS INT 10H	NAME	DESCRIPTION
			VioSetANSI	Set ANSI mode on or off
			VioSetCp	Set video code page ID
F		02H	VioSetCurPos	Set cursor position
F		01H	VioSetCurType	Set cursor type
			VioSetFont	Set font
F		00H	VioSetMode	Set display mode
		0BH	VioSetState	Set video state
F			VioShowBuf	Display logical buffer
F		09H	VioWrtCellStr	Write cell string
F		0AH	VioWrtCharStr	Write character string
F			VioWrtCharStrAttr	Write character string with attribute
F			VioWrtNAttr	Write N attributes
F			VioWrtNCell	Write N cells
F			VioWrtNChar	Write N characters
F	02H,09H	0EH	VioWrtTTY	Write a TTY string

DosAllocHuge

```
DosAllocHuge(size,seg,max,flags);

unsigned long size;        number of bytes
unsigned far *seg;         segment selector
short max;                 maximum number of segments
short flags;               flag bits, as follows
                             bit 0 = sharable via DosGiveSeg
                                 1 = sharable via DosGetSeg
```

Allocates a "huge block" containing one or more segments. The selector for the first segment is returned in *seg*, and information about the segment separation can be obtained via *DosHugeshift*. The *max* parameter indicates the maximum growth potential for the huge block via *DosReallocHuge*.

DosAllocseg

```
DosAllocseg(size,seg,flags);

unsigned size;             number of bytes
unsigned far *seg;         segment selector
short flags;               flag bits, as follows
                             bit 0 = sharable via DosGiveSeg
                                 1 = sharable via DosGetSeg
                                 2 = discardable
```

Allocates a segment, returning the selector in *seg*. If *size* is 0, then a complete 64-kilobyte segment is allocated.

DosAllocShrSeg

```
DosAllocShrSeg(size,name,seg);

unsigned size;             number of bytes
char far *name;            segment name
unsigned far *seg;         segment selector
```

Allocates a shared segment and gives it the specified name, which must begin with the prefix *\sharemem*. Other processes can access this segment via *DosGetShrSeg*. If *size* is 0, then a complete 64-kilobyte segment is allocated.

DosBeep

```
DosBeep(frequency,duration);

unsigned frequency;      frequency in Hertz
unsigned duration;       duration in milliseconds
```

Emits a console sound of the specified frequency and duration. Does not return until the operation is completed.

DosBufReset

```
DosBufReset(fh);

unsigned fh;             file handle
```

Completes all pending write operations for the specified file handle and updates the file's directory record.

DosCaseMap

```
DosCaseMap(size,codes,string);

unsigned size;           number of bytes in string
unsigned far *codes;     mapping codes, as follows
                           codes[0] = country code
                           codes[1] = code page
char far *string;        string to be mapped
```

Case-maps the string in place, using the specified country code and code page. If the former is 0, then the default country code is used. If the latter is 0, then the current code page is used. See Chapter 13 for a description of case mapping.

DosChDir

```
DosChDir(name,0L);

char far *name;          directory path
```

Changes the current directory in the requesting process to the specified path.

DosChgFilePtr

```
DosChgFilePtr(fh,distance,mode,newpos);

unsigned fh;        file handle
long distance;      distance in bytes
unsigned mode;      move mode, as follows
                      0 = relative to beginning of file
                      1 = relative to current position
                      2 = relative to end of file
long far *newpos; new file position
```

Moves the file pointer for the specified handle to a new position and reports the new position relative to the beginning of the file.

DosCLIAccess

```
DosCLIAccess();
```

Used in an IOPL process to request the use of CLI and STI instructions.

DosClose

```
DosClose(fh);

unsigned fh;             file handle
```

Closes the specified file.

DosCloseQueue

```
DosCloseQueue(qh);

unsigned qh;                queue handle
```

Closes the specified queue. If the calling process owns the queue, then the queue is removed from the system, and all other users will receive error codes if they attempt to access it. If the calling process does not own the queue, only that process's access to the queue is terminated.

DosCloseSem

```
DosCloseSem(sh);

long sh;                    semaphore handle
```

Closes the specified semaphore. After all processes using the semaphore close it or terminate, the semaphore is deleted.

DosCreateCSAlias

```
DosCreateCSAlias(ds,cs);

unsigned ds;                data selector
unsigned far *cs;           code selector
```

Creates a code segment alias for the specified data segment, which must be exclusively accessible by the calling process. Once the CS alias has been assigned, the process can execute code in the segment by placing the alias in the CS register. Call *DosFreeSeg* to discard the CS alias.

DosCreateQueue

```
DosCreateQueue(qh,order,name);

unsigned far *qh;           queue handle
unsigned order;             queue order, as follows
```

```
                              0 = FIFO (first in, first out)
                              1 = LIFO (last in, first out)
                              2 = user priority (0 to 15)
char far *name;             queue name
```

Creates a queue and assigns a handle to it. The queue name must include the prefix *\queues*. Only the process which creates the queue can access or remove queue elements. Any process can open the queue and add elements to it.

DosCreateSem

```
DosCreateSem(share,sh,name);

unsigned share;             sharing mode, as follows
                              0 = exclusive
                              1 = shared
long far *sh;               semaphore handle
char far *name;             semaphore name
```

Creates a system semaphore and assigns a handle so it can be used by the calling process. The name string must begin with *\sem*.

DosCreateThread

```
DosCreateThread(start,id,stack);

void (far *start)();        starting address
unsigned *id;               thread identifier
short far *stack;           thread stack
```

Creates a new execution thread in the calling process. The thread begins execution at the specified starting address and inherits all resources of the process. The *stack* argument must point to the high end of an area in a writable segment. You must provide enough stack space to satisfy the thread's needs; a minimum of two kilobytes is recommended.

DosCWait

```
DosCWait(action,wait,ret,cpid,pid);

unsigned action;   action code, as follows
                      0 = wait for child only
                      1 = wait for child and descendants

unsigned wait;     wait code, as follows
                      0 = wait if child has not yet ended
                          of until all children end
                      1 = return if child has not ended

long far *ret;     return codes

unsigned far *cpid;  child process id

unsigned pid;      target process id, or 0
```

Waits for one or more child processes to terminate. If *pid* is 0, the wait is for any child process; otherwise *pid* specifies the particular child process whose termination is awaited. The *ret* argument is treated as a two-word array. The low-order word contains a termination code, as follows:

CODE	MEANING
0	Normal exit
1	Hard error abort
2	Trap
3	DosKillProcess

The high-order word contains the return code passed by the process whose identifier is returned in *cpid*.

DosDelete

```
DosDelete(name,0L);
```

```
char far *name;  file name
```

Deletes the specified file, if possible. If the file is read-only, you must first call *DosSetFileMode* to make it writable.

DosDevConfig

```
DosDevConfig(info,item,0);

unsigned far *info;     device information
unsigned item;          item code, as follows
                          0 = number of printers
                          1 = number of serial ports
                          2 = number of diskette drives
                          3 = math coprocessor flag
                          4 = PC submodel
                          5 = PC model
                          6 = display adaptor type
```

Returns basic system configuration information. The math coprocessor flag is 1 if the coprocessor is present; otherwise it is 0. The display adaptor type is 0 for monochrome and 1 for any other type.

DosDevIOCtl

```
DosDevIOCtl(data,args,function,category,fh);

unsigned far *data;     data area
unsigned far *args;     argument area
unsigned function;      function code
unsigned category;      category code
unsigned fh;            file handle
```

Performs a control operation on the device associated with the file handle.

DosDupHandle

```
DosDupHandle(oldfh,newfh);
```

```
unsigned oldfh;          old file handle
unsigned far *newfh;     new file handle
```

Duplicates a file handle. If *newfh* contains 0xFFFF when the function is called, OS/2 assigns the new file handle. Any other value is the actual file handle that OS/2 should assign; if that handle is open, OS/2 closes it.

DosEnterCritSec

```
DosEnterCritSec();
```

Disables thread switching for the current process and increments the critical section counter.

DosErrClass

```
DosErrClass(code,class,action,locus);

unsigned code;           error code

unsigned far *class;     error class code, as follows
                           01 = out of resources
                           02 = temporary situation
                           03 = authorization failure
                           04 = internal error
                           05 = hardware failure
                           06 = system failure
                           07 = application failure
                           08 = item not found
                           09 = bad call format
                           10 = resource is locked
                           11 = media error
                           12 = already used or completed
                           13 = unclassified
                           14 = cannot perform request
                           15 = timeout

unsigned far *action;    action code, as follows
                           01 = retry immediately
                           02 = delay and then retry
                           03 = supply new values
                           04 = clean up and terminate
```

```
                        05 = terminate immediately
                        06 = ignore error
                        07 = retry after user action

unsigned far *locus;    locus code, as follows
                          01 = unknown
                          02 = block device (e.g. disk)
                          03 = network
                          04 = serial device
                          05 = memory
```

Obtains the class, action, and locus codes for the specified OS/2 error code.

DosError

```
DosError(action);

unsigned action;    action flags, as follows
                      Bit 0 = disable error display
                          1 = disable exception display
```

Enables or disables the pop-up displays for hard errors and exceptions occurring in a process. When a display is disabled and the condition occurs, the process is terminated.

DosExecPgm

```
DosExecPgm(obj,objlen,mode,args,env,term,progname);

char far *obj;          object name buffer
unsigned objlen;        object name buffer length
unsigned mode;          execution mode, as follows
                          0 = synchronous execution with
                              termination codes returned
                          1 = asynchronous execution with
                              termination codes discarded
                          2 = asynchronous execution with
                              termination codes saved
                          3 = trace mode
                          4 = detached mode
                          5 = frozen mode
```

```
char far *args;           argument strings, or NULL

char far *env;            environment strings, or NULL

unsigned far *term;       termination codes, as follows
                            Word 0 = 0 for normal exit
                                   = 1 for hard error
                                   = 2 for trap
                                   = 3 for killed process
                            Word 1 = process return code

char far *progname;       program file name
```

Creates a new process as a child of the current process unless the detached mode is specified. For mode 0, OS/2 does not return until the child process terminates, in which case the termination information is placed into *term*. For modes 1, 2, and 4, OS/2 returns after launching the child process. In those cases, word 0 of *term* contains the child process identifier. For mode 2, this identifier can be passed to *DosCWait* in order to obtain the child-process termination codes.

If the function fails, *obj* will contain the name of the object that contributed to the failure.

DosExit

```
DosExit(action,result);

unsigned action;          action code, as follows
                            0 = terminate current thread
                            1 = terminate current process

unsigned result;          result code
```

Terminates the current thread or process. In the latter case, the result code is passed back to the parent process.

DosExitCritSec

```
DosExitCritSec();
```

Decrements the critical section counter for the current process and enables thread switching if the counter reaches zero.

DosExitList

```
DosExitList(mode,func);

unsigned mode;              mode, as follows
                              1 = add function to list
                              2 = remove function from list
                              3 = advance to next function

void (far *func)();         function address, or zero
```

Adds or removes a function from the exit list for the current process. All exit functions are invoked during process termination, but not necessarily in the order that they were added to the list. Invocation is made via a JMP instruction, and the exit routine must return by calling *DosExitList* with mode 3. Upon entry, the word at SP+4 contains the termination code as specified for word 0 of *term* in the *DosExit* function.

DosFileLocks

```
DosFileLocks(fh,unlock,lock);

unsigned fh;                file handle
long far *unlock;           unlock range, or NULL
long far *lock;             lock range, or NULL
```

Locks and/or unlocks a region in the specified file. Each range argument points to a pair of 32-bit integers which specify the first and last byte of the range, relative to the beginning of the file.

DosFindClose

```
DosFindClose(dh);

unsigned dh;                directory handle
```

Closes the directory identified by the handle, which was previously provided by *DosFindFirst*.

DosFindFirst

```
DosFindFirst(name,dh,attr,result,length,entries,0L);

char far *name;             file name or pattern
unsigned far *dh;           directory handle
unsigned attr;              search attribute (see Chapter 6)
struct FILEDESC far *result;  result area (see Chapter 6)
unsigned length;            result area length
unsigned entries;           number of entries to find
```

Finds the first set of directory entries that match the specified file name or pattern, and returns their file descriptors in the *result* area. If the directory handle is specified as 0xFFFF, then OS/2 assigns a new directory handle and returns it in *dh*. If you are only searching one directory at a time, set *dh* to 1 before calling this function, because handle 1 is always available.

DosFindNext

```
DosFindNext(dh,result,length,entries);

unsigned dh;                directory handle
struct FILEDESC far *result;  result area (see Chapter 6)
unsigned length;            result area length
unsigned entries;           number of entries to find
```

Finds the next set of directory entries that match the file name or pattern that was specified on a prior call to *DosFindFirst*.

DosFlagProcess

```
DosFlagProcess(pid,action,flag,arg);

unsigned pid;               process identifier

unsigned action;            action code, as follows
                               0 = flag process and descendants
                               1 = flag process only
```

```
unsigned flag;            flag number (0, 1, or 2)

unsigned arg;             flag argument
```

Sets the event flag for the specified process and, if *action* is 0, for its attached descendants. The target processes can detect event flags via *DosSetSigHandler*.

DosFreeModule

```
DosFreeModule(mh);

unsigned mh;              module handle
```

Frees a dynamic link module currently being used by the calling process. When the last process frees a module, the module is removed from memory.

DosFreeSeg

```
DosFreeSeg(selector);

unsigned selector;        segment selector
```

Frees a segment previously obtained via *DosAllocSeg*, *DosAllocHuge*, or *DosCreateCSAlias*.

DosGetCollate

```
DosGetCollate(bsize,codes,buffer,asize);

unsigned bsize;           buffer size in bytes
unsigned far *codes;      mapping codes, as follows
                            codes[0] = country code
                            codes[1] = code page

char far *buffer;         collation table buffer
unsigned far *asize;      actual size of table
```

Gets a collation table that can be used for sorting the character codes from 0 through 255. The buffer size should be at least 256 bytes.

DosGetCP

```
DosGetCP(bsize,buffer,asize);

unsigned bsize;           buffer size in bytes
unsigned far *buffer;     buffer for code page identifiers
unsigned far *asize;      actual size of code page list
```

Obtains the current code page identifier if the buffer contains only one word (i.e., if *bsize* is 2). Otherwise, obtains the identifiers of all prepared system code pages, or as many as will fit in the buffer.

DosGetCtryInfo

```
DosGetCtryInfo(bsize,codes,buffer,asize);

unsigned bsize;           buffer size in bytes

unsigned far *codes;      mapping codes, as follows
                            codes[0] = country code
                            codes[1] = code page

struct CDI             country-dependent information
  {
  unsigned cc;         country code
  unsigned cp;         code page
  unsigned fdate;      date format, as follows
                         0 = mm/dd/yy
                         1 = dd/mm/yy
                         2 = yy/mm/dd
  char curr[5];        currency symbol
  char sthou[2];       thousands separator
  char sdec[2];        decimal separator
  char sdate[2];       date separator
  char stime[2];       time separator
  char fcurr;          currency format, as follows
                         Bit 0 = 0 if symbol precedes value
                               = 1 if symbol follows value
                         Bit 1 = number of spaces
                         Bit 2 = replace decimal symbol
```

```
    char dcurr;       number of decimals in currency
    char ftime;       time format, as follows
                        Bit 0 = 0 if 12-hour clock
                              = 1 if 24-hour clock

    long r1;          reserved
    char sdata[2];    data list separator
    unsigned r2[5];   reserved
    } far *buffer;

  unsigned far *asize;    actual size of data
```

Gets the country-dependent information for the specified country and code page.

DosGetDateTime

```
DosGetDateTime(dt);

struct DateTime
  {
  char hour;                  hour (0 to 23)
  char minute;                minute (0 to 59)
  char second;                second (0 to 59)
  char frac;                  fractional second (0 to 99)
  char day;                   day of month (0 to 31)
  char month;                 month (1 to 12)
  unsigned year;              year
  int zone;                   minutes from UTC
  char dow;                   day of week (0 to 6)
  } far *dt;
```

Gets the current date and time, together with information about the time zone. The latter is provided as a signed number of minutes relative to the Universal Time Coordinate (UTC), also called Greenwich Mean Time (GMT). This value is positive if the time is earlier than UTC. For example, the *zone* value for Eastern Standard Time is 300, indicating that New York is five hours behind UTC.

DosGetDBCSEv

```
DosGetDBCSEv(bsize,codes,buffer);

unsigned bsize;            buffer size in bytes
unsigned far *codes;       mapping codes, as follows
                             codes[0] = country code
                             codes[1] = code page

char far *buffer;          buffer
```

Gets the dual-byte character set vector for the specified country and code page. The vecton consists of byte pairs, with each pair indicating a range of values that begin dual-byte characters. The vector ends with a pair of zero bytes.

DosGetEnv

```
DosGetEnv(env,cmd);

unsigned far *env;         environment selector
unsigned far *cmd;         command line offset
```

Gets the selector for the environment segment and the offset to the command line within the segment.

DosGetHugeShift

```
DosGetHugeShift(shift);

unsigned far *shift;
```

Gets the "huge shift" value, which indicates the bit that must be incremented when stepping from one selector to another within a block obtained via *DosAllocHuge*. For example, if *shift* is returned as 4, then you must add 0x10 when advancing from one segment to the next.

DosGetInfoSeg

```
DosGetInfoSeg(global,local);

unsigned far *global;   global segment selector
unsigned far *local;    local segment selector
```

Gets the selectors for the global and local information segments maintained by the operating system.

DosGetMachineMode

```
DosGetMachineMode(mode);

char far *mode;         0 for DOS (real mode)
                        1 for OS/2 (protected mode)
```

Gets current machine mode.

DosGetMessage

```
DosGetMessage(var,nvar,buffer,bsize,msg,file,asize);

char far *(far *var);   list of variables
unsigned nvar;          number of variables
char far *buffer;       message buffer
unsigned bsize;         buffer size
unsigned msg;           message number
char far *file;         message file name
unsigned far *asize;    actual message size
```

Gets a message from a message file and inserts variable information into the message. The *var* argument is a 32-bit pointer to an array of 32-bit pointers, each of which refers to a null-terminated string which may include DBCS data if appropriate. This array can contain no more than nine pointers. Within the message, the variable insertion points are identifed by %n, where n is a digit from one to nine that refers to an entry in the variable array.

DosGetModHandle

```
DosGetModHandle(name,mh);

char far *name;           module name
unsigned far *mh;         module handle
```

Gets the handle of a dynamic link module if that module is currently in memory.

DosGetModName

```
DosGetModName(mh,buffer,bsize);

unsigned mh;              module handle
char far *buffer;         module name buffer
unsigned bsize;           buffer size
```

Gets the name of the dynamic link module corresponding to the specified module handle. The name is returned as a null-terminated string.

DosGetPID

```
DosGetPID(pid);

unsigned far *pid;        process id array, as follows
                            Word 0 = current process ID
                                 1 = current thread ID
                                 2 = parent process ID
```

Gets three words of process identification information.

DosGetProcAddr

```
DosGetProcAddr(mh,name,address);

unsigned mh;              module handle
char far *name;           procedure name
long far *address;        procedure address
```

Gets the address of the specified procedure name in the specified dynamic link module.

DosGetPrty

```
DosGetPrty(scope,priority,id);

unsigned scope;           scope of request, as follows
                            0 = first thread of process
                            1 = specific thread
unsigned far *priority;   priority code
unsigned id;              process or thread identifier
```

Gets the priority code for a specific thread or for the first thread in a process. On a successful return, the high-order byte of *priority* contains the priority class, while the low-order byte is the priority level.

DosGetSeg

```
DosGetSeg(seg);

unsigned seg;             segment selector
```

Gets access to a segment that was shared via *DosGiveSeg*.

DosGetShrSeg

```
DosGetShrSeg(name,seg);

char far *name;           segment name
unsigned far *seg;        segment selector
```

Gets access to a segment that was shared via *DosAllocShrSeg*.

DosGetVersion

```
DosGetVersion(version);
```

```
unsigned far *version;  OS/2 version code
```

Gets the version code, consisting of the minor release number in the low-order byte and the major release number in the high-order byte. OS/2 SE 1.0 has a major release number of 10.

DosGiveSeg

```
DosGiveSeg(oseg,pid,rseg);

unsigned oseg;          owner's segment selector
unsigned pid;           process ID of recipient
unsigned far *rseg;     recipient's segment selector
```

Gives a recipient process access to a shared segment. The *rseg* selector must be passed to the recipient via some form of interprocess communication.

DosHoldSignal

```
DosHoldSignal(action);

unsigned action;        action code, as follows
                          0 = enable signals
                          1 = disable signals
```

Enables or disables signals. While signals are disabled, they are latched up and will be recognized if signals are later enabled. This function maintains an up-down counter to allow for nested disable requests.

DosInsMessage

```
DosInsMessage(var,nvar,buffer,bsize,msg,file,asize);

char far *(far *var);   list of variables
unsigned nvar;          number of variables
char far *msg;          unedited message
unsigned msglen;        unedited message length
char far *buffer;       message buffer
unsigned bsize;         buffer size
unsigned far *asize;    actual message size
```

Inserts variables into a message. See *DosGetMessage* for a description of the variable list.

DosKillProcess

```
DosKillProcess(action,pid);

unsigned action;        action code, as follows
                          0 = kill process and children
                          1 = kill process only
unsigned pid;           process identifier
```

Sends the *SIGTERM* signal to the specified process and, optionally, to all of its attached descendants.

DosLoadModule

```
DosLoadModule(obj,objlen,name,mh);

char far *obj;          object name buffer
unsigned objlen;        object name buffer length
char far *name;         module name
unsigned far *mh;       module handle
```

Loads a dynamic link module into memory and assigns a module handle to it. If the loading operation fails, the name of the failing object is returned in *obj*.

DosLockSeg

```
DosLockSeg(seg);

unsigned seg;           segment selector
```

Locks a discardable segment so that it will not be discarded. Also increments the lock counter for that segment.

DosMakePipe

```
DosMakePipe(rh,wh,size);

unsigned far *rh;          read handle
unsigned far *wh;          write handle
unsigned size;             pipe buffer size
```

Creates a pipe that can be used to pass a serial stream of data from one process to another. If the *size* argument is 0, then the default size of 512 bytes is used.

DosMemAvail

```
DosMemAvail(size);

long far *size;            number of bytes available
```

Gets the size of the largest free memory block.

DosMkDir

```
DosMkDir(name,0L);

char far *name;            directory name
```

Creates a directory.

DosMonClose

```
DosMonClose(dh);

unsigned dh;               device handle
```

Closes a device monitor connection that was previously established via *DosMonOpen*;

DosMonOpen

```
DosMonOpen(name,dh);

char far *name;          device name
unsigned far *dh;        device handle
```

Opens a connection to a device driver so that the current process can register itself as a monitor.

DosMonRead

```
DosMonRead(input,wait,data,size);

char far *input;         monitor input buffer
unsigned wait;           wait code, as follows
                           0 = wait until data available
                           1 = return if data not available
char far *data;          data record buffer
unsigned far *size;      data buffer size
```

Moves one data record from the monitor input buffer to the data buffer. The *size* argument must contain the data buffer size when the function is called, and the function returns the record size in that argument. The monitor buffer must have been previously set up via *DosMonReg*.

DosMonReg

```
DosMonReg(dh,input,output,pos,index);

unsigned dh;             device handle
char far *input;         input buffer
char far *output;        output buffer
unsigned pos;            position code, as follows
                           0 = no preference
                           1 = prefer start of chain
                           2 = prefer end of chain
unsigned index;          data stream index
```

Registers the calling process as a monitor for the specified device. The first word of each buffer must contain the buffer length in bytes, including the length word. These sizes are usually the same and must be at least 20 bytes larger than the devices monitor chain buffer. This value varies from one device driver to another. The *index* argument is used by some device drivers to indicate which of their data streams is being monitored.

DosMonWrite

```
DosMonWrite(output,data,size);

char far *output;        monitor output buffer
char far *data;          data record
unsigned size;           data record size
```

Moves one data record from the data buffer to the monitor output buffer. The output buffer must have been previously set up via *DosMonReg*.

DosMove

```
DosMove(old,new,0L);

char far *old;           old file name
char far *new;           new file name
```

Renames a file and/or moves it to another directory on the same drive. That is, the *old* and *new* file names can be in different directories, but they must be on the same drive.

DosMuxSemWait

```
DosMuxSemWait(index,list,timeout);

unsigned far *index;     event index number
unsigned far *list;      event descriptor list
long timeout;            timeout value, as follows
                           -1 = wait indefinitely
                            0 = return if no events occurred
                           +n = return after n milliseconds
                                if no events have occurred
```

Waits until one of the specified events has occurred. The event descriptor list begins with a word specifying the number of events that are described. Then, each event is described by six bytes. The first two are reserved and must be 0; the next four contain the semaphore handle. *DosMuxSemWait* waits until any of the semphores in the list is cleared, and it then returns the index number of that semaphore. The first entry in the list has index number 0, the second is index 1, and so on.

DosNewSize

```
DosNewSize(fh,size);

unsigned fh;              file handle
long size;                file size
```

changes the size of a file. The file must not be marked as "read only." OS/2 attempts to add space in a contiguous area, but this is not guaranteed. The value of bytes added to the file is undefined.

DosOpen

```
DosOpen(name,fh,action,size,attr,type,mode,0L);

char far *name;        file name
unsigned far *fh;      file handle

unsigned far *action; action code, as follows
                         1 = file already exists
                         2 = file was created
                         3 = file was replaced

long size;             requested size

unsigned attr;         file attribute, as follows
                         Bit 00 = read only file
                             01 = hidden file
                             02 = system file
                             04 = directory
                             05 = archive flag

unsigned type;         function type, as follows
                         Low nibble...
```

```
                          0 = fail if file exists
                          1 = open if file exists
                          2 = replace if file exists
                        High nibble...
                          0 = fail if file doesn't exist
                          1 = create if file doesn't exist

unsigned mode;        open mode, as follows
                        Bits 00:02 = access mode
                                       0 = read
                                       1 = write
                                       2 = read/write
                             04:06 = sharing mode
                                       1 = deny read/write
                                       2 = deny write
                                       3 = deny read
                                       4 = deny none
                             07    = private file
                             13    = suppress error display
                             14    = write through cache
                             15    = open volume
```

Opens a file and assigns a file handle for use by the calling process.

DosOpenQueue

```
DosOpenQueue(pid,qh,name);

unsigned far *pid;      owner's process identifier
unsigned far *qh;       queue handle
char far *name;         queue name
```

Opens a queue that was previously created via *DosCreateQueue*. The queue name must begin with the prefix *\queue*.

DosOpenSem

```
DosOpenSem(sh,name);

long far *sh;           semaphore handle
char far *name;         semaphore name
```

Opens a semaphore that was previously created via *DosCreateSem*. The semaphore name must begin with the prefix *\sem*.

DosPeekQueue

```
DosPeekQueue(qh,rid,dsize,daddr,code,nowait,prty,sh);

unsigned qh;               queue handle
long far *rid;             request identification
unsigned far *dsize;       data size
long far *daddr;           data address
unsigned far *code;        search code
unsigned nowait;           0 to wait, else 1
unsigned far *prty;        priority code (0 to 15)
long sh;                   semaphore handle
```

Gets an element from a queue without dequeueing it. The request identification contains two 16-bit components. The low-order word is the process identifier of the process which added the element to the queue. The high-order word is application-dependent and is supplied by the process which placed the element in the queue. The data address is returned by OS/2 and points to the queue element in a shared segment. The search code should be set to 0 if you want to start at the beginning of the queue; OS/2 then sets it to a non-zero value so that a subsequent call to *DosPeekQueue* will get the next element.

DosPFSActivate

```
DosPFSActivate(sfh,size,name,cp,font,pid,0L);

unsigned sfh;              spool file handle
long far *size;            number of bytes written
char far *name;            printer name
unsigned cp;               code page identifier
unsigned font;             font identifier
unsigned pid;              process identifier
```

Used by a spooling monitor process to activate a code page for a printer. Normal processes should use *DosDevIOCtl* to change code pages.

DosPFSCloseUser

```
DosPFSCloseUser(name,pid,0L);

char far *name;  printer name
unsigned pid;  process ide
```

Used by a spooling monitor process to deactivate a printer code page previously activated via *DosPFSActivate.*

DosPFSInit

```
DosPFSInit(hfonts,sfonts,type,name,n,0L);

unsigned far *hfonts; hard font list
char far *sfonts; soft font file name
char far *type;  printer type
char far *name;  printer name
unsigned n;  maximum number of users
```

Used by a spooling monitor process to initialize the Font Manager for printer font switching.

DosPFSQueryAct

```
DosPFSQueryAct(name,cp,font,pid,0L);

char far *name;  printer name
unsigned far *cp; code page identifier
unsigned far *font; font identifier
unsigned pid;  process identifier
```

Used by a spooling monitor process to discover the font that is currently active for the specified process.

DosPFSVerifyFont

```
DosPFSVerifyFont(name,cp,font,0L);

char far *name;  printer name
unsigned cp;  code page identifier
unsigned font;  font identifier
```

used by a spooling monitor process to check if a specified font is available for a printer.

DosPhysicalDisk

```
DosPhysicalDisk(type,data,dsize,parm,psize);

unsigned type;   function type, as follows
                           1 = get number of disks
                           2 = get disk handle
                           3 = release disk handle

unsigned far *data; data buffer address
unsigned dsize;   data buffer size

unsigned far *parm; input parameter buffer
unsigned psize;   parameter buffer size
```

Obtains information about partitionable disks. For function types 1 and 2, the data buffer size must be 2. Type 1 returns the total number of partitionable disks in the system, while type 2 returns a disk handle that can be used in certain *DosDevIOCtl* calls. For type 3, the data buffer size must be 0, and the data buffer pointer should be null. No input parameters are required for function type 1. For type 2, the parameter buffer must contain a null-terminated string consisting of the partition number (1-based) followed by a colon. For type 3, the input parameter is the 16-bit handle returned by a previous type 2 call.

DosPortAccess

```
DosPortAccess(0,type,first,last);

unsigned type;   function type, as follows
                          0 = request access
                          1 = release access
unsigned first;  first port number
unsigned last;   last port number
```

Used by IOPL processes to request or release access to a range of I/O ports. CLI access is also granted, so there is no need to call *DosCLIAccess*.

DosPtrace

```
DosPtrace(buffer);

struct Ptrace far *buffer; trace buffer
```

Used by debuggers to control the execution of processes under test. See the *OS/2 Technical Reference* for details.

DosPurgeQueue

```
DosPurgeQueue(qh);

unsigned qh;   queue handle
```

Removes all elements from the specified queue.

DosPutMessage

```
DosPutMessage(fh,size,msg);

unsigned fh;   file handle
unsigned size;  message size
char far *msg;  message
```

Writes a message to a file, editing the message so that words and dual-byte characters are not split when the messge is displayed on a screen with 80-character lines.

DosQCurDir

```
DosQCurDir(drive,dir,size);

unsigned drive;  drive number
char far *dir;  directory name buffer
unsigned far *size; buffer size
```

Gets the full path name of the current directory for the specified drive. If *drive* is 0, then the current drive is queried. Otherwise, drive A is number 1, drive B is number 2, and so on.

The *size* argument must be set to the buffer size when the function is called; upon return, it will contain the directory path name. The directory name that is returned does not begin with a drive letter or a leading backslash.

DosQFHandState

```
DosQFHandState(fh,state);

unsigned fh;            file handle
unsigned far *state;    file state
```

Returns the file state, which is a bit-encoded word identical to the *mode* argument supplied to *DosOpen*.

DosQFileInfo

```
DosQFileInfo(fh,level,buffer,size);

unsigned fh;            file handle
unsigned level;         information level (must be 1)
struct FILEDESC far *buffer;  file descriptor
unsigned size;          descriptor size
```

Gets the descriptor for the specified file. See Chapter 6 for the file descriptor format.

DosQFileMode

```
DosQFileMode(name,attr,0L);

char far *name;          file name
unsigned far *attr;      file attribute
```

Gets the attribute word for the specified file name. See Chapter 6 for the layout of this word.

DosQFsInfo

```
DosQFsInfo(drive,level,buffer,size);

unsigned drive;          drive number
unsigned level;          information level
char far *buffer;        information buffer
unsigned size;           buffer size
```

Gets information about the file system on the specified drive. Drive 0 is the current drive, 1 is drive A, 2 is drive B, and so on.

Level 1 information is returned in the following format:

```
struct FSINFO1
  {
  long fsid;               file system identification
  long spau;               sectors per allocation unit
  long nau;                number of allocation units
  long fau;                free allocation units
  unsigned bps;            bytes per sector
  };
```

The level 2 information consists of a 32-bit reserved area, followed by a 1-byte length specifying the size of the volume label. The label follows this length byte and is a null-terminated string.

DosQHandType

```
DosQHandType(fh,type,dattr);

unsigned fh;            file handle

unsigned far *type;     handle type, as follows
                          Low byte:
                            0 = disk file
                            1 = character device
                            2 = pipe file
                          High byte:
                            Bit 7 = remote file

unsigned far *dattr;    device attribute flags
```

Indicates whether the specified file handle refers to a disk file, a character device, or a pipe. Also indicates whether this is a local file or one that is accessed on a remote machine via a network. Returns the device attribute flags for character device files.

DosQueryQueue

```
DosQueryQueue(qh,size);

unsigned qh;            queue handle
unsigned far *size;     number of queue elements
```

Gets the number of elements currently in the specified queue.

DosQVerify

```
DosQVerify(vfy);

unsigned far *vfy;      verify flag
```

Returns the state of disk write verification. A value of 0 indicates that verification is not active.

DosRead

```
DosRead(fh,buffer,size,asize);

unsigned fh;              file handle
char far *buffer;         input buffer
unsigned size;            buffer size
unsigned far *asize;      actual size
```

Reads up to *size* bytes from the specified file and returns the actual number of bytes read in *asize*. Control does not return until the input operation is finished.

DosReadAsync

```
DosReadAsync(fh,sem,rc,buffer,size,asize);

unsigned fh;              file handle
long far *sem;            local semaphore
unsigned far *rc;         return code
char far *buffer;         input buffer
unsigned size;            buffer size
unsigned far *asize;      actual size
```

Same as *DosRead* except that control returns immediately so that the calling process can continue while the input operation is in progress. The local semaphore must be set via *DosSemSet* before *DosReadAsync* is called. Before checking the return code or the actual size, you must wait on the semaphore by calling *DosSemWait*.

DosReadQueue

```
DosReadQueue(qh,rid,dsize,daddr,code,nowait,prty,sh);

unsigned qh;              queue handle
long far *rid;            request identification
unsigned far *dsize;      data size
long far *daddr;          data address
unsigned far *code;       search code
unsigned nowait;          0 to wait, else 1
```

```
unsigned far *prty;        priority code (0 to 15)
long sh;                   semaphore handle
```

Same as *DosPeekQueue* except that the element is removed from the queue.

DosReallocHuge

```
DosReallocHuge(size,seg);

long size;                 new size
unsigned seg;              segment selector
```

Reallocates a huge block previously created via *DosAllocHuge*. The selector must refer to the first segment in the huge block.

DosReallocSeg

```
DosReallocSeg(size,seg);

unsigned size;             new size
unsigned seg;              segment selector
```

Reallocates a segment. A *size* value of 0 indicates 64 kilobytes. The size of a shared segment cannot be decreased.

DosResumeThread

```
DosResumeThread(tid);

unsigned tid;              thread identifier
```

Restarts a thread that was previously stopped via *DosSuspendThread*.

DosRmDir

```
DosRmDir(name,0L);

char far *name;            directory name
```

Removes the specified directory, which must be empty. You cannot remove the root directory or the current directory.

DosScanEnv

```
DosScanEnv(name,value);

char far *name;          environment variable name
long far *value;         environment variable pointer
```

Scans the environment area for the specified variable name and returns a pointer to the value associated with that name.

DosSearchPath

```
DosSearchPath(mode,paths,name,buffer,size);

unsigned mode;           search mode, as follows
                           Bit 0 = search current directory
                           Bit 1 = environment path

char far *paths;         search paths or variable name

char far *name;          file name

char far *buffer;        result buffer

unsigned size;           buffer size
```

Searches for a file in one or more directories. If bit 1 of *mode* is reset, then *paths* is a list of path names with a semicolon between names. If bit 1 is set, then *paths* is an environment variable name, and that variable contains a list of paths. Bit 0 of *mode* indicates whether the current directory should be searched first.

If the search is successful, then the result buffer will contain the file name preceded by the path in which it was found. Wildcard characters are allowed in the file name.

DosSelectDisk

```
DosSelectDisk(drive);

unsigned drive;          drive number
```

Makes the specified disk drive the current one for the calling process. Drive A is number 1, B is number 2, and so on.

DosSelectSession

```
DosSelectSession(sid,0L);

unsigned sid;            session identifier
```

Used by a parent session to switch itself or one of its child sessions to the foreground.

DosSemClear

```
DosSemClear(sh);

long sh;                 semaphore handle
```

Clears a semaphore and unblocks any threads that are waiting for it.

DosSemRequest

```
DosSemRequest(sh,timeout);

long sh;          semaphore handle
long timeout;     timeout value, as follows
                    -1 = wait indefinitely
                     0 = return if semaphore is owned
                    +n = return after n milliseconds
                         if semaphore is still owned
```

Checks if a semaphore is clear and, if so, seizes it until it is released via *DosSemClear*. If the semaphore is already in use by another thread, the caller either waits or receives an immediate error return, depending on the *timeout* value.

DosSemSet

```
DosSemSet(sh);

long sh;            semaphore handle
```

Unconditionally sets a semaphore. This function should be used only in special cases when the semaphore is being used for event signaling. In resource control situations, use *DosSemRequest* instead.

DosSemSetWait

```
DosSemSetWait(sh,timeout);

long sh;            semaphore handle
long timeout;       timeout value, as follows
                      -1 = wait indefinitely
                       0 = return if semaphore is owned
                      +n = return after n milliseconds
                           if semaphore is still owned
```

Same as *DosSemSet* followed by *DosSemWait*.

DosSemWait

```
DosSemWait(sh,timeout);

long sh;            semaphore handle
long timeout;       timeout value, as follows
                      -1 = wait indefinitely
                       0 = return immediately
                      +n = return after n milliseconds
                           if semaphore is still set
```

Checks if the specified semaphore is set and returns immediately if it is not. If it is set and *timeout* is nonzero, then the current thread is blocked until the semaphore is cleared. If *timeout* is zero, then the function returns immediately.

DosSendSignal

```
DosSendSignal(pid,signal);

unsigned pid;            process identifier
unsigned signal;         signal number, as follows
                           1 = SIGINTR (CTRL-C)
                           4 = SIGBREAK (CTRL-BREAK)
```

Sends a signal to the most recent child process having a handler installed for that signal.

DosSetCP

```
DosSetCP(cp,0);

unsigned cp;             code page identifier
```

Sets the code page for the current process. The print spooler is notified to use this code page for all subsequent print files generated by the process. This function also sets the keyboard and display code pages for the session to which the process belongs, thereby overriding previous settings made in the session via *DosSetCP*, *KbdSetCP*, and *VioSetCP*.

DosSetCP

```
DosSetDateTime(dt)

struct DateTime far *dt;        date/time structure
```

Sets the system date and time, using a data structure as defined for *DosGetDateTime*.

DosSetFHandState

```
DosSetFHandState(fh,state);

unsigned fh;              file handle
unsigned far *state;      file state
```

Sets the file state, which is a bit-encoded word identical to the *mode* argument supplied to *DosOpen*.

DosSetFileInfo

```
DosSetFileInfo(fh,level,buffer,size);

unsigned fh;              file handle
unsigned level;           information level (must be 1)
struct FILEDESC far *buffer;  file descriptor
unsigned size;            descriptor size
```

Sets the descriptor for the specified file. See Chapter 6 for the file descriptor format.

DosSetFileMode

```
DosSetFileMode(name,attr,0L);

char far *name;           file name
unsigned far *attr;       file attribute
```

Sets the attribute word for the specified file name. See Chapter 6 for the layout of this word.

DosSetFSInfo

```
DosSetFSInfo(drive,level,buffer,size);

unsigned drive;           drive number
unsigned level;           information level, must be 2
char far *buffer;         data buffer
```

```
unsigned size;              buffer size
```

Sets the file system information for the specified drive. Drive number 0 is the default drive, 1 is drive A, and so on. The buffer must contain a null-terminated ASCII string, which is the new volume label. This string must be preceded by a byte giving the length of the string, not including the null terminator.

DosSetMaxFH

```
DosSetMaxFH(maxfh);
unsigned maxfh;             maximum number of file handles
```

Sets the maximum number of file handles for the current process.

DosSetProcCP

```
DosSetProcCP(cp,0);
unsigned cp;                code page
```

Same as *DosSetCP*, but does not change the code page for the keyboard and display.

DosSetPrty

```
DosSetPrty(scope,class,change,id);
unsigned scope;  scope of change, as follows
                    0 = change the process and its threads
                    1 = change the process, its threads,
                        and its descendant processes and
                        threads
                    2 = change the thread

unsigned class;  new priority class, as follows
                    0 = no change
                    1 = idle time
                    2 = regular
```

```
                        3 = time critical

int change;         priority change (-31 to +31)

unsigned id;        process or thread identifier
```

Sets the priority class and/or level for processes and threads. If the class is changed, then the new priority level is set to 0, and the *change* parameter should not be negative.

DosSetSession

```
DosSetSession(sid,status);

unsigned sid;              session identifier
unsigned far *status;      status information, as follows
                             Word 0 = length (6)
                             Word 1 = select indicator
                                      0 = no change
                                      1 = selectable
                                      2 = not selectable
                             Word 2 = bond indicator
                                      0 = no change
                                      1 = bond
                                      2 = no bond
```

Sets the status for a child session. If the session is selectable, then it can appear in the Session Manager switch list so that the user can select it for the foreground. If the session is bonded, then it will come to the foreground whenever its parent session is selected. When this call is used to bond a session, the previous bond (if any) to the parent is broken.

DosSetSigHandler

```
DosSetSigHandler(addr,paddr,paction,action,signal);

void (far *addr)();               new handler address
unsigned long far *paddr;         previous handler address
unsigned far *paction;            previous action code
unsigned action;                  new action code, as follows
                                    0 = system default
                                    1 = ignore
```

```
                                  2 = call handler
                                  3 = no signal allowed
                                  4 = reset
unsigned signal;                 signal number
```

Sets the status of the specified signal in the calling process. The valid signal numbers are:

NUMBER	NAME	DESCRIPTION
1	SIGINTR	User interrupted via CTRL-C
3	SIGTERM	Program was terminated
4	SIGBREAK	User interrupted via CTRL-BREAK
5		Process flag A
6		Process flag B
7		Process flag C

The signal names are often used when programming, just in case the signal numbers get changed in some future release of OS/2.

The *paddr* and *paction* items allow you to save the previous signal status so that it can be restored later. Notice that even though *paddr* is declared here as an *unsigned long*, it will actually contain the address of a function.

Action codes 0 through 3 indicate how future occurrences of the signal are to be handled. Code 4 simply resets the signal without affecting the current handling method. Only code 2 requires a handler address; *addr* should be 0 for the other codes.

DosSetVec

```
DosSetVec(vecnum,addr,paddr);

unsigned vecnum;                 interrupt vector number
void (far *addr)();              interrupt handler address
unsigned long far *paddr;        previous handler address
```

Registers an address to serve as an interrupt handler for the current process. The valid vector numbers are:

NUMBER	DESCRIPTION
00	Divide overflow
04	Overflow
05	Boundary error
06	Invalid operation
07	Process extension not available
16	Processor extension error

Registered interrupt handlers are entered as if the handler address were actually hooked into the processor interrupt vector table, except that interrupts remain enabled. Handlers must return be executing an IRET instruction.

For interrupt 16, the floating-point status word is pushed onto the stack before the interrupt handler is entered, and the handler must pop this word before the IRET.

If a handler is registered for vector 7, then any attempt to use the floating point hardware in this process will cause that interrupt to occur. This allows for the activation of a floating-point simulator on systems where the actual hardware is not present.

DosSetVerify

```
DosSetVerify(state);

unsigned state;          verify switch state, as follows
                           0 = deactive
                           1 = active
```

Sets the state of the verify switch. When active, this switch causes each disk write operation to be verified, which is slower than unverified operation but safer in certain critical environments.

DosSleep

```
DosSleep(time);

unsigned long time;     sleep time in milliseconds
```

Suspends the current thread for the specified time period, which is rounded up to the next timer tick. Because of rounding and scheduling delays, this function should not be used for precise timing.

If the time value is 0, then this function simply checks if there are any higher priority threads to run. If not, control returns immediately.

DosStartSession

```
DosStartSession(info,sid,pid);

struct SessInfo
  {
  unsigned length;         structure length (24)
  unsigned relation;       session relation, as follows
                             0 = not related
                             1 = child session
  unsigned mode;           initial mode, as follows
                             0 = foreground
                             1 = background
  unsigned trace;          trace option, as follows
                             0 = no trace
                             1 = trace
  char far *title;         session title
  char far *name;          program name
  char far *args;          program argument string
  char far *queue;         termination queue name
  } far *info;

unsigned far *sid;         session identifier
unsigned far *pid;         base process identifier
```

Starts a new session, which can be a child of the current session or can run independently. The base process within the new session runs the specified program. The session and process identifiers are returned only if the new session is started as a child.

If the *queue* item points to a valid queue name, then the session manager returns the result code of the base process when the child session terminates. This is placed into a two-word queue element containing the child session identifier in the first word and the result code in the second. The parent session must use *DosFreeSeg* to release the queue element. If you do not want to obtain the result code, set *queue* to zero.

DosStopSession

```
DosStopSession(mode,sid,0L);

unsigned mode;          termination mode, as follows
                          0 = one session
                          1 = all children and descendants

unsigned sid;           session identifier
```

Terminates one child session or all children and their descendants. In the latter case, *sid* is ignored.

DosSubAlloc

```
DosSubAlloc(seg,offset,size);

unsigned seg;            segment selector
unsigned far *offset;    offset of new block
unsigned size;           block size in bytes
```

Allocates a block from a segment that was previously prepared via *DosSubSet*. The size must be a multiple of four bytes and cannot be larger than the segment size less eight bytes. The segment must have been previously allocated via *DosAllocSeg* or *DosAllocShrSeg*.

DosSubFree

```
DosSubFree(seg,offset,size);

unsigned seg;            segment selector
unsigned offset;         block offset
unsigned size;           block size
```

Frees a block of memory that was previously allocated via *DosSubAlloc*.

DosSubSet

```
DosSubSet(seg,mode,size);

unsigned seg;           segment selector
unsigned mode;          initialization mode, as follows
                          0 = increasing segment size
                          1 = initializing a segment
unsigned size;          segment size in bytes
```

Initializes a segment so that blocks can be allocated and released via *DosSubAlloc* and *DosSubFree*. Also used to increase the size of a segment that was previously initialized.

DosSuspendThread

```
DosSuspendThread(tid);

unsigned tid;           thread identifier
```

Suspends a thread at the first opportunity, until *DosResumeThread* is called. The thread must be within the current process.

DosTimerAsync

```
DosTimerAsync(time,sh,th);

unsigned long time;     time in milliseconds
unsigned long sh;       semaphore handle
unsigned far *th;       timer handle
```

Starts a one-shot asynchronous timer which clears the semaphore after the specified time has elapsed. The semaphore should be set via *DosSemSet* before this function is called. You can use the timer handle in conjunction with *DosTimerStop* to stop the timer before the interval is over.

DosTimerStart

```
DosTimerStart(time,sh,th);

unsigned long time;      time in milliseconds
unsigned long sh;        semaphore handle
unsigned far *th;        timer handle
```

Starts a periodic timer which clears the semaphore periodically, using the specified time period. The semaphore should be set via *DosSemSet* before this function is called and after each time period. The timer can be turned off by passing the timer handle to *DosTimerStop*.

DosTimerStop

```
DosTimerStop(th);

unsigned th;             timer handle
```

Stops a one-shot or a periodic timer and releases all system resources associated with it. This function does not affect the semaphore that is tied to the timer.

DosUnlockSeg

```
DosUnlockSeg(seg);

unsigned seg;            segment selector
```

Unlocks a discardable segment that was previously locked via *DosLockSeg*.

DosWrite

```
DosWrite(fh,buffer,size,asize);

unsigned fh;             file handle
char far *buffer;        input buffer
unsigned size;           buffer size
unsigned far *asize;     actual size
```

Writes up to *size* bytes to the specified file and returns the actual number of bytes written in *asize*. Control does not return until the input operation is finished.

DosWriteAsync

```
DosWriteAsync(fh,sem,rc,buffer,size,asize);

unsigned fh;              file handle
long far *sem;            local semaphore
unsigned far *rc;         return code
char far *buffer;         input buffer
unsigned size;            buffer size
unsigned far *asize;      actual size
```

Same as *DosWrite* except that control returns immediately so that the calling process can continue while the output operation is in progress. The local semaphore must be set via *DosSemSet* before *DosWriteAsync* is called. Before checking the return code or the actual size, you must wait on the semaphore by calling *DosSemWait*.

DosWriteQueue

```
DosWriteQueue(qh,rid,dsize,daddr,prty);

unsigned qh;              queue handle
long far *rid;            request identification
unsigned far *dsize;      data size
long far *daddr;          data address
unsigned far *prty;       priority code (0 to 15)
```

Adds an element to a queue. The request identification is a value that identifies the element to the queue reader. That is, the writer and reader must agree in advance on the *rid* codes. The priority code is used to order the elements in priority queues. Elements with priority 0 go at the end of the queue, while those with priority 15 go at the beginning. Elements with the same priority are in FIFO order.

KbdCharIn

```
KbdCharIn(data,wait,kh);

struct KbdData               keyboard data structure
  {
  char acode;                ASCII code
  char scode;                scan code
  char status;               status flags, as follows
                               Bit 7: final character
                                   6: interim character
                                   5: immediate conversion
                                   0: shift status only
  char nls;                  NLS status
  unsigned shift;            shift state flags, as follows
                               Bit 00: right shift down
                                   01: left shift down
                                   02: either CTRL down
                                   03: either ALT down
                                   04: ScrollLock on
                                   05: NumLock on
                                   06: CapsLock on
                                   07: Insert on
                                   08: Left CTRL down
                                   09: Left ALT down
                                   10: Right CTRL down
                                   11: right ALT down
                                   12: ScrollLock down
                                   13: NumLock down
                                   14: CapsLock down
                                   15: SysReq down
  long time;                 time stamp
  } far *data;

unsigned wait;               0 to wait, else 1
unsigned kh;                 keyboard handle
```

Gets the next keyboard data record, which records a single keystroke. If "shift report" has been activated by *KbdSetState*, then a data record will also be generated each time the user changes the shift state.

KbdClose

```
KbdClose(kh);
unsigned kh;                keyboard handle
```

Close a logical keyboard.

KbdDeRegister

```
KbdDeRegister();
```

De-registers a replacement keyboard subsystem that was previously installed via *KbdRegister*.

KbdFlushBuffer

```
KbdFlushBuffer(kh);
unsigned kh;                keyboard handle
```

Flushes all data records from the specified keyboard buffer.

KbdFreeFocus

```
KbdFreeFocus(kh);
unsigned kh;                keyboard handle
```

Frees the logical-to-physical keyboard linkage that was created by a previous call to *KbdGetFocus*.

KbdGetCP

```
KbdGetCP(0L,cp,kh);
```

```
unsigned far *cp;            code page identifier
unsigned kh;                 keyboard handle
```

Gets the identifcation number of the keyboard code page that is currently in use. Valid identification numbers in OS/2 SE 1.0 are:

CODE	DESCRIPTION
0000	Resident code page
0437	IBM PC USA
0850	Multilingual
0860	Portuguese
0863	Canadian-French
0865	Nordic

KbdGetFocus

```
KbdGetFocus(wait,kh);

unsigned wait;               0 to wait, else 1
unsigned kh;                 keyboard handle
```

Makes a logical-to-physical connection for the specified keyboard handle. If another handle has the keyboard focus and the *wait* argument is 0, the function will not return until the request can be granted.

KbdGetStatus

```
KbdGetStatus(s,kh);

struct KbdStat              keyboard status structure
  {
  unsigned length;          structure length (10)
  unsigned fmask;           function mask, as follows
                              Bit 00: echo on
                                  01: echo off
                                  02: binary mode on
                                  03: ASCII mode on
                                  04: modify shift state
                                  05: modify interim flags
                                  06: modify turnaround char
```

```
                              07: set for 2-byte turnaround
                              08: shift report on
    unsigned tchar         turnaround character
    char status;           status, as in KbdData
    char nls;              NLS state, as in KbdData
    unsigned shift;        shift state, as in KbdData
    } far *s;
  unsigned kh;             keyboard handle
```

Gets the keyboard status.

KbdOpen

```
KbdOpen(kh);

unsigned far *kh;              keyboard handle
```

Creates a new logical keyboard and returns its handle in *kh*.

KbdPeek

```
KbdPeek(data,kh);

struct KbdData far *data;      keyboard data record
chort kh;                      keyboard handle
```

Gets the next data record from the specified logical keyboard without removing it from the buffer. If a valid record is present, bit 7 of the *status* item in *KbdData* will be set.

KbdRegister

```
KbdRegister(name,kbd,mask);

char far *name;                module name
char far *kbd;                 entry point name
unsigned long mask;            function mask, as follows
                                 bit 00 = KbdCharIn
                                     01 = KbdPeek
                                     02 = KbdFlushBuffer
                                     03 = KbdGetStatus
```

```
04 = KbdSetStatus
05 = KbdStringIn
06 = KbdOpen
07 = KbdClose
08 = KbdGetFocus
09 = KbdFreeFocus
10 = KbdGetCP
11 = KbdSetCP
12 = KbdXlate
13 = KbdSetCustXt
```

Attaches a replacement keyboard subsystem which handles the *Kbd* functions identified in the *mask* argument.

When the alternate function specified by *kbd* is called, five additional words will have been pushed on the stack. The first two (lowest) are the return address to the KBD router in the operating system. The third word is the caller's DS register. The fourth word is an internal pointer, and the fifth word is the keyboard function index, with values from 0 to 31 corresponding to the mask bits.

When the alternate keyboard routine returns to the operating system, the AX register contains a code informing the keyboard router what should be done next. If the code is 0, then the operation was successful and control passes back to the caller with AX set to 0. If the value is -1, then the base keyboard subsystem is invoked and its return code is passed back to the caller. Any other value returned from the alternate keyboard routine is passed back to the caller as an error code.

KbdSetCP

```
KbdSetCP(0L,cp,kh);

unsigned far *cp;          code page identifier
unsigned kh;               keyboard handle
```

Changes the keyboard code page. Set *KbdGetCP* for a list of the valid code page identifiers.

KbdSetCustXt

```
KbdSetCustXt(tt,kh);

struct CodePage far *tt;          translation table
unsigned kh;                      keyboard handle
```

Installs a custom code page. See Chapter 13 for information about the *CodePage* structure.

KbdSetStatus

```
KbdSetStatus(s,kh);

struct KbdStatus far *s;          keyboard status structure
unsigned kh;                      keyboard handle
```

Sets the status of the logical keyboard. See *KbdGetStatus* for a definition of the keyboard status structure.

KbdStringIn

```
KbdStringIn(buff,size,wait,kh);

char far *buff;                   buffer
unsigned size;                    buffer size
unsigned wait;                    0 to wait, else 1
unsigned kh;                      keyboard handle
```

Gets a character string from the logical keyboard. If ASCII mode is active, the string is returned when the buffer is full or when the turnaround character is typed. In binary mode, the string is returned only when the buffer is full.

KbdSynch

```
KbdSynch(wait);
```

```
unsigned wait;                    0 for no wait, else 1
```

Synchronizes a replacement keyboard subsystem with the keyboard driver so that the subsystem can issue a *DosDevIOCTL* call.

KbdXlate

```
KbdXlate(xdata,kh);

struct KbdXdata                   translation structure
  {
  struct KbdData data;            keystroke data
  unsigned mflags;                monitor flags
  unsigned xflags;                translation flags
  unsigned state[2];              translation state
  } far *xdata;
unsigned kh;                      keyboard handle
```

Translates a scan code and shift state into an ASCII code, which is placed into the keyboard data record. Because of NLS processing, several calls may be needed to complete the translation. Completion is indicated when bit 0 in the *xflags* word is set. This function is normally used by keyboard monitors as described in Chapter 8.

MouClose

```
MouClose(mh);

unsigned mh;              mouse handle
```

Closes a mouse device for the current session.

MouDeRegister

```
MouDeRegister();
```

Deregisters an alternate mouse subsystem that was previously registered via *MouRegister*.

MouDrawPtr

```
MouDrawPtr(mh);
unsigned mh;              mouse handle
```

Redraws the mouse pointer after it was removed or restricted via *MouOpen* or *MouRemovePtr.*

MouFlushQue

```
MouFlushQue(mh);
unsigned mh;              mouse handle
```

Flushes the mouse event queue.

MouGetDevStatus

```
MouGetDevStatus(status,mh);
unsigned far *status;   status word, as follows
                          Bit 00 = event queue busy
                              01 = block read in progress
                              02 = flush in progress
                              03 = pointer draw disabled
                                   by unsupported video mode
                              08 = pointer draw disabled by
                                   user program
                              09 = mouse data in mickeys
unsigned mh;            mouse handle
```

Gets the status flags from the mouse driver.

MouGetEventMask

```
MouGetEventMask(mask,mh);
```

```
unsigned far *mask;      event mask, with bits set to
                         receive following events
                           Bit 0 = motion
                               1 = button 1, with motion
                               2 = button 1
                               3 = button 2, with motion
                               4 = button 2
                               5 = button 3, with motion
                               6 = button 3
unsigned mh;             mouse handle
```

Gets the mouse event mask, which determines which events are reported through the mouse event queue. The button numbers are 1 for left, 2 for center, and 3 for right.

MouGetNumButtons

```
MouGetNumButtons(buttons,mh);

unsigned far *buttons;  number of buttons
unsigned mh;            mouse handle
```

Gets the number of buttons on the mouse.

MouGetNumMickeys

```
MouGetNumMickeys(mickeys,mh);

unsigned far *mickeys;  number of mickeys
unsigned mh;            mouse handle
```

Gets the number of mickeys per centimeter. A mickey is the smallest unit of motion that the mouse can register.

MouGetNumQueEl

```
MouGetNumQueEl(meq,mh);

unsigned far *meq;      event queue information, as follows
                          Word 0 = current number of queue
                                   elements
```

```
                          Word 1 = maximum number of queue
                                   elements
unsigned mh;            mouse handle
```

Gets the current number of mouse event queue elements and the maximum number.

MouGetPtrPos

```
MouGetPtrPos(pos,mh);

unsigned far *pos;      position information, as follows
                          Word 0 = current row
                          Word 1 = current column
unsigned mh;            mouse handle
```

Gets the current mouse position in either pixel or character units, depending on the video display mode. The upper left corner of the screen is row 0, column 0.

MouGetPtrShape

```
MouGetPtrShape(image,def,mh);

char far *image;        pointer bit image buffer
unsigned far *def;      pointer definition, as follows
                          Word 0 = buffer length
                          Word 1 = number of columns
                          Word 2 = number of rows
                          Word 3 = hotspot column offset
                          Word 4 = hotspot row offset
unsigned mh;            mouse handle
```

Gets information that defines the shape of the mouse pointer. The caller must place the image buffer length in bytes into word 0 of the definition array, and the function returns information in words 1 through 4 and in the buffer.

For text display modes, words 1 through 4 are in character units. Furthermore, words 1 and 2 will always contain 1, and words 3 and 4 will contain 0.

For graphics display modes, words 1 through 4 are in pixel units.

MouGetScaleFact

```
MouGetScaleFact(scale,mh);

unsigned far *scale;     scale factor, as follows
                           Word 0 = row scaling
                           Word 1 = column scaling
unsigned mh;             mouse handle
```

Gets the current row and column scaling factors, which are numbers between 1 and 32,767. The scaling factors indicate the number of mickeys required to move 8 pixels or 1 character. The default for both factors is 8. Higher values result in slower response, while lower values give faster response.

MouInitReal

```
MouInitReal(name);

char far *name;          pointer draw driver name
```

Called by the Session Manager to specify the pointer draw driver that should be used in the DOS session. If *name* is null, then the default driver is used. Otherwise, *name* must be the name of a driver that was installed during initialization via the *config.sys* file.

MouOpen

```
MouOpen(name,mh);

char far *name;          pointer draw driver name
unsigned far *mh;        mouse handle
```

Opens the mouse device for the current session. The *name* pointer should be null to use the default pointer draw driver. Otherwise, it must point to the name of a pointer draw driver that was installed via *config.sys*.

MouReadEventQue

```
MouReadEventQue(buffer,wait,mh);

struct MouEvent           mouse event
  {
  unsigned state;         mouse state, as follows
                            Bit 0 = motion, no buttons down
                            Bit 1 = motion, button 1 down
                            Bit 2 = no motion, button 1 down
                            Bit 3 = motion, button 2 down
                            Bit 4 = no motion, buttion 2 down
                            Bit 5 = motion, button 3 down
                            Bit 6 = no motion, button 3 down
  unsigned long time;     event time in milliseconds
  unsigned row;           row position
  unsigned col;           column position
  } far *buffer;

unsigned wait;            Wait (1) or no-wait (0)
unsigned mh;              mouse handle
```

Reads the mouse event queue. If the queue is empty and *wait* is 0, then a null event record is returned, with its *time* item cleared. Otherwise, the *state* bits indicate the current status of the mouse. If these bits are all reset, then the mouse is at rest with no buttons pressed. Bits 1, 3, and 5 are set if the mouse moves while the corresponding button is pressed. Bits 2, 4, and 6 indicate that a button was pressed before motion began.

MouRegister

```
MouRegister(name,mou,mask);

char far *name;           module name
char far *mou;            entry point name
unsigned long mask;       function mask, as follows
                            Bit 00 = MouGetNumButtons
                                01 = MougetNumMickeys
                                02 = MouGetDevStatus
                                03 = MouGetNumQueEl
                                04 = MouReadEventQue
                                05 = MouGetScaleFact
```

```
06 = MouGetEventMask
07 = MouSetScaleFact
08 = MouSetEventMask
11 = MouOpen
12 = MouClose
13 = MouGetPtrShape
14 = MouSetPtrShape
15 = MouDrawPtr
16 = MouRemovePtr
17 = MouGetPtrPos
18 = MouSetPtrPos
19 = MouInitReal
20 = MouSetDevStatus
```

Attaches a replacement mouse subsystem which handles the *Mou* functions identified in the *mask* argument.

When the alternate function specified by *mou* is called, five additional words will have been pushed on the stack. The first two (lowest) are the return address to the MOU router in the operating system. The third word is the caller's DS register. The fourth word is an internal pointer, and the fifth word is the mouse function index, with values from 0 to 31 corresponding to the mask bits.

When the alternate mouse routine returns to the operating system, the AX register contains a code informing the mouse router what should be done next. If the code is 0, then the operation was successful and control passes back to the caller with AX set to 0. If the value is -1, then the base mouse susbsystem is invoked and its return code is passed back to the caller. Any other value returned from the alternate mouse routine is passed back to the caller as an error code.

MouRemovePtr

```
MouRemovePtr(box,mh);

unsigned far *box;      collision area, as follows
                          Word 0 = upper left row
                          Word 1 = upper left column
                          Word 2 = lower right row
                          Word 3 = lower right column
unsigned mh;            mouse handle
```

Defines a rectangular "collision area" on the screen and removes the mouse pointer if it is in this area. The mouse pointer is not allowed to move into the collision area until *mouDrawPtr* is called. If a previous collision area was defined, the new definition replaces it. The row and column coordinates should be expressed in pixels or in characters, depending on whether the current display mode is graphics or text.

MouSetDevStatus

```
MouSetDevStatus(status,mh);

unsigned status;            status word, as follows
                              Bit 08 = disable pointer draw
                              Bit 09 = mouse data in mickeys
unsigned mh;                mouse handle
```

Sets the status flags from the mouse driver. If bit 8 is set, then the calling program assumes all responsibility for drawing the mouse pointer. If bit 9 is set, then mouse information is returned as the number of mickeys relative to the last report. Normally, the mouse position is returned as pixels or characters, depending on the video mode.

MouSetEventMask

```
MouSetEventMask(mask,mh);

unsigned mask;              event mask, with bits set to
                            receive following events
                              Bit 0 = motion
                                  1 = button 1, with motion
                                  2 = button 1
                                  3 = button 2, with motion
                                  4 = button 2
                                  5 = button 3, with motion
                                  6 = button 3
unsigned mh;                mouse handle
```

Sets the mouse event mask, which determines which events are reported through the mouse event queue. The button numbers are 1 for left, 2 for center, and 3 for right.

MouSetPtrPos

```
MouSetPtrPos(pos,mh);

unsigned far *pos;       position information, as follows
                           Word 0 = current row
                           Word 1 = current column
unsigned mh;             mouse handle
```

Sets the current mouse position in either pixel or character units, depending on the video display mode. The upper left corner of the screen is row 0, column 0.

MouSetPtrShape

```
MouSetPtrShape(image,def,mh);

char far *image;         pointer bit image buffer
unsigned far *def;       pointer definition, as follows
                           Word 0 = buffer length
                           Word 1 = number of columns
                           Word 2 = number of rows
                           Word 3 = hotspot column offset
                           Word 4 = hotspot row offset
unsigned mh;             mouse handle
```

Sets the shape of the mouse pointer. For text display modes, words 1 through 4 are in character units. Words 1 and 2 must contain 1, and words 3 and 4 must contain 0. For graphics display modes, words 1 through 4 are in pixel units.

MouSetScaleFact

```
MouSetScaleFact(scale,mh);

unsigned far *scale;     scale factor, as follows
                           Word 0 = row scaling
                           Word 1 = column scaling
unsigned mh;             mouse handle
```

Sets the current row and column scaling factors, which are numbers between 1 and 32,767. The scaling factors indicate the number of mickeys required to move 8 pixels or 1 character. The default for both factors is 8. Higher values result in slower response, while lower values give faster response.

MouSynch

```
MouSynch(wait);
unsigned wait;              Wait (1) or no-wait (0)
```

Used by an alternate mouse subsystem to synchronize with the mouse driver before calling *DosDevIOCtl*.

VioDeRegister

```
VioDeRegister ();
```

Deregisters a replacement video subsystem that was previously registered by the calling process.

VioEndPopUp

```
VioEndPopUp(vh);
unsigned vh;                video handle
```

Ends the use of the temporary video buffer that was previously activated by a call to *VioPopUp*.

VioGetANSI

```
VioGetANSI(ind,vh);
unsigned far *ind;          ANSI mode indicator
unsigned vh;                video handle
```

Returns the ANSI mode indicator in the word whose address is specified as *ind*. A value of 1 indicates that ANSI translation is active, while 0 means that it is not active.

VioGetBuf

```
VioGetBuf(buff,length,vh);

unsigned far * (far *buff);address of buffer pointer
unsigned far *length;      address of buffer length
unsigned vh;               video handle
```

Gets the pointer to the logical video buffer and the length of the buffer in bytes. Note that the first argument must be the address of the 32-bit area where the buffer pointer is to be returned.

VioGetConfig

```
VioGetConfig(0,config,vh);

struct ConfigData            configuration data structure
  {
  unsigned length;           structure length in bytes
  unsigned adaptor;          adaptor type, as follows:
                              1 = color graphics adaptor (CGA)
                              2 = enhanced graphics adaptor
(EGA)

                              3 = video graphics array (VGA)
                              7 = IBM 8514/A

  unsigned display;          display type, as follows:
                              1 = color (CGA)
                              2 = enhanced color (EGA)
                              3 = monochrome (IBM 8503)
                              4 = IBM 8512 or 8513 (VGA)
                              9 = IBM 8514

  long memory;            size of adaptor memory in bytes
  } far *config;
unsigned vh;                 video handle
```

Returns information about the display adaptor and the display type currently being used by the video subsystem. Note that you must load the *length* item in the *ConfigData* structure with the structure length before calling the function. This value is 10.

VioGetCp

```
VioGetCp(0,cpid,vh);

unsigned far *cpid;          code page identifier
unsigned vh;                 video handle
```

Returns the current code page identifier which was inherited from the parent process or set via *VioSetCp*. An identifier of 0 means that the active code page is the one in ROM that is provided with the system hardware.

VioGetCurPos

```
VioGetCurPos(row,col,vh);

unsigned far *row;           row number
unsigned far *col;           column number
unsigned vh;                 video handle
```

Gets the current cursor position. The upper left corner of the screen is at row 0 and column 0. This is often called the home position.

VioGetCurType

```
VioGetCurType(curdata,vh);

struct CursorData            cursor data structure
  {
  unsigned start;            start line
  unsigned end;              end line
  unsigned width;            width
  unsigned attr;             attribute
  } far *curdata;
unsigned vh;                 video handle
```

Returns information about the cursor. The cursor height can be no greater than the number of scan lines in each character cell, which varies from one display adaptor to another. The topmost scan line is line 0. The cursor width in the base video subsystem can be no greater than one cell. The attribute will be 0 if the cursor is visible or -1 if it is hidden.

VioGetFont

```
VioGetFont(fontdata,vh);

struct FontData                  font data structure
  {
  unsigned length;               structure length in bytes
  unsigned type;                 request type
  unsigned cols;                 pixel columns per character
  unsigned rows;                 pixel rows per character
  char far *font;                font table pointer
  unsigned size;                 font table size in bytes
  } far *fontdata;
unsigned vh;                     video handle
```

Returns information about the current font if the request type is 0. The returned information includes the dimensions of a character cell in the *cols* and *rows* fields. If the *font* field contains an address, then the font is copied into that area, whose length is given by *size*. However, if the address is 0, then it is replaced with the address of a system-supplied segment that contains the font.

If the request type is 1, the function returns information about the ROM font whose character dimensions are specified in the *cols* and *rows* fields. The *font* field is treated as previously described.

VioGetMode

```
VioGetMode(mode,vh);

struct ModeData                  mode data structure
  {
  unsigned length;               structure length in bytes
  char type;                     type flags, as follows:
                                      bit 0 = 0 for monochrome
                                            = 1 for other
```

```
                                     bit 1 = 0 for text mode
                                             1 for graphics mode
                                     bit 2 = 0 to enable color
  burst
                                             1 to disable color
  burst

    char color;                  color mask, as follows:
                                      1 for 2 colors
                                      2 for 4 colors
                                      4 for 16 colors

    unsigned tcols;                 text columns
    unsigned trows;                 text rows
    unsigned pcols;                 pixel columns
    unsigned prows;                 pixel rows
    } far *mode;
  unsigned vh;                      video handle
```

Returns information about the current video mode.

VioGetPhysBuf

```
VioGetPhysBuf(buf,vh);

struct BufData                 physical buffer data
  {
  unsigned long real;          real address of physical buffer
  unsigned long length;        buffer length in bytes
  unsigned unsigned prots[?]; selector array
  } far *buf;                 address of BufData structure
unsigned vh;                   video handle
```

Maps the specified physical video buffer into the protected address space and returns one or more selectors for addressing the buffer. The *real* and *length* items must be initialized before the function is called. The former should contain the *segment:offset* address of the physical buffer, and the latter should contain the buffer length in bytes. The *prots* array must contain one word for each 64 kilobytes in the buffer.

VioGetState

```
VioGetState(state,vh);

struct Vstate far *state;  video state structure
unsigned vh;               video handle
```

Returns information about the current video state. The *Vstate* structure varies, depending on the type of state information being requested. The first word is always the structure length, and the second is the request type.

Request type 0 gets some or all of the palette registers, and in that case the request structure has the following format:

```
struct VioState0
  {
  unsigned length;            structure length in bytes
  unsigned type;              request type = 0
  unsigned reg;               first palette register (0 to
15)
  unsigned regs[?];           pallette register array
  };
```

The *regs* item should contain 16-*reg* words.

Request type 1 gets the border color. The structure size is six bytes, and the third word receives the color value.

Request type 2 gets the blink switch value in the third word of a 6-byte structure. The switch is 0 if blinking foreground colors are enabled. If it is 1, then high-intensity foreground colors are enabled.

VioModeUndo

```
VioModeUndo(owner,killer,0);

unsigned owner;               owner code, as follows:
                                0 = reserve ownership
                                1 = give up ownership

unsigned killer;              killer code, as follows:
                                0 = return error code
```

```
                                    1 = terminate thread
```

Cancels a mode wait previously established by another thread within the same process.

VioModeWait

```
VioModeWait(type,notify,0);

unsigned type;                  request type, must be 0
unsigned far *notify;           address of notify code
```

Causes the calling thread to wait until the video mode must be restored by a graphically-oriented process. When the thread wakes up, the notify code specifies what operation should be performed. Notify code 0 is the only one defined in OS/2 SE 1.0.

VioPopUp

```
VioPopUp(options,vh);

unsigned far *options;          option flags, as follows:
                                  bit 0 = 0 for immediate
return
                                        = 1 to wait for pop-up
                                  bit 1 = 0 to clear screen
                                        = 1 to preserve screen

unsigned vh;                    video handle
```

Temporarily assigns the physical screen and keyboard to the calling process, even if it is running in the background. Normally called to notify the user of a condition that requires manual intervention.

VioPrtSc

```
VioPrtSc(vh);

unsigned vh;                    video handle
```

Copies the screen to the printer if the video mode is 0, 1, 2, 3. or 7.

VioPrtScToggle

```
VioPrtScToggle(vh);

unsigned vh;                    video handle
```

This function is normally called only by the Session Manager when the user presses CTRL-PRTSC to toggle the "screen logging" mode. When this mode is active, all video lines sent by the foreground session via *VioWrtTTY* are copied to the printer.

VioReadCellStr

```
VioReadCellStr(b,size,row,col,vh);

unsigned far *b;                buffer
unsigned far *size;             buffer size in bytes
unsigned row,col;               starting row and column
unsigned vh;                    video handle
```

Reads *size/2* cells from the logical screen into buffer *b*. If the end of the screen is reached before the buffer is full, then *size* is set to the number of bytes actually read.

VioReadCharStr

```
VioReadCharStr(b,size,row,col,vh);

char far *b;                    buffer
unsigned far *size;             buffer size in bytes
unsigned row,col;               starting row and column
```

```
unsigned vh;                    video handle
```

Reads *size* characters from the logical screen into buffer *b*. If the end of the screen is reached before the buffer is full, then *size* is set to the number of bytes actually read.

VioRegister

```
VioRegister(mod,ent,mask1,mask2);

char far *mod;                  module name
char far *vio;                  entry point name
long mask1;                     function mask 1
long mask2;                     function mask 2
```

Registers function *vio* in the module named *mod* to receive control whenever a process in the current session calls one of the *Vio* functions specified by *mask1* and *mask2*. The bits in these masks are assigned as follows:

BIT	MASK 1	MASK 2
00	VioGetCurPos	VioModeWait
01	VioGetCurPos	VioModeUndo
02	VioGetMode	VioGetFont
03	VioGetBuf	VioGetConfig
04	VioGetPhysBuf	VioSetCp
05	VioSetCurPos	VioGetCp
06	VioSetCurType	VioSetFont
07	VioSetMode	VioGetState
08	VioShowBuf	VioSetState
09	VioReadCharStr	
10	VioReadCellStr	
11	VioWrtNChar	
12	VioWrtNAttr	
13	VioWrtNCell	
14	VioWrtTTY	
15	VioWrtCharStr	
16	VioWrtCharStrAttr	
17	VioWrtCellStr	

18	VioScrollUp	
19	VioScrollDn	
20	VioScrollLf	
21	VioScrollRt	
22	VioSetANSI	
23	VioGetANSI	
24	VioPrtSc	
25	VioScrLock	
26	VioScrUnlock	
27	VioSavRedrawWait	
28	VioSavRedrawUndo	
29	VioPopUp	
30	VioEndPopUp	
31	VioPrtScToggle	

When the alternate function specified by *vio* is called, five additional words will have been pushed on the stack. The first two (lowest) are the return address to the VIO router in the operating system. The third word is the caller's DS register. The fourth word is an internal pointer, and the fifth word is the video function index, with values from 0 to 31 corresponding to the first mask and values from 32 corresponding to the second mask.

When the alternate video routine returns to the operating system, the AX register contains a code informing the video router what should be done next. If the code is 0, then the operation was successful and control passes back to the caller with AX set to 0. If the value is -1, then the base video subsystem is invoked and its return code is passed back to the caller. Any other value returned from the alternate video routine is passed back to the caller as an error code.

VioSavRedrawUndo

```
VioSavRedrawUndo(owner,term,vh);

unsigned owner;          ownership indicator
                           0 = reserve ownership
                           1 = give up ownership
unsigned term;           termination indicator
                           0 = notify thread
                           1 = kill thread
```

```
unsigned vh;                video handle
```

Cancels a redraw wait established by another thread in the same process.

VioSavRedrawWait

```
VioSavRedrawWait(type,action,vh);

unsigned type;              wait type
                              0 = save and redraw
                              1 = redraw only
unsigned far *action;       action
                              0 = save
                              1 = redraw
unsigned vh;
```

Waits until the screen must be saved or redrawn because of a session switch (redraw only if *typ* is 1). When the function returns, *action* indicates what operation must be performed.

VioScrLock

```
VioScrLock(wait,state,vh);

unsigned wait;              wait mode
                              0 = return if lock fails
                              1 = wait if lock fails
unsigned far *state;        lock state
                              0 = locked
                              1 = not locked
unsigned vh;                video handle
```

Locks the physical screen to prevent session switches while the current session uses the physical video buffer.

VioScrollDn

```
VioScrollDn(ulr,ulc,lrr,lrc,rows,fill,vh);
```

```
unsigned ulr,ulc;        upper left row and column
unsigned lrr,lrc;        lower right row and column
unsigned rows;           number of rows or -1 for all
unsigned fill;           fill value
unsigned vh;             video handle
```

Scrolls a region of the screen downward, replacing empty rows at the top with the fill value.

VioScrollLf

```
VioScrollLf(ulr,ulc,lrr,lrc,rows,fill,vh);

unsigned ulr,ulc;        upper left row and column
unsigned lrr,lrc;        lower right row and column
unsigned rows;           number of rows or -1 for all
unsigned fill;           fill value
unsigned vh;             video handle
```

Scrolls a region of the screen to the left, replacing empty columns at the right with the fill value.

VioScrollRt

```
VioScrollRt(ulr,ulc,lrr,lrc,rows,fill,vh);

unsigned ulr,ulc;        upper left row and column
unsigned lrr,lrc;        lower right row and column
unsigned rows;           number of rows or -1 for all
unsigned fill;           fill value
unsigned vh;             video handle
```

Scrolls a region of the screen to the right, replacing empty columns at the left with the fill value.

VioScrollUp

```
VioScrollUp(ulr,ulc,lrr,lrc,rows,fill,vh);
```

```
unsigned ulr,ulc;           upper left row and column
unsigned lrr,lrc;           lower right row and column
unsigned rows;              number of rows or -1 for all
unsigned fill;              fill value
unsigned vh;                video handle
```

Scrolls a region of the screen upward, replacing empty rows at the bottom with the fill value.

VioScrUnlock

```
VioScrUnlock(vh);

unsigned vh;
```

Unlocks the screen after it was locked by *VioScrLock*.

VioSetANSI

```
VioSetANSI(mode,vh);

unsigned mode;              ANSI mode
                              0 = ANSI off
                              1 = ANSI on
unsigned vh;                video handle
```

Activates or deactivates ANSI mode.

VioSetCp

```
VioSetCp(resv,cp,vh);

unsigned resv;              reserved
unsigned cp;                code page identifier
unsigned vh;                video handle
```

Sets the code page used by the current process to display text on the screen.

VioSetCurPos

```
VioSetCurPos(row,col,vh);

unsigned row;              row
unsigned col;              column
unsigned vh;               video handle
```

Sets the cursor position.

VioSetCurType

```
VioSetCurType(curdata,vh);

struct CursorData far *curdata;
unsigned vh;               video handle
```

Sets the cursor type, using a cursor data structure as defined for *VioGetCurType*.

VioSetFont

```
VioSetFont(fontdata,vh);

struct FontData far *fontdata;
unsigned vh;
```

Downloads a display font to the video adaptor, using a font data structure as defined for *VioGetFont*.

VioSetMode

```
VioSetMode(mode,vh);

struct ModeData far *mode;
unsigned vh;
```

Sets the video mode, using a mode data structure as defined for *VioGetMode*.

VioSetState

```
VioSetState(state,vh);

struct Vstate far *state;
unsigned vh;
```

Sets the video state, using the structures defined for *VioGetState*.

VioShowBuf

```
VioShowBuf(offset,length,vh);

unsigned offset;          offset into buffer
unsigned length;          number of bytes
unsigned vh;              video handle
```

Updates a portion of the screen from the logical video buffer if the process is in the foreground session.

VioWrtCellStr

```
VioWrtCellStr(b,size,row,col,vh);

unsigned far *b;          buffer
unsigned size;            buffer size in bytes
unsigned row,col;         starting row and column
unsigned vh;              video handle
```

Writes *size/2* cells to the logical screen from buffer *b*. If the end of the screen is reached before the buffer is exhausted, then the operation terminates.

VioWriteCharStr

```
VioWriteCharStr(b,size,row,col,vh);
```

```
char far *b;             buffer
unsigned size;           buffer size in bytes
unsigned row,col;        starting row and column
unsigned vh;             video handle
```

Writes *size* characters to the logical screen from buffer *b*, leaving the attributes unchanged. If the end of the screen is reached before the buffer is exhausted, then the operation terminates.

VioWrtCharStrAttr

```
VioWrtCharStrAttr(b,size,row,col,attr,vh);

char far *b;             buffer
unsigned size;           buffer size in bytes
unsigned row,col;        starting row and column
unsigned far *attr;      attribute
unsigned vh;             video handle
```

Writes *size* characters to the logical screen from buffer *b*, setting their attributes to the value specified by *attr*. If the end of the screen is reached before the buffer is exhausted, the operation terminates.

VioWrtNAttr

```
VioWrtNAttr(attr,n,row,col,vh);

char far *attr;          address of attribute
unsigned n;              number of positions
unsigned row,col;        starting row and column
unsigned vh;             video handle
```

Writes an attribute into the specified number of positions, beginning at the specified row and column coordinate. The character part of each position is unchanged.

VioWrtNCell

```
VioWrtNCell(cell,n,row,col,vh);

unsigned far *cell;          address of cell
unsigned n;                  number of positions
unsigned row,col;            starting row and column
unsigned vh;                 video handle
```

Writes a cell into the specified number of positions, beginning at the specified row and column coordinate.

VioWrtNChar

```
VioWrtNChar(chr,n,row,col,vh);

char far *chr;               address of character
unsigned n;                  number of positions
unsigned row,col;            starting row and column
unsigned vh;                 video handle
```

Writes the character into the specified number of positions, beginning at the specified row and column coordinate. The attribute part of each position is unchanged.

VioWrtTTY

```
VioWrtTTY(str,size,vh);

char far *str;               character string
unsigned size;               size of string
unsigned vh;                 video handle
```

Writes the character string in TTY mode, wrapping at the end of the line and scrolling at the end of the screen. Carriage returns, line feeds, backspaces, tabs, and bells are treated as special characters. The attribute for each character is set to 7 if ANSI mode is not active. Otherwise, the current ANSI attribute is used.

INDEX

A

B

C

D

E

F

L

M

N

O

P

Q

R

S

W